Creating and Recovering Experience

Creating and Recovering Experience

Repetition in Tolstoy

Natasha Sankovitch

STANFORD UNIVERSITY PRESS
STANFORD, CALIFORNIA

Stanford University Press
Stanford, California
© 1998 by the Board of Trustees of the
Leland Stanford Junior University
Printed in the United States of America
CIP data appear at the end of the book

To mama and papa

Acknowledgments

I owe an incalculable debt of gratitude to those who have given me help and encouragement in undertaking and completing this project, including but my no means limited to the few individuals named below. To Irwin Weil, my first and most sincere mentor in Russian literature; to Gary Saul Morson for generously sharing his knowledge, his imagination, and his wisdom with me; to Andrew Wachtel for his thoughtful and timely suggestions and, even more, his friendship; to Gregory Freidin for his capable advice and assistance and helpful criticism; to Jehanne Gheith, Tom Hodge, Judith Kalb, Rachel May, and Richard Sperling, for their constant encouragement and affection; to Catalina Ilea for her patience, competence, and most of all her kindness; to Donald Lateiner, the kind of colleague-friend I'd always hoped to have; to my sisters Anne-Marie and Nina, who probably don't realize how much strength I draw from their love and their example; and to my extraordinary parents Anatol and Tilde, for a love and friendship that transcends ordinary bounds and to whom this work is dedicated.

N.S.

Contents

Creating and Recovering Experience

Introduction

My earliest recollections of my grandmother, before our move to Moscow and our life there, reduce to three strong impressions connected with her. The first is how grandmother used to wash and with some kind of special soap set free on her hands astonishing bubbles, which, it seemed to me, only she alone could make. We were brought on purpose to her—probably our delight and astonishment at her soap bubbles amused her—in order to see how she washed. I remember her white blouse and skirt, her white elderly hands and the enormous bubbles rising on them, and her satisfied, smiling white face.[1]

For Lev Tolstoy, it is our perception of the particular, unremarkable, and seemingly unmotivated details of our experience that can bestow on us a sense, an intuition, of some ultimate harmony. Those details acquire their significance through our gaze and recollection and it is by means of them that we structure and give meaning to our lives. Believing as he did that knowledge is a process of relating different elements together and giving unity to them, Tolstoy explores in his fictions how knowledge of the self and of the world is acquired. The role of

[1] Tolstoy quoted in P. I. Biriukov's 1921 biography of him, p. 28. All translations into English are my own unless otherwise noted. Unless specified, translations of Tolstoy are based on the Jubilee edition of his works, *Polnoe sobranie sochinenii* (Moscow, 1928–58), 90 volumes. Parenthetical references refer to the volume and page, except in the case of quotations from *War and Peace*, in which case they refer to volume, part, and chapter, and in the case of quotations from *Anna Karenina* and *Resurrection*, in which case they refer to part and chapter, so that citations can be found easily in any edition of these novels. Unless otherwise speci-

repetition in Tolstoy's endeavor is the focus of my inquiry. In the course of studying Tolstoy's use of repeated elements in his narratives, I am led also to ponder questions of broader implication such as how repetition affects the processes of reading and of perception in general; how repetition functions as an aid to or influence on memory formation and retention; and what the limits and possible dangers might be of viewing life via the regularity, uniformity, and certitude that repetition can imply.

Tolstoy was born in 1828 at a time when the patriarchal gentry in Russia was still dominant and died a sage in 1910 in an age of unprecedented technological, industrial, and economic development. For Tolstoy, and others too, the age was one of fragmentation and disenchantment. And like many nineteenth-century writers, Tolstoy tried to make sense in his works of the socially and historically fast-changing world and the confrontation of the individual and the social in that world. His search for understanding combines two seemingly conflicting impulses: a desire for universal truths and values and a recognition of the variability and relativity of human perceptions and responses. He was both hedgehog and fox, a product of both the Enlightenment, which he loved, and the nineteenth-century obsession with historicism, which he continually re-examined.[2]

---

fied, all emphases have been added by me. Also note that spaced dots indicate an ellipsis in the original.

I adhere to the Library of Congress system of transliteration, although I preserve the common English spellings of well-known proper names (e.g. Tolstoy, Gogol, Alexander) and transliterate a common ending of Russian surnames as "-sky," not "-skii."

[2] I allude here to Isaiah Berlin's well-known essay *The Hedgehog and the Fox: An Essay on Tolstoy's View of History*, in which he distinguishes between two kinds of personality: "For there exists a great chasm between those, on one side, who relate everything to a single central vision, one system . . . in terms of which they understand, think and feel—a single, organizing principle in terms of which alone all that they are and say has significance—and, on the other side, those who

His simultaneously held beliefs in an essential, all-embracing unity and in the radical significance of the minute and ordinary particulars of experience need to be seen in the context of the general epistemological revolution taking place in nineteenth-century Europe. The widespread belief in the possibility of a positivist and scientific synthesis of all knowledge, which reached its height from the 1850s to the 1880s, had among its detractors Tolstoy, who objected that science could not teach people how to live.[3] There was at this time a continuum of attitudes toward science that ran from the conviction that science would lead to greater understanding of the mind, a new morality, and an eventual reconstruction of society, to the belief that science could never replace traditional Christian values and teaching. Tolstoy's position in this debate is not on the continuum, but rather to the side of it. Rejecting both science and the established Church as sources of moral knowledge, Tolstoy put his faith in a kind of ethical consciousness, which in his view would give human beings the ability to join a sense of the harmony and unity associated with some higher and unfathomable general purpose with the discontinuities and multiplicities of everyday life. Addressing all who would call themselves civilized, Tolstoy's narrator in "From the Notes of Prince D. Nekhliudov, Lucerne" asserts:

> And who is able to tear himself away so completely from life with his mind, even for a moment, so as to look upon it independently

---

pursue many ends, often unrelated and even contradictory, connected, if at all, only in some *de facto* way. . . . The first kind of intellectual and artistic personality belongs to the hedgehogs, the second to the foxes" (1–2). Also, note that the word "historicism" is not a transparent concept. See Lee and Beck, "The Meaning of 'Historicism.'" In the context of Tolstoy and his objections to those who would propose universal laws of history and progress, "historicism" refers to the belief that the truth, meaning, and value of anything are to be found in history.

[3] Joravsky, pp. 11–13.

from above? One, we have only one infallible instructor, a Universal Spirit, penetrating all of us together and each of us as individuals, endowing each of us with a yearning for that which ought to be; that same Spirit which tells the tree to grow towards the sun, tells the flower to scatter its seed in autumn, and tells us to draw unconsciously closer to one another.

And this one infallible, beatific voice muffles the loud, hurried development of civilization [5, 25].[4]

Tolstoy vacillates between an intuitive belief in the possibility of unified and complete wholes and an empirical recognition of the fragmentary, discrete nature of observation and hence of knowledge.[5] His desire, it would seem, was to comprehend life in a single glance in all its detail and entirety. But he knew, of course, that such an understanding was not possible. So he worked instead to achieve that intuition of life and to convey it to his readers by paying attention to and piecing together the parts, the particulars, in a way that would not compromise or artificially reduce their unity or multiplicity.

Already obsessively self-observant as a youth, Tolstoy became more and more interested in how human beings acquire knowledge of themselves and of the world. He came to view life as an infinite "calculus" of moments and saw the extent to which countless past events, feelings, and thoughts, as well as expectations for the future, can influence and shape an individual's life in the present.[6] He viewed life as temporal to the core, with pastness and futurity, recollections and anticipations,

[4]Note the affinity for eighteenth-century conceptions Tolstoy expresses in this passage: his use of the phrase "Universal Spirit" in particular.

[5]In *War and Peace* Tolstoy argues that a complete and continuous understanding of history would require an integration of the infinitely small and numerous events that determine it (3, 3, 1). As Berlin points out, Henri Bergson's discussion of "pure duration" has some parallels with Tolstoy's notion of calculation by infinitesimals as a means of overcoming the distortions of fragmentation (31).

[6] For Tolstoy's "calculus" see *War and Peace*, 3, 3, 1.

shaping each present experience. Self-knowledge and knowledge of the world seemed to be a matter of making connections, understanding changing relations, and moving between the particular and the universal. Repetition, or the ability to recognize similarities, was fundamental to these processes. In repetition, Tolstoy discovers a device that can negotiate between discreteness and wholeness, that can help to illuminate the interrelation between the meaning of the part and the meaning of the whole. Repetition reminds us of wholes by intimating rhythms and patterns, but it also calls attention to specificities because it is never *perfect* repetition. Tolstoy's use of repetition in his novels and short stories is related to his view of consciousness as the continuous interplay between similarity and difference and ever-changing relations between parts and the whole.

Again and again through the ages, philosophers, theorizers, and thinkers have seen repetition as offering a clue to unlocking the significance of human experience and the problem of the self.[7] Writers have made use of repetition as a device to represent or encourage these efforts. Tolstoy's repetition of distinct verbal phrases in representations of characters' thoughts, mental processes, and interrelationships corresponds directly to his understanding of the self's engagement with life. Repetition in Tolstoy's fictions is more than a mere stylistic device, for its

[7] As J. Hillis Miller notes in his book on repetition in seven English novels: "The history of Western ideas of repetition begins ... with the Bible on the one hand and with Homer, the Pre-Socratics, and Plato on the other.... The modern history of ideas about repetition goes by way of Vico to Hegel and the German Romantics, to Kierkegaard's *Repetition* to Marx (in *The Eighteenth Brumaire*), to Nietzsche's concept of the eternal return, to Freud's notion of the compulsion to repeat, to the Joyce of *Finnegan's Wake*, on down to such diverse present-day theorists of repetition as Jacques Lacan or Gilles Deleuze, Mircea Eliade or Jacques Derrida" (5).

use is fundamentally related to his understanding of human psychology and experience.[8] Essentially, repetition for Tolstoy is the way the mind works: in perception the mind seizes on a detail that is familiar or striking, assigns a verbal form to the detail, which could be an object, an action, a concept, or a feeling, and reiterates this form as it brings the rest of experience—past, present, or anticipated—into focus around the key detail. This mental process is at work whether characters are trying to make sense of their experience, the narrator is trying to depict relationships among characters, the author is trying to establish certain themes, or readers are trying to shape multiple and various details into a coherent narrative.

For Tolstoy, repetition constitutes a principle or force of order imposed upon disorder. His characterizations suggest that he recognized the enormous psychological need for order and fear of chaos that makes human beings draw boundaries, make distinctions, repeat what is familiar. And it is not just order in immediate experience that is sought and valued, but also order over time: hence, we witness a complex and nearly indissoluble link between repetition and memory. Recurrences and meanings generated by recurrences are central to achieving a sense of continuity in history, the self, and in each text. Repetition in Tolstoy's fictions serves obvious narratological purposes: it contributes to characterization, plays a role in thematic and plot development, and can act as a mnemonic aid to readers, to list a few. But it is also fundamental to Tolstoy's exploration of philosophical questions, including how we ac-

---

[8] Cf. Paul Friedrich: "when we talk about craft we must distinguish between devices, rules, and tricks of the trade, as an inventory of means, and the psychological integration of these things with more deeply rooted intentions and designs" (156). Consider also Paolo Vivante's understanding of style "in its broadest and truest sense—not as a manner of saying things but as at once a way of perceiving, conceiving, expressing" (57).

quire knowledge and how we ought to live. Repetition plays a critical role in his analysis of how human beings impose design on the seemingly endless continuum of their own and all physical nature. Tolstoy's literary aim, as Viktor Shklovsky notes, was ambitious: "He wanted literature to attain greater heights of morality and knowledge, through analysis."[9] Tolstoy takes advantage of the fact that repetition signals both sameness and difference, essence and relation, in order to depict perception and thought as mutually determining, continuous processes.

My study of how Tolstoy uses the device of repetition in his fictions to represent, call attention to, and provoke the processes by which human beings structure and give meaning to their experience is divided into four parts. The first part is intended to sketch broadly the narratological and epistemological concerns repetition helps Tolstoy to address, the second and third to examine *intra*textual repetition in his fiction, and the fourth to consider *inter*textual ones. My focus throughout is on the repetition of discrete verbal elements, as opposed, for instance, to the repetition of character types or plot structures, because the former seems to offer the clearest picture of the relation between Tolstoy's thought and his method.

In Chapters 2 and 3 I draw most heavily from *War and Peace* and *Anna Karenina* for my examples. Repetition plays a critical role in much of Tolstoy's fiction (and in much of his nonfiction as well), but these two novels are perhaps his best known works, and I found it was possible to illustrate everything I discovered about Tolstoy's use of this device as it relates to his understanding of human psychology and experience through these two familiar books. It is difficult to say whether there was any development—in the sense of obvious new de-

---

[9] Shklovsky, *Lev Tolstoy*, p. 197.

ployments—in Tolstoy's use of repetition. Different works afforded him different opportunities depending on the particular work's scale, characters, and themes. Thus, given the rich and lengthy complexity of both *War and Peace* and *Anna Karenina*, it is no surprise that these two works contain many of Tolstoy's most striking and effective uses of the device.

Chapter 1, "Repetition in Tolstoy," begins with a discussion of what critics and scholars, both contemporaneous with Tolstoy and of a later age, have had to say about his use of repetition and how translators have handled his difficult, because often wordy and convoluted, prose. Translators have usually eliminated many repetitions in order to make Tolstoy's works "read smoothly" according to English literary conventions. Next I outline the philosophical and novelistic foundations of Tolstoy's use of the device, which rest on three main points: (1) the development of character, plot, and theme as a process, that is, as an end in itself, (2) the reader's experience as a cocreator of the literary work and (3) a multiplicity and diversity of perspectives in a text that creates an irony that urges comparison of competing values, motives, beliefs, and emotions. Each of these concerns has to do with how order and meaning are created, and repetition proves critical to Tolstoy's representation of these processes. With repetition he can suggest the overlapping cognitive, aesthetic, and ethical energies that complicate efforts to structure and give meaning to experience, and can underscore the continuous nature of such efforts. Tolstoy's depiction of these efforts is at least partly responsible for the length of his novels. Thus also in this first chapter, I develop the concept of "novels of length," which are distinguished from ordinary "long novels" in that length is essential to their themes and purposes.

Chapter 2, "The Structure of Characters' Experience," explores Tolstoy's use of repetition in the representation of characters' attempts to make sense of both the separate moments of their lives and their experience as some kind of whole. Repetitions in characters' inner speech, in their remembered experience, and in the narrator's descriptions of what characters do not or cannot observe about themselves are key to Tolstoy's depictions of characters' psychology. Readers observe characters working to make sense of their experiences. Simultaneously readers themselves participate in a parallel process as they continually recast past knowledge of the text in the light of present experience and alter expectations of textual outcomes while responding to the passages they are reading. Throughout my study I assume a careful and competent reader, one for whom both form and content matter and who responds positively to the demands Tolstoy places on his readers. A complex dynamic of memory, forgetting, and reminders (repetitions) structures both the characters' evolving identities and the readers' changing apprehension of the text. A deep concern with the dynamics of memory, which involves both repetition and alteration, is in fact central to Tolstoy's art. Here and in the third chapter as well, I show that Tolstoy also uses repetition to illuminate a process that is at the very core of human understanding and acquisition of knowledge: the appropriation and transformation by individuals of public social, cultural, and historical forms and symbols.

Chapter 3, "Relationships Among Characters," examines how repetition functions in various ways to structure and give meaning to connections among characters. Here repeated elements serve the development of both character and theme. Sometimes a repeated word or phrase is used to call attention to the continuous interplay between individual and communal interests and emotions that characterizes participation in a group. Tolstoy uses repetition to expose the conventions or codes of behavior that operate in group activity. Other times the repeated element sheds light on the relationships—the similarities and differences—between just two characters. In both cases, repetition also serves to define and illuminate particular themes or ideas in the book. By repeating the same thematic phrase in the quoted or narrated monologue of various characters in various contexts, Tolstoy depicts differing perspectives on the same issue. As readers sift through these perspectives, they acquire a kind of ethical education—an education in sympathy, understanding, and humility. Here especially repetition reflects Tolstoy's moral and sympathetic imagination: the depth and breadth of his conception of the complexities that constitute human experience and his ability to imagine and enter into positions other than his own. The repetitions considered in this chapter tend to be outside of characters' consciousness. That is, these words and phrases are not spoken (or thought) repeatedly by the same character, but occur in the words and thoughts or in the description of more than one character. With these repetitions Tolstoy encourages the active participation of his readers in piecing together the details of the text and makes an argument for thought as a form of active and consequential, rather than merely passive, engagement with life.

Chapter 4, "Intertextual Repetition in Tolstoy," considers repetitions that occur across the boundaries of separate works written over the course of Tolstoy's long career. For me, as for any dedicated student of his, Tolstoy is ultimately the sum of his works. Tolstoy wrote that if he wanted to say in words all that he had meant to express in his novel *Anna Karenina*, he would have to write the entire novel all over again word for word.[10] And, similarly, for me to say who Tolstoy is would be to reprint all of his texts. But intertextual repetitions seem to offer insight into the essential Tolstoy, into the themes and motifs that for Tolstoy are basic to all human experience. Tolstoy as the sum of his literary and nonliterary, fictional and nonfictional texts is the ultimate whole his dedicated readers pursue. Throughout the vast body of his work—only a portion of which is considered in this study—Tolstoy uses the device of repetition over and over again. And over and over again repetition in Tolstoy has to do with the processes by which people structure and give meaning to their experience. Repetition becomes the means for the achievement of a sense of continuity and wholeness, a sense of harmony, without which the world seemed to Tolstoy hopelessly contingent, ephemeral, fragmented, and meaningless.[11] For Tolstoy repetition is the key to how human beings create and recover experience.

[10]See Tolstoy's letter to N. N. Strakhov around Apr. 23, 1876 (62, 268–69).

[11]By referring to Tolstoy's concern with the opposition between continuity, wholeness, and harmony on the one hand, and contingency, ephemerality, and fragmentation on the other—an opposition often associated these days with postmodernist thought—I do not mean to imply that Tolstoy was a postmodernist thinker before his time. On the contrary, if postmodernism can be said to celebrate contingency, ephemerality, and fragmentation, Tolstoy believes in the possibility of transcending a view of life that rests on these terms through increased understanding and empathy. For a clear and intelligent study of postmodernity see Harvey, *The Condition of Postmodernity*.

1. Repetition in Tolstoy

> When one does not possess the categories of recollection or of
> repetition, the whole of life is resolved into a void and empty noise.
> —Kierkegaard's Constantine Constantius, *Repetition: An Essay in*
> *Philosophy*
>
> Endless repetition threatens sanity.
> —Saul Bellow's Herzog, *Herzog*

Repetition occurs in both time and space and marks human experience of these categories by establishing patterns and
symmetries. By nature paradoxical and ubiquitous, repetition
in culture can imply sameness and difference, continuity and
discontinuity, change and stasis, meaning and disruption of
meaning, parts and wholes. But wherever and however it
manifests itself, repetition can be both a communicative and a
cognitive strategy. As such it is a key technique in belles lettres. Repetition as a literary device, that is, the intentional and
purposeful use of repeated elements in narratives and descriptions, can take many different forms and serve various functions according to the author's intentions within a particular
genre or tradition. All writers rely on repetition to a greater or
lesser extent, because it is fundamental to the creation of simili-
tude and therefore of meaning, especially in belles lettres.

Repetition of key elements of character, plot, and theme is
certainly one of the most obvious devices in Tolstoy's prose.
Critics in Tolstoy's time tended to decry his unconventional

style. The aristocratic self-assuredness with which he rejected many traditional literary values and techniques in his attempt to achieve more "truthful" depictions of human experience in literature was a source of irritation to many of his contemporaries. Later, in our own century, when Tolstoy had become the yardstick, as it were, of Russian literature, scholars began to interpret his literary strategies, including repetition, in terms of their own theories about literature. Repetition in Tolstoy now became a viable topic of discussion.

American readers may often be unaware of Tolstoy's repetition because translators have been tempted to improve on Tolstoy by eliminating many of his repetitions, apparently in the hope of making his texts more "readable." But such efforts are misguided, since in Tolstoy the device is foregrounded and is itself a subject of his thought and thematics. We can think of repetition in Tolstoy as a device that encodes information about values, beliefs, emotions, and motives into characters' and the narrator's discourse. Repetition in his fiction becomes a means of both conveying (communicating) and achieving (cognizing) experience and meaning. A brief overview of how earlier critics and scholars have viewed Tolstoy's use of repetition, and how translators have dealt with what some view as mere repetitiousness, paves the way for a discussion of the main epistemological underpinnings of Tolstoy's use of repetition.

Critics and Translators

Before the early 1900s, Tolstoy's use of repetition is rarely singled out for mention by reviewers.[1] But we may conjecture

---

[1] For a good discussion of the range of views expressed by contemporary critics on *War and Peace*, *Anna Karenina*, and *Resurrection*, see Babaev, *Lev Tolstoi*.

that when critics dwell upon his carelessness and overuse of detail, they were responding in part to what they perceived as repetitiveness. One early critic who did explicitly disapprove of his repetitions is I. S. Turgenev. Sharing his impressions of *War and Peace* with P. V. Annenkov in an 1868 letter, Turgenev wrote in apparent exasperation: "And how tortuous are these deliberate, stubborn repetitions of one and the same trait: the little mustache on the upper lip of Princess Bolkonskaia, etc."[2] Nor were such reactions confined to Russians. In an unsigned review of *Anna Karenina*, which appeared in the *Nation* in 1886, Tolstoy's repetitions are taken as evidence of the creatively unruly spirit that distinguishes his prose:

> How Count Tolstoi writes we are not informed, but anyone who reads him in the original soon becomes breathless at the earnestness and rapidity with which chapter after chapter seems to have been dashed off and never afterwards revised.... This dash results in an apparent indifference to some of the commonest rules of writing and of novel manufacture, in which far inferior performers excel. It is not uncommon for him to repeat himself on the same page, to begin several consecutive sentences with the same name in the most awkward manner, to contradict his own statements.... But his habitual disregard for nice points does not detract from the effect, and it serves to accentuate still more strongly the contrast between Tolstoy's artistic temperament and Turgeneff's phlegmatic nature.[3]

[2] Turgenev, *Pis'ma*, 8: 129. Two years earlier after reading only the first two parts of the book, Turgenev had made the same complaint in separate letters written on the same day (Mar. 25, 1866) to both Annenkov and A. A. Fet.

[3] Cited in Knowles, p. 344. Note that the contrasting of Tolstoy (or Dostoevsky) with Turgenev was quite commonplace at this time: Tolstoy and Dostoevsky were seen as the unruly spirits, while Turgenev was considered the real artist. Of course, the other tradition of Tolstoy versus Dostoevsky is still with us today.

But N. N. Strakhov's recollections of his collaboration with Tolstoy in preparing *Anna Karenina* for publication in book form contradict this anonymous reviewer's comments:

> As far as my corrections went, which concerned only language, I noticed one peculiarity which, although it wasn't unexpected to me, nevertheless was very pronounced. Leo Nikolaevich firmly defended every last word he had written and did not agree even to what seemed to be the most innocent changes. From his explanations, I became convinced that he values his language to an unusual degree, in spite of the apparent nonchalance and unevenness of his style. He thinks about every single word, every single turn of phrase no less than the most punctilious poet.[4]

It is evident, therefore, that the repetitions were deliberate and that the violation of the "nice points" arose not from disregard but from a conscious strategy. While some critics saw his disregard of narrative conventions, style, structure, and even content as deliberate means to achieve calculated ends, others saw these "deviations" as the sign of Tolstoy's incompetence as a writer of fiction. This disparity of opinion made any relation between Tolstoy's particular use of repetition and his ideas difficult to perceive. Further obscuring the significance of repetition in Tolstoy was the fact that during the age of realism, discussion of literary technique was held in low esteem. Only with the advent of the modernist interest in language and the relation between form and content did Tolstoy's use of repetition become a focal point for theoretical inquiry.

The earliest critic to pay attention to repetition in Tolstoy's work was D. S. Merezhkovsky, whose three-volume work comparing and contrasting Dostoevsky and Tolstoy as men,

[4] Cited in the Norton Critical Edition of *Anna Karenina*, p. 753.

artists, and religious thinkers appeared in 1901 and 1902. In *L. Tolstoy and Dostoevsky* Merezhkovsky draws mostly on examples from *War and Peace* to show how Tolstoy uses repetition to represent and underscore themes, and more importantly in Merezhkovsky's analysis, to strengthen readers' impressions of both the physical and related spiritual traits of individual characters. According to Merezhkovsky, repetition is critical to Tolstoy's artistic method of moving from the external to the internal, from the bodily to the spiritual.[5] On the murder of Vershchagin in *War and Peace*, Merezhkovsky writes: "Not a word about the inward, psychic state of the victim, but in five pages the word thin is repeated eight times in various combinations—thin neck, thin legs, thin boots, thin arms—and this outward sign fully depicts the inward state of Vereshchagin, his relation to the crowd."[6]

Like Merezhkovsky in his analysis, Viktor Shklovsky also focuses attention on Tolstoy's epithet-like repetitions in *War and Peace*; he even discusses many of the same examples, including Princess Bolkonskaia's downy little lip, Vereshchagin's thin neck and fox fur, and Speransky's white hands. In his study, written during the 1920s, entitled *Material and Style in Lev Tolstoy's Novel "War and Peace,"* Shklovsky, a leading formalist theoretician and critic, discusses Tolstoy's use of repetition as primarily a device of characterization and defamiliarization (Shklovsky's designation for an artistic technique that renews perception of familiar objects by removing them from their usual contexts). Also writing on the murder of Vereshchagin, Shklovsky observes: "Let us notice here the repetition

---

[5] Cf. Boris Sorokin's discussion of Merezhkovsky's comments on repetition in Tolstoy in his *Tolstoy in Prerevolutionary Criticism*, pp. 215–19.
[6] Merezhkovsky, p. 144.

of the phrase, 'the young man in the fox fur'—it is repeated eight times. The phrase, 'slash him!' is repeated four times. Already the very fact of the repetition of a thing, the repetition of a word removes it from the line and estranges it."[7]

A broader look at the various roles repetition plays in *War and Peace* is taken by R. F. Christian in his *Tolstoy's War and Peace: A Study* (1962). Christian, whose approach is descriptive rather than empirical, examines repetition in *War and Peace* as a mnemonic, structural, and characterological device, and notes that in his novel Tolstoy repeats themes, aspects of characterization, and situations from his earlier works. Sydney Schultze, in his 1982 study entitled *The Structure of "Anna Karenina,"* devotes a chapter to a discussion of Tolstoy's use of language, including his use of repetition. Schultze points to Tolstoy's use of repetition to connect clauses and sentences; to explain, simplify or contrast terms or concepts; and to rivet the reader's attention to the concept expressed. He also notes that the repetition of verbs like "to know," "to feel," and "to remember" is characteristic of Tolstoy's style, but he does not try to explain what substantive significance these particular repetitions might have. For Schultze, it is Tolstoy as hedgehog who relies on repetition, along with metonymy and accretion, to create "a certain world in *Anna Karenina*" and Tolstoy as fox who uses contrast and irony to "provide counterpoint on all levels."[8] For me, repetition, which often works side-by-side with these other devices, reflects both of Tolstoy's impulses.

Repetition as the embodiment of these dual impulses seems to be at the root of Sergei Bocharov's view as laid out in his 1987 study, *Roman L. Tolstogo "Voina I Mir."* Bocharov shows

[7] Shklovsky, *Mater'ial i stil'*, p. 96.
[8] Schultze, p. 158. For the hedgehog/fox dichotomy see Introduction, note 2.

how in *War and Peace* Tolstoy uses repetition to connect separate episodes and characters in order to illuminate fundamental human situations. Thus, Bocharov seems to appreciate the unity in diversity that Tolstoy tries so hard to represent and that George Steiner, in his *Tolstoy or Dostoevsky*, sees as the link between Tolstoy's poetics and metaphysics. The reason for the recurrence in Tolstoy's oeuvre of decisive motifs, themes, and actions, Steiner asserts, is that "the quest for unity, for the revelation of total meaning, underlies Tolstoy's art even where his sensuous perception is most enthralled by the boundless diversity of life."[9] Repetition, which suggests a unity where other elements of the narrative emphasize diversity, helps Tolstoy create artistic representations that capture both universal and particular aspects of human experience.

These artistic representations have been compromised at times by translators. Repetitions in Tolstoy are considerably greater in number, and therefore more compelling, when reading his works in the original Russian. If we believe Strakhov's assertion that Tolstoy "thinks about every single word, every single turn of phrase," it becomes particularly lamentable that translators have tended to smooth over his at times awkward and ungrammatical prose by, among other editorial gestures, removing many of his repetitions. Both interesting and amusing in this context are Iurii Olesha's comments concerning Tolstoy's infamous style:

> It's strange that, existing in plain view, so to speak, of everyone, Tolstoy's style with its piling up of coordinating subordinate clauses (several "thats" ensuing from a single "that"; several subsequent "whiches" from a single "which") is, in essence, the only style in Russian literature characterized by freedom and by a dis-

[9] Steiner, p. 243.

tinctive incorrectness, and up to the present time, despite the demand that young writers write in a so-called correct way, no one has yet given an explanation of just why Tolstoy wrote incorrectly. It would be necessary (and it's odd that up to the present time it hasn't been done) to write a dissertation about the distinctive "ungrammaticalness of Tolstoy." Someone observed that Tolstoy knew about his violation of syntactic rules (he spoke constantly of having a "bad style") but that he felt no need whatsoever to avoid these violations—he wrote, it's said in this observation, as if no one had ever written before him, as if he were writing for the first time. Thus, even Tolstoy's style is an expression of his rebellion against all norms and conventions.[10]

Following the famous steeplechase scene in *Anna Karenina*, in which Vronsky breaks the back of his horse, Anna tells Karenin about her involvement with Vronsky. Later she tries to convince herself that with the truth out in the open things will become easier for her:

> After her husband left her, she told herself she was glad that everything would now be *defined*, and at least there would be no lies and deceit. There seemed to her to be no doubt that her situation would now be *defined* for good. It might be a bad one, this new situation, but it would be *definite*, and there would be no vagueness and lies. The pain she had caused herself and her husband by having said these words would now, she thought, be compensated for by the fact that everything would be *defined*. That evening she saw Vronsky, but did not tell him what had passed between her and her husband, although for the situation to be *defined* it would be necessary to tell him [3, 15].

In this passage the word "defined" (*opredelitsia*) is repeated four times and a related form, "definite" (*opredelenno*), appears once.

---

[10] Olesha, pp. 402-3.

As all too often happens, well-intentioned translators "improve" on Tolstoy by substituting synonyms for his repetitive use of the same word. Here, for example, is Alymer Maude's translation of the passage just cited:

> After he left her, she told herself that she was glad she had told him, that now everything would be *definite*—at any rate, the falsehood and deception would no longer exist. She thought it quite certain that her position would be *cleared up* for good. Her new position might be a bad one but it would be *definite*, and there would be no vagueness or falsehood. The pain she had inflicted on her husband would now, she thought, be compensated for by the fact that the matter would be *settled*. She saw Vronsky that same evening, but did not tell him what had passed between her and her husband, though he would have to be told before her position could be *settled*.[11]

[11] Here is the passage in the original Russian: "Posle togo kak muzh ostavil ee, ona govorila sebe, chto ona rada, chto teper' vse *opredelitsia*, i po krainei mere ne budet lzhi i obmana. Ei kazalos' nesomnennym, chto teper' polozhenie ee navsegda *opredelitsia*. Ono mozhet byt' durno, eto novoe polozhenie, no ono budet *opredelenno*, b nem ne budet neiasnosti i lzhi. Ta bol', kotoruyu ona prichinila sebe i muzhu, vyskazav eti slova, budet voznagrazhdena teper' tem, chto vse *opredelitsia*, dumala ona. V etot zhe vecher ona uvidalas' s Vronskim, no ne skazala emu o tom, chto proizoshlo mezhdu eiu i muzhem, xotia, dlia togo chtoby polozhenie *opredelilos'*, nado bylo skazat' emu."

David Magarshack translates the passage this way: "After he left her she told herself that she was glad, that now everything would be *resolved* and at least there would be no more lying and deception. It seemed to her absolutely certain that her position would now be *cleared up* for good. It might be bad, this new position of hers, but it would be *clear*; there would be no vagueness or falsehood about it. The pain she had inflicted on herself and her husband in uttering those words would be compensated for now by the fact that everything would be *settled* unequivocally. She saw Vronsky the same evening, but did not tell him what had passed between her and her husband, though *to clear up* the position she should have told him."

Constance Garnett is the most true to the original repetition with her translation: "After her husband had left her, she told herself that she was glad, that now everything was made *clear*, and at least there would be no more lying and decep-

In this version the key repeated phrase is translated three different ways. The force of Anna's efforts to persuade herself that the situation will straighten itself out and our sense that these words express Anna's own thoughts, rather than the narrator's, are thus diminished. Eliminating the repetition obscures not only Tolstoy's use of narrated monologue, but the incantatory nature of Anna's words as well.[12] Because of this kind of "correction" by a good stylist, readers of Tolstoy's works in English are less likely to appreciate the significant role repetition plays in Tolstoy's writing. Repetitions in Tolstoy figure not only as important details of the narrative—of plot, character, and theme development—but constitute notions of how the world in which we find these details works, as well.

Development as an End in Itself

In a draft introduction to *War and Peace* Tolstoy writes: "No matter how much I tried at first to devise a novelistic plot and denouement, I became convinced that it was not within my means and decided, in describing these characters, to surrender to my habits and strengths. I tried only to give each part of my work its own independent interest [which was contained not in the development of events, but in the development]"(13,

---

tion. It seemed to her beyond doubt that her position was now made *clear* forever. It might be bad, this new position, but it would be *clear*; there would be no indefiniteness or falsehood about it. The pain she had caused herself and her husband in uttering those words would be rewarded now by everything being made *clear*, she thought. That evening she saw Vronsky, but she did not tell him of what had passed between her and her husband, though, to make the position *definite*, it was necessary to tell him."

[12] I return to this passage for further analysis in Chapter 2. See also Gary Saul Morson's explanation for this sort of repetition in *Mikhail Bakhtin: Creation of a Prosaics*, pp. 335–37.

55). Tolstoy subsequently crossed out the bracketed part of this quotation;[13] apparently dissatisfied with his articulation of his thought, Tolstoy nevertheless seems to want to suggest that the interest of his fiction is contained not in the events themselves, but in how these events are narrated, in the process of development. Tolstoy sees a world in which "events" do not neatly divide into discrete and unified wholes, but have ineradicable roots in the past and certain, if not always clear, implications for the future. Meaning is generated by relations, by similitudes, which are the effect of repetition. The real life of any individual, for Tolstoy, is not composed of events with determinable beginnings and endings, as conventional novelists and historians would have it, but is an ongoing stream of experience, thoughts, emotions, and memories ordered, to a greater or lesser extent, by human consciousness. N. G. Chernyshevsky in a review article entitled "Childhood and Boyhood: The

[13] Throughout my book I make use of Tolstoy's letters, diaries, and drafts (and here even a crossed-out portion of a draft). I am, of course, aware of Tolstoy's concern for his "unpublished" papers. On Aug. 25, 1909, he made the following request in his diary: "Something very important. Although this is very immodest, I can't help writing down that I earnestly beg my friends, who collect my notes and letters and write down my words, not to attach any significance to what I have deliberately not committed to print.... Every person is weak and at times expresses things that are downright stupid, but people write them down and then make too much of them, as though they were a most important authority" (57, 124). I am also aware of Nabokov's scathing remarks in the introduction to his translation of Pushkin's *Eugene Onegin* concerning the use of manuscript materials: "Rough drafts, false scents, half-explored trails, dead ends of inspiration, are of little intrinsic importance. An artist should ruthlessly destroy his manuscripts after publication, lest they mislead academic mediocrities into thinking that it is possible to unravel the mysteries of genius by studying canceled readings. In art, purpose and plan are nothing; only the result counts" (15). Notwithstanding his comments, Nabokov does discuss the draft variants of many lines and stanzas in *Eugene Onegin*, leading me to believe that they must have had some meaning for him. As for my own use of Tolstoy's letters, diaries, drafts, etc., I rely on them as support, not as primary evidence, for interpretations based on my reading of his fictions.

Military Tales," which appeared in the *Contemporary* in 1856, was the first to call attention to Tolstoy's skill at communicating the dynamic workings of the human psyche, which he termed "the dialectic of the soul [mind]":

> He [Tolstoy] is interested in observing how an emotion, which has arisen directly from a given situation or impression, submitting to the influence of memories and to the power of associations, both supplied by the imagination, turns into other emotions, again returns to the former initial point and again and again wanders, changing along the entire chain of memories.[14]

Throughout his life Tolstoy's artistic commitment, which expressed his belief that the aesthetic and the ethical are conjoined in "good" art, was to the truthful depiction of life with all its loose ends, chance occurrences, and prosaic details.[15] In a letter to the prolific novelist, short-story writer, and critic P. D. Boborykin in July or August of 1865, Tolstoy wrote: "The goal of an artist is not indisputably to resolve a question, but to compel a love of life in all its innumerable, inexhaustible manifestations" (61, 100). His ambition to depict life "in all its innumerable, inexhaustible manifestations" led Tolstoy to what might be called novels of length.

[14]Chernyshevsky, pp. 246–47.

[15]My use of the word "prosaic" here is directly related to the concept of prosaics as developed by Gary Saul Morson and Caryl Emerson in their book *Mikhail Bakhtin: Creation of a Prosaics*. Morson and Emerson use this term to refer to both an approach to prose and a view of the world focusing on the prosaic and messy events of daily life. See also Morson, *Hidden in Plain View*; "Prosaics: An Approach to the Humanities"; "Prosaics in *Anna Karenina*"; and "Prosaic Chekhov: Metadrama, the Intelligentsia, and *Uncle Vanya*."

Novels of Length

By "a novel of length" I mean something more than merely a long novel. A novel of length is one that does not just happen to be long, but one for which length is essential because of the particular nature of the themes and ideas that structure its plot. *Remembrance of Things Past* is clearly a novel of length, and so is *Anna Karenina*, but *Les Misérables*, which is longer than *Anna*, is not. In novels of length characters' mental actions and reactions are not merely the machinery that propels the plot, but are themselves the subject of the narrative. The effects of memory, imagination, and awareness over time on understanding as a continual process are foregrounded. Gary Saul Morson makes a similar observation when he explains that "[o]ne of the reasons Tolstoy's novels are so long is precisely that his art is centered on the depiction of minute changes in consciousness, on the tiny alterations that ultimately determine everything."[16]

Tolstoy himself spoke on at least two known occasions of his desire to write a *roman de longue haleine*, literally, a "novel of long breath." In an 1862 letter to Sonya's sisters, Tolstoy wrote: "To tell the truth, my little journal is beginning to be a burden, especially its requirements: students, corrections, et cet. And so I long now [to write] a free work *de longue haleine*—a novel or something" (60, 451). And many years later in an 1891 diary entry he wrote: "and then I began to think how good it would be to write a novel *de longue haleine*, illuminating it with my present view on things. And I thought that I could unite in it all my projects which I regret not having executed" (52, 5). As E. G. Babaev explains, for Tolstoy the "novel

---

[16]Morson, *Hidden in Plain View*, p. 221.

of long breath" was not so designated because of the number of volumes it contained, but because of the substance and precision of its creative conception.[17]

One of Tolstoy's artistic concerns as a novelist of length is to make room in his narratives for the details of the continuous stream of life that many conventional narratives ignore: details that have no apparent consequences or further implications, but for Tolstoy have their own intrinsic value as part of this stream. And Tolstoy is particularly intrigued by how our minds choose among, shape, and recall the details that translate into our very identities. These mental processes involve the interplay of experience both as a storehouse of remembered impressions, feelings, and thoughts, and as direct participation in present events. It is in part the recording of this interplay and of the ongoing change and development to which it leads in characters that necessitates the length of *War and Peace, Anna Karenina,* and *Resurrection.* Repetition helps Tolstoy in the successful creation of novels of length by offering readers memorable scenes that relate to each other in complex and decisive ways. These scenes are memorable not only because of the particular effectiveness of the repetition in the context of the scene, but also because of the relation between the scene and the larger text, a relation suggested or emphasized, at least in part, by the repetition.

When, in a famous scene from *War and Peace,* Prince Andrei Bolkonsky travels to his Riazan estates, he is less morbidly dissatisfied with life than he had been one year earlier. But he remains cynical about the possibility of ever again experiencing love and happiness. Along the way he passes a gigantic oak, which alone among the trees in the forest has not yet begun to

[17]Babaev, p. 137.

turn green and whose aspect seems to confirm Andrei's somber thought:

> This was a huge oak, double the compass of both arms, with branches evidently long ago broken, and broken bark overgrown with old defects. With its huge, awkwardly and unsymmetrically sprawling and gnarled arms and fingers, it stood like an old, angry, and scornful monster among the smiling birches. Only it alone didn't want to submit to *spring's* charm and didn't want to see either *spring* or the *sun*.
>
> "*Spring*, and love, and happiness!" this oak seemed to say, "Aren't you tired of that same stupid, senseless *deception*! Always the same and always a *deception*! There is no *spring*, no *sun*, no happiness.... And so I stand and don't believe in your hopes and *deceptions*" [2, 3, 1].

The narrator begins this passage with apparently objective description of an oak tree, then moves almost imperceptibly into subjective description that seems to capture Andrei's point of view, and this description is followed by the direct quotation of what the tree, in Andrei's imagination, is thinking and feeling. Andrei identifies with the tree and the attitude it seems to express as if it offers independent confirmation of the soundness of his attitude: "'Yes, this oak is right, a thousand times right,' thought Prince Andrei. 'Let others, young people, fall for this *deception*, but we know life—our life is finished!'" The repetition, however, of the words "spring" and "sun," linking the subjective description with the quotation, and later "deception," linking what are ostensibly the tree's sentiments with Andrei's, suggests the extent to which Andrei projects on to the tree his own thoughts and feelings.

Tolstoy shows us in this scene how one's mood alters the point of view with which one interprets experience. Our emo-

tions and images, he suggests, are not separate from our interpretations of the world: they are critical to the way we think
about experience. Here, as is often the case, repetition is both
cognitively significant, since it helps readers to understand
what Andrei has renounced and why, and affectively significant, since it imitates the intensity of his emotion. Andrei's
conclusion, reached as he stands before the tree, that he should
just live out his life (*dozhivat' svoiu zhizn'*) without causing any
harm, repeats a declaration he made to Pierre a year ago: "I am
alive and that's no fault of mine, and so I have somehow to live
out my life as best I can until death [*dozhit' do smerti*] without
disturbing anyone" (2, 2, 11). By means of this repetition, Tolstoy joins a present moment with a moment in the past, helping readers to perceive the separate links in the chain that is
Andrei's life. Whether or not Andrei himself is recalling the
words he spoke to Pierre, readers are reminded of that momentous exchange between the two friends about the value and
meaning of life: an exchange which ended with the narrator's
assertion that "the meeting with Pierre marked an epoch in
Prince Andrei's life: though outwardly his life was the same,
inwardly a new life began for him" (2, 2, 12). Paradoxically, we
are allowed to sense that newness through repetitions.

   About a month after his first encounter with the oak tree,
on his return journey, Andrei passes the same tree now thick
with foliage: "The old oak, wholly transformed, spreading out
a tent of lush, dark green, was drooping and slightly swaying in
the rays of the evening sun. Neither the gnarled fingers, nor
the defects, nor the old sorrow and distrust—none of this was
visible" (2, 3, 3). Significantly, the season is spring, and Easter,
the central feast of the Russian Orthodox Church, is not long
past. Indeed, it may be close to Trinity Week, which was the

most important celebration of spring vegetation in Russia.[18] Both spring and Easter, of course, are symbolic of renewal, resurrection, rebirth, as well as of the cyclical repetition, in nature or through sacrament, that sustains life. At first Andrei does not recognize the oak, since he is expecting to find the dour and scarred tree whose image he carries in his memory. Then he realizes that the tree he is now admiring is the very oak he passed on that day in May:

> "Yes, this is that same oak," thought Prince Andrei, and there came upon him *suddenly [vdrug]* a groundless vernal feeling of joy and renewal. All the best moments of his life *suddenly* and at the same time came to his mind. Austerlitz with its lofty sky, the lifeless, reproachful face of his wife, Pierre on the ferry, the girl thrilled by the beauty of the night, and that night, and the moon—all this *suddenly* came to his mind.
>
> "No, life *is not finished* at thirty-one years of age," *suddenly*, definitively, and irrevocably decided Prince Andrei.

The repetition of "suddenly" four times in this passage strongly communicates the great impact the recognition of the oak tree has on Andrei, as well as the extraordinarily rapid and involuntary activity of his mind. Andrei does not consciously and deliberately cull this list of memorable events from the vast contents of his memory; associative mechanisms not under his conscious control are imperceptibly at work. Here and in countless other passages, Tolstoy successfully communicates the existence of mental processes of which we cannot be aware, but whose results do become the object of our awareness. Once the list is made not only Andrei, but readers too, can reflect on what the connection among these events might be.

[18] Ivanits, p. 9.

Tolstoy wisely leaves it to readers to articulate for themselves an answer to this question.

When Andrei comes upon the oak tree for the second time, the tree has undergone an actual physical transformation, but Andrei's experience of the tree on both occasions is a function not only of the tree's objective physical appearance, but also of the thoughts, memories, and feelings that course through his mind as he gazes upon it. This time, the tree's vernal regeneration is in accord with Andrei's own sense of rejuvenation. Once again, he projects his own feelings—renewed energy and hope—onto the tree, and once again the tree acts as a stimulus to his thought and emotion. The oak tree becomes for Andrei, and for readers, too, a kind of symbol of his own transformation.

If Andrei's earlier pessimistic perception of the tree confirmed his conviction that for him "life is finished," his optimistic perception now of the transformed tree lets him assert unequivocally that his "life is not finished." Here Tolstoy uses repetition *with a difference* to mark changes in Andrei that have occurred slowly over time. The differences between what are recognizable as two opposing faces of a single term—between the exhausted tree and the revived tree, between the denial of life and the affirmation of life—serve as the correlative of the shift in Andrei's attitude. By repeating the images of the tree and of life as something that is either finished or not finished in these two separate passages, Tolstoy concretizes Andrei's change of heart in a way that would not be possible if he simply told us of this change without relating it to Andrei's own perceptions. Repetitions that allow readers to see the connections among separate scenes demonstrate Tolstoy's concern with depicting the development of character, plot, and theme as a process. The two scenes in which Andrei sees the oak tree form a kind of unity, but both resonate with other scenes as well. Repetition, which allows us to join separate moments by similarity rather than contiguity, plays a crucial role in the movement of the narrative. Something must be ended before it can be repeated, and yet the fact of repetition, of memory, ensures a living on, so that repetition implies both continuity and discontinuity.[19] Tolstoy uses repetition to suggest a continuum of related experiences that have no identifiable beginning or end and of whose relation Andrei only gradually becomes aware. Recognizing and understanding the connections among the details of experience is as much a task for readers as it is for Andrei.

The Experience of the Reader

In formulating basic principles for the composition of short prose narratives, Edgar Allan Poe relates the writer's aims directly to the brevity of the form: "If any literary work is too long to be read at one sitting, we must be content to dispense with the immensely important effect derivable from unity of impression—for, if two sittings be required, the affairs of the world interfere, and everything like totality is at once destroyed."[20] Poe stipulates that readers' memory is responsible for securing a "unified impression," but adds that when memory fails, the poet is to be blamed for creating a work of exces-

---

[19] Regina M. Schwartz identifies this double aspect as "one of the chief ironies that inhere in the notion of repetition" (122).

[20] Poe, p. 365.

sive length. In the *Poetics* Aristotle similarly states: "As therefore, in the case of animate bodies and pictures a certain magnitude is necessary, and a magnitude which may be easily embraced in one view; so in the plot, a certain length is necessary, and a length which can be easily embraced by the memory."[21] Tolstoy would probably have agreed that a single impression is suitable for a short work and requires brevity. In a draft for an introduction to *War and Peace* Tolstoy tries to explain the generic nature of his composition:

> the offered work is not a tale. In it no single thought is being adhered to; nothing is being proved; no single event is being described; even less could it be called a novel, with a plot, an interest that becomes more and more complicated, and a happy or unhappy denouement with which the interest of the narrative is destroyed [13, 54].[22]

He goes on to say that he tried to give each part of his work its own independent interest, and in another draft asserts:

> My aim is to describe the life and encounters of certain people in the period 1805 to 1856. I know that if I were exclusively occupied with this task and if my task were executed under the most advantageous conditions, I should still hardly be in a position to fulfill my aim. But were I fulfilling it as I would like, I am convinced and would strive to ensure that interest in my narrative would not end with the achievement of the intended epoch. It seems to me that if

[21] Aristotle, p. 24.

[22] In a letter to his editor M. N. Katkov, Tolstoy writes: "As much as I tried, I couldn't write an introduction that I liked. The essence of what I wanted to say lies in the fact that this work is not a novel and not a tale and does not have the kind of plot whose interest is destroyed with its denouement" (Jan. 3, 1865; 61, 67). Note also Tolstoy's criticism of *Boyhood* in a diary entry for December 19 and 20, 1853: "For a work to be attractive it is not enough that it be governed by a single thought; it must be wholly imbued with a single feeling. That wasn't the case with my *Boyhood*" (46, 214–15).

my work has interest, then it will continue, and will be satisfied in each part of this work, and that owing to this peculiarity it cannot be called a novel [13, 56].

Here and in his execution not only of *War and Peace*, but of *Anna Karenina* and *Resurrection* too, Tolstoy seems to amend Poe's argument: brevity is suitable for creating a single impression, but *length is suitable for conveying a sense of the world that requires multiple impressions*. It is needed to evoke the experience of development in process and over long periods of time. After all, "the affairs of the world intervene" not only between sections of reading but also in the concerns of our real life. We follow no concern, however important, without interruptions, whether for other concerns or for sleep. A novel of length makes this experience of continuity across interruptions part of its own prosaics.

Just as characters must work to connect the details or parts of their experience in order to achieve an understanding of their lives as wholes that are never quite whole, readers, too, as co-creators of the literary text, must work to make sense of the continuously developing whole of the text. Tolstoy demonstrates the importance for both his characters and his readers of a constant double vision backward and forward in order to achieve a sense of the continuity and potential wholeness of experience. Tolstoy uses repetition to depict the experience of his characters as they undergo this process of development that involves perceiving the relations that constitute the whole and to ensure that his readers will have a similar experience. Repetition for both characters and readers brings order into something which may in immediate experience be largely disordered.

In his description of the retreat of the Russian army after the loss at Shevardino in *War and Peace,* Tolstoy uses a cluster of repeated images to follow the course of Pierre's thoughts as he participates in and observes the preparations for the next battle. As we read this scene, we watch Pierre make connections among, and begin to draw conclusions from, his impressions and thoughts. Leaving Mozhaisk in order to press closer to the field of action, Pierre walks past the cathedral set at the top of a hill "where a service was taking place and *the bells for church were ringing*" (3, 2, 20). As he begins to descend out of town, Pierre finds himself caught between a fresh cavalry regiment also descending the hill and a train of carts carrying the wounded ascending the hill. Studying the wounded men, Pierre notices that "almost all of them *stared* with naive, childlike curiosity at [his] *white hat and green swallow-tailed coat*." He is forced to stop and observe the scene from the side of the hill as the "cavalry regiment with its songs" goes by: "Because of the slope of the hill the sun did not reach the hollow of the road and it was cold, damp here; above Pierre's head was the bright August morning and the *ringing of the bells* resounded cheerfully."

The sights and sounds, especially of the wounded, suggest to Pierre that here he may find the answer to the question that has been occupying him. To understand what question this is, readers have to return, as Pierre's thoughts have returned, to the events of the previous day. Upon his arrival the day before in Mozhaisk, Pierre had been amazed at the number of soldiers in the town and had been caught up by the mood of restless agitation and anticipation. Looking about, he had recalled the feeling of wishing to sacrifice something that had overcome him ten days earlier when the Tsar had made an appearance at the Sloboda Palace, and he had experienced again a pleasant feeling of consciousness that everything that constituted people's happiness, the comforts of life, wealth, even life itself, was nonsense which one would gladly throw away in comparison with what . . . With what, Pierre couldn't give himself an answer, but he didn't even try to understand for whom and for what he found a special charm in sacrificing everything. He was not concerned with why he wanted to sacrifice; the sacrifice itself afforded him a new joyous feeling [3, 2, 18].

This is not the first time, nor is it the last, that Pierre wonders about what seems to him to be something profoundly and eternally significant "in comparison with" other more trivial, ephemeral, or finite matters. The phrase "in comparison with" (*v sravnenie s*) becomes a repeated sign of his yearning for sure answers to the seemingly unanswerable questions that life continually poses.

Pierre's recall of his question, as the fresh troops pass in one direction and the wounded in the other, sets in motion both in his mind and readers' minds a train of related thoughts and images. Notably, Tolstoy does not explicitly restate the question in this scene; he leaves it to readers to figure out what Pierre is thinking about at this moment. From their first introduction to Pierre, readers have watched as he has struggled to articulate what it is he needs to know and understand in order to live life with some degree of contentment. The repetition of key phrases such as "in comparison with" and "for what reason" (*zachem*), and of other details that are part of Pierre's memory and thought, is both the form and content of the depiction of Pierre's journey towards greater knowledge and understanding. So now on the morning of the 25th of August, one day after his arrival in Mozhaisk and ten days after the Tsar's appearance at the Sloboda Palace in Moscow, Pierre stands against the side of the hill and becomes totally immersed in the multiple and varied sensations that surround him:

> The cavalry singers were passing close by the cart. "Akh, za-pro-pa-la . . ." They made up a soldier's dance song. As if echoing them, but with a different kind of cheer, the metallic sounds of the bell ringing clanged from on high. And with yet a different kind of cheer, the hot rays of the sun spilled over the top of the opposite slope. But under the slope, by the cart with the wounded, alongside the little horse, next to which stood Pierre, it was damp, gloomy, and sad.

The same contrast of light and dark, warmth and cold that was noted earlier is evoked again here. It is not just the sights and sounds, but the contrasting sensations that create the atmosphere in which Pierre and readers, vicariously, find themselves.

After the road has cleared Pierre continues on his way:

> Pierre drove on, looking along both sides of the road, searching for familiar faces and encountering everywhere only the unfamiliar military faces of men from various branches of the service, uniformly *staring with surprise at his white hat and green swallow-tailed coat.*

At last Pierre recognizes an acquaintance, a doctor, coming along the road from the opposite direction. The doctor's dire predictions for the upcoming battle act as a catalyst for Pierre's thoughts:

> Pierre was struck by the strange notion that of the thousands of men, alive, well, young and old, who had *stared with cheerful surprise at his hat*, twenty thousand, probably, were doomed to be wounded or die (maybe those same he had seen).
> "They may die tomorrow; why do they think about something other than death?" And suddenly by some mysterious association

of thoughts, the descent from the Mozhaisk hill, the carts with the wounded, the ringing of the bells, the slanting rays of the sun, and the songs of the cavalrymen vividly recurred to him.

"The cavalrymen go into battle and meet the wounded and never for a minute think about what awaits them, but pass and wink at the wounded. And of all of them, twenty thousand are doomed to die, yet they are *surprised at my hat!* Strange!" thought Pierre as he continued on his way to Tatarinovo.

Pierre is puzzled by the soldiers' ability to think of something other than the possibility of their own death. Continually returning in his mind to the image of their amused surprise at his hat and coat, he tries to understand what accounts for this apparent lack of fear and concern. Because we as readers have experienced along with Pierre, and through his perspective, the sights, sounds, and sensations of the troop movements, Pierre's "mysterious association of thoughts" seems to catch an experience familiar to us all. Tolstoy's careful and precise repetition of the details of Pierre's perception ensures that we not simply read about Pierre's mental replay of these details, but re-enact it. Throughout this scene repetition serves not only to trace the movement of Pierre's memory and thought, but to reinforce in readers' own minds the images that so impress Pierre. The repetitions seem to slow down perception of details that are set before readers' analytical attention and help Pierre's and their imaginations alike integrate experience. By means of repetition both Pierre and readers apprehend meaning as both construct and process.

As the chapter ends Pierre watches a group of peasant-soldiers work to secure their positions on the battlefield: "seeing these peasants, obviously still amused by their new military positions, Pierre again recalled the wounded soldiers in Mozhaisk, and he understood what the soldier wanted to express when he'd said, 'They want to attack with the whole nation.'" Earlier in the day a wounded soldier had expressed this view to Pierre and "in spite of the incoherence of the soldier's words, Pierre understood everything he wanted to say and nodded his head in agreement." Twice we read that Pierre understands the soldier's words, but never are we told exactly what it is he understands.

The work readers must do to make sense of Pierre's ongoing experience deepens their understanding of the questions Tolstoy explores through Pierre and increases their sense of involvement with the text. At the end of this scene questions remain unanswered for both Pierre and readers, but as events continue to unfold both will also find that the impressions that were gained and the ideas that began to take shape in this experience figure prominently in their ever-evolving sense of the whole. Within this scene repetition is a means of focusing readers' attention on objective facts that become full of subjective emotional and psychological significance for Pierre. Repetition also connects the scene back to earlier scenes, and later, future scenes will connect back to this one. The total effect is to keep readers continually involved with Pierre's continually developing thoughts and emotions.[23]

Pierre's experience on the Mozhaisk hill both triggers memories of earlier experiences and plays a role in shaping

[23] In her study of devices that create involvement in discourse Deborah Tannen writes: "The varied purposes simultaneously served by repetition can be subsumed under the categories of production, comprehension, connection, and interaction. The congruence of these functions of discourse provides a fourth and over-arching function in the establishment of coherence and interpersonal involvement" (48).

later experiences. Repetition of details from one scene to another indicates to readers the connections that Pierre makes among his separate experiences, and demonstrates Pierre's effort to achieve a sense of the whole by relating separate moments. Within an individual scene, repetition establishes the separate moments as significant, distinctive, and memorable in their own right. Operating on the principles of emphasis and relation, repeated elements help to create, call attention to, and underscore the relations that structure not only the text as an ensemble of characters, events, motifs, and themes, but individual scenes as micro-ensembles as well. Repetition in Tolstoy effects the continual knitting together, by readers as well as characters, of the new and the old, the familiar and the strange, the past and the present, in ongoing processes of development. And repetition plays another key role: for reading itself, as Tolstoy understood, partakes of repetition.

Reading as a Kind of Repetition

For Tolstoy each experience in the world is irreducibly particular, and the true artist—like Mikhailov and unlike Vronsky in *Anna Karenina*—sees the particularity of the experience, what makes it not just a repetition of other experiences. That is why what one needs to be an artist is not mechanical talent, but an eye, a keenly sensitive and discerning awareness: "If what he saw had been revealed to a little child or to his cook, they too would have been able to remove the shell from what they saw," thinks Mikhailov (5, 11). And with regard to his picture of Pilate's admonition, Mikhailov is quite certain and pleased that "no one had ever painted a picture like it" (5, 10).

Why is he so sure? Because his work is so irreducibly particular in the feelings and situation conveyed.[24]

Of course, the generalities of experience are rather easily conveyed in discursive language with all its abstractions; whereas particularities, if they are not to become mere instances of well-known generalities, can only be conveyed by the artist who is alert to them. If properly conveyed, readers will feel that the experience has happened to them and that it had to be that way. Recall Vronsky's reaction to Mikhailov's portrait of Anna:

> "One needed to know and love her as I love her to find that most sweet soulful expression of hers," thought Vronsky, though he had only come to know that sweet soulful expression of hers through the portrait. But that expression was so true that it seemed to him and to others, that they had known it for a long time [5, 13].

Readers will experience something new because they repeat more or less the author's experience. More or less, because they relate that experience to their own earlier ones, and so the meaning of the same experience is different for each reader. This feeling on the part of readers that they have not merely perceived, but experienced, even created, something new is what Tolstoy calls aesthetic feeling and attributes to the "infectiousness of art." Art is infectious when "it evokes in the spectator, the hearer, or the reader, those feelings which the artist experiences" (29, 13). Tolstoy's theory of infection is

---

[24] In his study of the relation of time to narrative form and to an ethical dimension of the literary experience, Gary Saul Morson notes Bakhtin's recognition that human conduct cannot adequately be transcribed in general terms because of its "irreducibly particular" and "unrepeatable" character (*Narrative and Freedom*, 22), and goes on to explain how this recognition ties in with Bakhtin's concept of eventness and account of creativity.

fully and clearly articulated in *What Is Art?* (which appeared in 1898), but the idea and its concomitant suggestion that art is essentially a matter of repetition (or something approaching it) are evident in Tolstoy's earliest writings about art.

Throughout his life, Tolstoy commented extensively in diaries, letters, prefaces and afterwords, drafts, notes, and articles on the relationship between authors and readers, or, more generally, between artists and audiences. Although he took no active part in the aesthetic disputes between the radical and conservative critics that raged especially virulently in the 1850s and 1860s, Tolstoy was critical of the radicals' demand that literature display themes of social and political relevance and shared the conservatives' belief in the autonomy of art. In an 1858 letter to his friend V. P. Botkin, a spokesman for art-for-art's-sake theory and an "aesthetic" critic, Tolstoy wrote:

> What would you say when at the present time a political, dirty stream wants resolutely to gather into itself everything and if not destroy, then dirty, art, what would you say about people who, believing in the independence and eternal nature of art, would make up their minds to prove by deed (that is, by art itself as word) and by word (criticism) this truth and save what is eternal and independent from the incidental, biased, and predatory political influence? Couldn't we be these people? That is, Turgenev, you, Fet, me, and all who share and *will* share our convictions [60, 248].

In the same year Tolstoy wrote in his diary, "The political excludes the artistic, since the former, in order to prove, must be one-sided" (48, 10). Tolstoy's letters and diaries from these years suggest that he was more influenced by what impressed him as art, whether Russian or European, than by any political or social tendency. While the focus of the aesthetic debates of the 1850s and 1860s was the nature of art and the proper relationship between art and reality,[25] Tolstoy's focus was and remained the relationship between artist and audience. As G. N. Ishchuk asserts: "Tolstoy always reflected a great deal on the reader, wrote much about him, and above all, always strove to imagine him as a participant in the creative process. That is why the problem of the reader's perception proves to be connected to his fundamental philosophical-aesthetic inquiries and constructions."[26]

Already in his first published work (*Childhood*, 1852), repetition emerges as a key ingredient in Tolstoy's efforts to guide readers' response and to involve them in the realization of his intention.[27] Repetition, for Tolstoy's readers as well as for his characters, involves recognition of the repeated and discovery of the new.[28] With repetition Tolstoy encourages independent, active readers whose own impressions and past experiences contribute to their understanding of characters and conflicts: he attempts in effect to construct his own ideal reader. As Seymour Chatman and Wolfgang Iser among others have pointed out, every text has its implied reader: that reader which, implied by the language the author uses, is an internal structure of the text. Chatman defines the implied reader as "the audience presupposed by the narrative itself."[29] The desired audience stance is made explicit when there is a narratee-

[25] Moser, p. xiv.

[26] Ishchuk, p. 17.

[27] See for example Gareth Williams's analysis of the repetition of the detail of Karl Ivanych's red cap (59–61).

[28] This phrase—recognition of the repeated and discovery of the new—is Mikhail Bakhtin's and is taken from a passage in "From Notes Made in 1970–71," in which Bakhtin is anxious to establish the ethical, as well as intellectual and emotional, nature of "understanding."

[29] Chatman, p. 150.

character, but can only be inferred on ordinary cultural and moral terms when there is no clearly depicted narratee. According to Iser, "the concept of the implied reader designates a network of response-inviting structures, which impel the reader to grasp the text."[30]

From the very beginning of his literary career Tolstoy envisioned an ideal reader, or what he called an "imaginary reader." His conception of this ideal, or imaginary, reader seems to have been shaped at least in part by his admiration for certain Enlightenment values, such as the improvement and welfare of the individual, respect for the power and limits of both reason and the emotions, and art as the transmitter of moral thought and feeling. Although in his later years Tolstoy conceived of the moral in more and more narrow terms, his literary works before 1880, and some even after this time, embody a broader view of the moral as that which guides people towards a humane and responsible reconciliation of their individual needs and desires, beliefs and ideals, with the inescapable fact of their communal nature. Confident throughout his life of the moral power of "good" art, Tolstoy sought a balance between controlling his readers and encouraging their free and active participation in the meaning of the text. Tolstoy's sense of the need to strike such a balance is curiously echoed by, on the one hand, Wayne C. Booth's observation that "every literary work of any power—whether or not its author composed it with his audience in mind—is in fact an elaborate system of controls over the readers' involvement and detachment along various lines of interest,"[31] and on the other, Iser's comment that "A literary text must ... be conceived in such a way that it will en-

[30] Iser, *The Act of Reading*, p. 34.
[31] Booth, *The Rhetoric of Fiction*, p. 123.

gage the reader's imagination in the task of working things out
for himself, for reading is only a pleasure when it is active and
creative."[32] For Tolstoy, as for other writers before and after
him, the problem was how to establish a mutual understanding, a reciprocity of emotional, intellectual, and moral response
with persons never seen.

In an address to his readers intended as a chapter for *Childhood* but omitted in later published editions, Tolstoy lists the
traits he requires in his readers and notes that the most important of these is that readers be "understanding":

> In order to be accepted among my chosen readers, I require very
> little: that you be sensitive, that is, you are able to feel pity from
> the heart and even shed a few tears for a fictional person whom
> you love, and to rejoice from the heart for him and not be
> ashamed of this; that you love your memories; that you be a relig-
> ious person; that you, reading my story, search for those places
> that touch you in the heart, and not those that make you laugh;
> that you not despise out of envy a good circle, even if you don't
> belong to it, but look on it calmly and impartially—I will accept
> you among the chosen. And the main thing is that you be an *un-
> derstanding* person, one of those people to whom, when you meet,
> you see that it is not necessary to explain your feelings and your
> inclinations, because you see that he understands you, that every
> sound in your soul is echoed in his.... The main indication of un-
> derstanding people is consonancy in relations—they don't need
> clarifications, explanations, but it is possible with complete confi-
> dence to communicate the most unclear, in terms of expression,
> thoughts. There are such subtle, elusive relations of feeling, for
> which there are no clear expressions, but which are understood
> very clearly. It is possible to speak boldly with them [understand-

[32] Iser, "The Reading Process," p. 51.

ing readers] about these feelings and relations by means of hints and agreed-upon words [1, 208].[33]

It would seem from reading Tolstoy's description that he seeks readers who are just like him: who share the same values and are as sensitive and reflective when they read as he is. Also discernible in this passage are two ideas which later became the basis of Tolstoy's aesthetic theory as expounded in *What Is Art?*: the idea of art as communication and the idea that what art communicates is feeling.[34] Or as Tolstoy put it in his treatise:

> art is one of the means of communion of people among themselves.... The peculiarity of this means of communion, distinguishing it from communion by means of words, consists in this, that by words a person communicates thoughts to another, by art people communicate their feelings to one another [30, 63–64].

But Tolstoy's concern went beyond readers' sensibility. About the same time that *Childhood* was published (in the fall of 1852 in the *Contemporary*) and having begun work on *The Raid*, the first of his Caucasian tales, Tolstoy articulated his ideas about other aspects of the author-reader relationship in an essay entitled "Notes About the Caucasus: A Journey to Mamakai Iurt," which was never published. In this essay Tolstoy recalls his first experience of the Caucasus and the tremendous gulf between the expectations, with which the Caucasian stories of Russian authors, such as Marlinksy and Lermontov, had filled

[33]Ishchuk aptly suggests that Tolstoy's term "understanding" (*ponimanie*) is the first phenomenological and terminological step towards the term he would later use to denote one of the characteristics of art, "infection" (*zarazhenie*) (22).

[34]Others, too, have noted the consistent line of attitudes from *Childhood* to *What Is Art?* See, for example, Edward Wasiolek, "A Paradox in Tolstoi's *What Is Art?*" and Rimvydas Silbajoris, *Tolstoy's Aesthetics and His Art*.

him and the reality. This gulf becomes the starting point for
Tolstoy's discussion of the effect of poetic images on readers,
the role of readers' imagination and memory in aesthetic perception, and the gap between language and what it seeks to express.

Tolstoy begins by describing how his earliest literary impressions of the Caucasus were transformed over time by his
imagination and memory into still more pleasurable impressions:

> But this was so long ago, that I remembered only that poetic feel-
> ing, which I had experienced while reading, and the poetic images,
> which were called up.... These images colored by memory took
> shape in a singularly poetic way in my imagination. I forgot al-
> ready long ago the poems of Marlinsky and Lermontov, but in my
> memory, other poems, a thousand times more captivating, have
> been formed from these images [3, 215].

Still recalling his own experience as a reader of romantic tales
of the Caucasus, Tolstoy describes the process of give-and-take
that constitutes the act of reading:

> Without trying to understand the sense of each phrase, you con-
> tinue to read, and from some words intelligible to you, a com-
> pletely different sense comes into your head; true, it is unclear,
> vague, and inexpressible in words, but therefore all the more beau-
> tiful and poetic [3, 215].

In other words, since he could not always receive an image, an
impression, directly from the author's words, his own creative
faculties came to his aid. But, Tolstoy continues, as difficult as
it is to convey poetic images via words, which he implies is
what the Romantics were trying to do, it is yet more difficult
to convey reality: "The true transmission of reality is the

stumbling stone of the word. Perhaps the imagination of the reader completes the insufficiencies of the author's expression. Without this assistance how commonplace and colorless all descriptions would be" (3, 216). And to transmit the reality of the Caucasus is Tolstoy's stated intention: "You will have to renounce many still resounding words and poetic images if you want to read my stories. I wish for you, as for me, that in place of what is lost there will arise new images, which will be closer to reality and not less poetic" (3, 216). Sensitive to the way readers recreate or formulate texts and aware of the role their reactions and judgments play in literary reception, Tolstoy asks for readers' conscious assistance in creating a new method of "realistic" representation.

Even as he recognizes and encourages the participatory role of readers' imagination, however, Tolstoy cautions authors about its volatility. In the second edition of *Childhood* Tolstoy writes: "The imagination is such a lively, capricious faculty that it is necessary to treat it very carefully. One unsuccessful hint, one incomprehensible image, and all the charm produced by a hundred beautiful, true descriptions, is ruined" (1, 178). For Tolstoy, a critical task of the writer is to find the right balance between too much detail and not enough: "The art of writing well for a sensitive and intelligent person consists not in knowing what to write, but in knowing what not to write. No brilliant additions can improve a composition as much as deletions can improve it" (Oct. 16, 1853; 46, 285). The author's sense of proportion is critical if readers are to feel that they participate in a work's creation: "About a sense of proportion in art: it's the absence of proportion that exposes to view the producer of art, and therefore destroys the illusion that I [that is, the reader] am not perceiving, but creating" (Nov. 1, 1908;

56, 156). Tolstoy is critical of Shakespeare in part because, he argues, Shakespeare denies spectators this feeling:

> One may, without breaking the illusion, not fill in a great deal: the reader or spectator himself will do the filling in, and sometimes as a result the illusion is even strengthened for him; but to say what is superfluous is like breaking up a statue made up of parts, or taking the lamp out of a magic lantern. The attention of the reader or spectator is distracted, the reader sees the author, the spectator the actor, the illusion disappears, and to restore the illusion again is sometimes already impossible. And that's why without a sense of proportion there cannot be an artist, especially a dramatist. Shakespeare is entirely devoid of this sense [35, 251].

In other words, it is the author's task, according to Tolstoy, to write in such a way that readers experience in reading a text what the author experienced in writing it: to create the illusion for readers that they are creating and not just perceiving.

At times, then, Tolstoy places the responsibility for the successful realization of a text squarely with the author, seeking to define as it were the ideal author. Other times, however, Tolstoy emphasizes the role of the ideal reader who is capable of experiencing what the author has experienced. Writing to his friend Botkin in the summer of 1857, Tolstoy explains what he hopes will occur between himself and his reader:

> You know my belief in the necessity of an imagined reader. You are my favorite imagined reader. Writing to you is as easy as thinking; I know that every one of my thoughts, every one of my impressions is apprehended by you more purely, more clearly, and more elevatedly than it is expressed by me.... I only wish that when I write, the other person, a kindred spirit, would rejoice at what I rejoice at, would be angry at what angers me, or would cry

with the same tears with which I cry. I don't know the need to say something to the whole world, but I know the pain of solitary pleasure, crying, suffering [60, 214].

From either perspective what Tolstoy seems to be saying is that readers' experience ought to repeat the author's experience. Reading becomes then, for Tolstoy, essentially a kind of repetition.

Barely perceptible in all of these passages is Tolstoy's anxiety about having control over his reader. But the tension between the reader's freedom and the author's control that hovers over Tolstoy's fictional works is precisely the force that maintains his labyrinthine architectonics;[35] it is a tension born of the author's pulling his reader along on a search where the main points along the way may be clearly indicated, but the paths between and among them must be newly charted with each reading. In a diary entry for December 19, 1900, Tolstoy observes: "An artist, in order to act upon others, must be a searcher, so that his work is a searching. If he had found everything and knows and teaches everything, or purposely interferes, he does not act [upon others]. Only if he searches does

---

[35] In a well-known letter to Strakhov about *Anna Karenina* in particular and art in general, Tolstoy himself uses the image of the labyrinth: "In everything, almost everything, I have written, I was guided by the need to bring together ideas linked among themselves in order to express myself, but every idea, expressed by itself in words, loses its meaning, is terribly debased, when taken alone out of that linkage in which it is found. The linkage itself is not constituted by an idea, I think, but by something else, and to express the basis of this linkage directly in words is quite impossible; but it is possible only indirectly—in words describing images, actions, situations.... Now, it is true, when nine-tenths of everything published is criticism, then for the criticism of art, people are needed who would show the senselessness of the search for ideas in an artistic work and would continually guide readers in this endless labyrinth of linkages in which the essence of art consists, and to those laws which serve as a foundation for these linkages" (Apr. 23, 1876; 62, 269).

the viewer, the listener, the reader merge with him in his searches" (54, 74).

Over and over again Tolstoy articulates his view that aesthetic perception involves the apprehension by the audience of
the artist's feeling such that the audience and artist become
one. As he explains in *What Is Art?*: "The main peculiarity of
this [aesthetic] feeling is that the perceiver merges with the artist to such a degree, that it seems to him that the perceived object has been made not by someone else, but by himself, and
that all that which is expressed by this object is exactly what he
had been wishing to express (30, 149).[36] We may recall that this
aesthetic feeling is exactly what Vronsky experiences when he
sees Mikhailov's portrait of Anna in *Anna Karenina*. And in a
1909 diary entry, just a year before he died, Tolstoy elaborates
this view further:

> A work of art is only real when the perceiver cannot imagine any
> more than that which he sees or hears or understands. When the
> perceiver experiences a feeling similar to reminiscence, that this,
> he says, already was many times, that he knew this long ago, only
> wasn't able to say, but now himself has said. Mainly, when he
> feels that that which he hears, sees, and understands could not be
> any different, but has to be just as he perceives it. If the perceiver
> feels that that which the artist shows him could be different, if he

[36] In the continuation of this passage the essentially religious function Tolstoy
was assigning to art by this time (1897) emerges: "A real work of art destroys in
the consciousness of the perceiver the division between himself and the artist, and
not only between himself and the artist, but also between him and all people who
perceive the same work of art. In this freeing of the individual from his separation
from other people, from his isolation, in this merging of the individual with others, lies the main attractive force and virtue of art" (30, 149). Richard Gustafson,
who argues for the predominance of a religious viewpoint in all of Tolstoy's writings, asserts that for Tolstoy aesthetic experience is a form of religious experience
to the extent that "in the aesthetic moment we all become aware that we belong
to each other right here, right now" (372).

sees the artist, sees his tyranny, then this is no longer art [Oct. 14; 57, 151].

The aesthetic feeling Tolstoy describes is similar to the feeling of free will he sets forth in the first epilogue of *War and Peace*: in each case external constraints and influences seem nonexistent and all power of creation or action seems to emanate from the self. That is, there are external constraints, but they are not sensed as such. Again we see that for Tolstoy aesthetic perception feels like a repetition: that which is perceived makes so much sense (not necessarily logical) that it seems familiar. This conception, which recreates the sense of recollection, is similar to Platonic idealism, in which true knowledge is apprehended by reminiscence. But whereas the Platonic experience is of something absolutely general, the Tolstoyan is of something irreducibly particular; the Platonic is of the timeless, the Tolstoyan of the timely and local. And whereas Plato literally believes that we knew mathematical knowledge, forgot it at birth, and then remember it, Tolstoy speaks of readers' *sense* of recollection, which is in fact an illusion. Readers have not remembered the author's experience, but they experience it *as if* they had.

According to Tolstoy real art can be distinguished from its counterfeit, because real art is always infectious. The infectiousness of art guarantees a union between artist and audience based on the feelings transmitted by the work of art. But just because all art is infectious does not mean that all art is good; Tolstoy sets as an important condition for "good" art that it communicate something "new." As Tolstoy's use of repetition in his fictions indicates, Tolstoy knew very well that repetition and novelty are not mutually exclusive. The novelty in repetition comes from that which is superadded by a different and unique perspective or point of view whether in time, place, or mental constitution. Infection theory posits that in reading, readers' experience repeats the author's experience, but not completely, since we relate what we read to our own compass of experience. Tolstoy's insistence upon the merging of audience and artist is important because it suggests the value he placed on readers' experience, on involving readers in the production of the text's potential.[37] In his critical and theoretical remarks Tolstoy continually refers to the feeling that is communicated by a work of art as the essential point of contact between artist and audience. Of course, Tolstoy's fictional works elicit an entire spectrum of human response—intellectual, psychological, moral as well as emotional. Once contact is established and as long as it is maintained, then, for Tolstoy, readers fill in as it were the shell of what is shared with that which is generated by the uniqueness and particularity of the individual.

Tolstoy knew from his own experience as a reader and a writer that the impressions and images called up during reading are mediated by imagination and memory, that readers bring

[37] In an article about the changes that Tolstoy made between the original version of Part One of *War and Peace* (published as *The Year 1805*) and its later revision, N. M. Fortunatov asserts, "Rejecting authorial explanations, Tolstoy strives to ensure that the reader's thought works strenuously. And, indeed, the reader co-supplies [*sopostavliaet*] the facts, gropes for the connection between them, guesses at the reasons for their being. At these moments of involvement with the book, the reader becomes, to a certain extent, the artist's 'co-author'" (73). And L. Kuzina and K. Tiun'kin cite Tolstoy in their assessment of his relationship with his reader: "Reflecting upon how to approach the sources of the psychic process, watching for the very moment of its conception and tracing it to its conclusion, not discarding everything that is pre-logical, unconscious, that has yet to become a thought or a word, wishing 'to tell those secrets, which it is impossible to tell by words alone' (53, 94), Tolstoy more and more often arrives at the notion of the 'reader-creator.'... Reading something artistic, he must not only perceive what is written, but also create together with the author, 'merging with him in inquiry' (54, 74)" (94).

their own experience, including knowledge of the conventions of reading and the literary tradition, to what they read and that a sense of any text as a whole rests upon a construct of these impressions and images mediated by individual experience and imagination. For Tolstoy, the imagination is the eye capable of perceiving the relations that constitute the whole. But he also maintained that the starting point for aesthetic perception was the reader's sympathy with the author (or with his/her characters): the reader's experience of the feelings experienced by the author (or his/her characters) such that a unity—a unity in diversity—would be established between reader and author. In an article entitled "The Tolstoy Connection in Bakhtin," Caryl Emerson uses this phrase—unity in diversity—to explain Bakhtin's distinction between monologism, which he associated with Tolstoy, and dialogism, which he associated with Dostoevsky:

> Dialogism alone allows for the restoration of a larger, inclusive unity in diversity.... In a dialogic universe, inclusive unity is celebrated by the fact that truth about the world is linked with specific position, with truth for the individual personality.[38]

A Bakhtinian unity in diversity stresses the potential for a mutually enriching exchange among multiple consciousnesses; a Tolstoyan unity in diversity stresses the potential for the human sympathy and understanding that derives from the sameness of experience. These conceptions are not in opposition to one another, but while the former emphasizes the unique and individual, the latter emphasizes the shared. If Bakhtin meant to oppose any insidious collective mentality that might swallow up the individual, Tolstoy was critical of what he per-

[38] Emerson, "The Tolstoy Connection in Bakhtin," p. 69.

ceived as a spreading egoistical individualism that threatened the fellowship of human beings. Both men were wary of the intolerant, absolutist, and reductionist points of view that either extreme tended to foster.

Tolstoy expects readers' experience to repeat that of the author in the sense that he expects them to recognize and sense the familiarity of the feelings being communicated. The commonality of experience, made possible by imagination, which allows us to see in the particular what is universal (that is, it allows us to recognize a cat as a cat or sadness as sadness), is the basis for the universality Tolstoy demanded of good art. This sameness, however, is not an objective fact: we cannot be certain that one person's experience of objects, qualities, or concepts is identical to that of another. And it is this uncertainty that guarantees the individuality which Tolstoy also demanded of good art.[39] Tolstoy's fictional works reveal repetition, and the perceptual parallax it embodies, to be the quintessential enactment of the paradox of universality and individuality.[40] The term "parallax" is more commonly associated with discussions of astronomy than of literature and refers to the apparent displacement of an object as seen from two different points. I use it here to refer to the difference in perceptions and memories that differences in perspective across time, space, and persons can make. Thus, the term "parallax" quite aptly captures the sameness and difference that repetition can embody and antici-

[39] Cf. Friedrich's intuition that it is the "dynamic verbal counterpoint between uncertainty and harmony [that] largely creates the sense of beauty" (22).

[40] Cf. Wasiolek, "A Paradox in Tolstoi's *What Is Art?*" in which the author explores the paradox underlying Tolstoy's conception of good art: "the paradox that art is universal, general and specific, and that it communicates what is the same and what is different" (586).

pates the discussion that follows on the diversity and multiplicity of perspectives. Repetition as the embodiment of sameness and difference is not only the underlying principle of Tolstoy's theory of reading, but is one of the key devices Tolstoy uses to stimulate readers' memories and imaginations and at the same time guide their response.

The Irony of Perspectives

Repetition seems indispensable to narrative texts since it is crucial to readers' being able to remember and piece together even the most basic elements of plot, character and theme. But some writers—Dickens, Trollope, Zola, and Tolstoy, for example—rely more heavily on the device of repetition than others. And for Tolstoy, recurrences, or repetitions, are more than just an artistic device, since, as I have already noted, the fact of repetition is directly related to his understanding of how human beings structure and give meaning to their experience. Perhaps the most remarked-upon kind of repetition in Tolstoy is the repetition of descriptive details of character: Princess Bolkonskaia's "downy upper lip" in *War and Peace* is as ubiquitous in the criticism on the novel as in the text itself. Other well-known examples include Princess Marya's luminous eyes, Anna Karenina's little hands, and Maslova's shiny black eyes and full bosom in *Resurrection*. The repetition of such physical details underscores their significance: readers are meant to read character from or into these attributes, which become synecdoches for characters' entire moral, intellectual, or spiritual being. In Tolstoy's fictional world, repeated physical traits, as Merezhkovsky observes, "superficial and insignificant as they may seem, are really bound up with deep-seated and important inner spiritual characteristics of the characters."[41]

The literary ancestry of this type of repetition goes back, of course, to the Homeric epithet.[42] In epic the source of authorial knowledge is not questioned and epithets are taken to designate permanent, objective, and general qualities. "The stability of epithets in epic works," suggests Boris Uspensky, "could be considered as a formal characteristic of the description of an object not simply as it appears, but as it really is (not of its appearance, but of its essence)."[43] According to Christian, Tolstoy's repeated attributes differ from Homeric epithets in that they are not intended as mnemonic aids and they are not mere generalizations.[44] The repeated reference to some external detail "is a combination of the assertion of a permanent, individualizing feature with the expression of a moral judgment. As well as suggesting what is most significant about his heroes, Tolstoy tries to evoke in the reader at the same time a positive or negative response to them."[45] Christian's account of this particular use of repetition in Tolstoy may be too simple: he does not, after all, seem to take into account the fact that an external attribute which becomes a repeated element of a character's representation is witnessed by other characters and the narrator, and that this act of witnessing is the starting point of evaluation or commentary, by means of which readers then arrive at a moral judgment. Usually this type of repetition in

---

[41] Merezhkovsky, p. 143.
[42] For an excellent discussion of the epithets in Homer, see Paolo Vivante, *The Epithets in Homer: A Study in Poetic Values.*
[43] Uspensky, p. 169.
[44] Christian, p. 148.
[45] Ibid., p. 149.

Tolstoy serves to bring out something about the relationship between one character and another or others, about the effect or influence of one character on another or others. Also, I believe these repetitions do serve as mnemonic aids in the sense that when they are spread over several chapters or even volumes, each particular instance recalls past instances to readers' mind, and it is readers' memory and imagination that draw connections and make comparisons among the separate instances. It may be true that repeated external attributes do not serve to remind readers of which character is which or who a character is, but they do play a role in readers' coming to know and understand characters in a deeper sense than mere identification. And this process of coming to know depends upon readers' memory and imagination.

Like Homeric epithets, Tolstoy's repeated physical traits seek to capture an essential attribute of a character and guide the attention of readers to a focus. But unlike Homeric noun-epithets, which tend to secure an image of a particular character or thing, Tolstoy's character-attribute complexes not only identify or evoke particular characters, but also play a role in reflecting how characters perceive one another. Repeated physical traits may be as significant for what they suggest to readers about the characters who bear them as about the characters, including the narrator, who observe them. Designation, impression, and moral judgment are all merged into a single form of expression. In fact, it is important to note the irony—the result of individual, subjective points of view—that often attaches to these Tolstoyan repetitions. The repeated element is sifted through numerous perspectives: through the perspective of one character, then another, with a changing role for the authorial perspective; and through a series of changing circumstances.

Because it depends on context for its meaning, a Tolstoyan epithet captures only one dimension of a character from one possible point of view at a time. This one dimension and this one point of view resonate in readers' memory with other dimensions and other points of view as they become known. The result is an irony of perspective that contributes to the complexity of the character. Readers are infected with—repeat—characters' experiences and learn from sharing their experiences. The repetitions allow for this sharing, but also for comparison. Differences among individual characters' perceptions of the same event or person create an irony of perspectives for readers. By means of this irony of perspectives, Tolstoy draws attention to the ineluctable link between point of view and understanding: understanding for Tolstoy is particular.

Princess Lise Bolkonskaia is introduced to readers at Anna Pavlovna's soiree in the opening chapters of *War and Peace* as the "most bewitching woman in Petersburg." Her one flaw—the shortness of her upper lip which causes her mouth always to appear half open—is also the distinctive feature of her beauty, according to the narrator whose "as always" claims a certain expertise in this area:

> Her pretty *little upper lip, just slightly blackened with tiny mustache hairs*, was short over her teeth, but was all the more charming when it was lifted and still more charming when sometimes it was drawn down and fell over her lower lip. *As always* with quite attractive women, her defect—the shortness of her lip and her half-open mouth—seemed to define her own particular beauty [1, 1, 2].[46]

[46] My translation of this passage seems to be unique, especially as regards the underlined portion of the first line. In the original Russian this line reads: "Ee xoroshen'kaia, s chut' chernevshimisia usikami verxniaia gubka byla korotka po

The narrator goes on to assert that "everyone" delights in watching Lise and "everyone" feels more amiable after talking to her. Readers, however, discover in the very next chapter that in fact not everyone is charmed by the Princess: her own husband, Prince Andrei, is bored and annoyed by her. In fact, later, when Andrei and Lise argue in front of Pierre about Andrei's intention to take a more active role in the war, her raised lip gives her face "not a joyful, but a bestial, squirrellike expression" (1, 1, 6). For the men who admire and flirt with Lise at social gatherings, her short upper lip with its tiny mustache hairs is a sign of her feminine and winsome charm and vitality. But Andrei, put off by the false and ostentatious show of Petersburg social life, finds her behavior exaggerated and unnatural. Each time readers encounter Lise's little lip, they see the same lively and pretty young woman, but in a new and different context. The sense of recognition and familiarity that readers experience encourages their involvement and interest in what is being portrayed, while taking account of changed circumstances adds to their understanding of and sympathy for Lise, who at first seems little more than the insipid and frivo-

---

zubam, no tem milee vytiagivalas' inogda i opuskalas' na nizhniuiu." Constance Garnett translates the first line this way: "Her pretty little upper lip, faintly darkened with down, was very short over her teeth, but was all the more charming when it was lifted, and still more charming when it was at times drawn down to meet the lower lip." And Ann Dunnigan translates it this way: "Her pretty little upper lip, shadowed with a barely perceptible down, was too short for her teeth and, charming as it was when lifted, it was even more charming when drawn down to meet her lower lip." If here and elsewhere these translators refer euphemistically to the hairs on Princess Bolkonskaia's lip as down, I prefer to render Tolstoy's "little mustache hairs" literally, not only because I want to preserve the diminutive and plural form of the word, which contributes to the mental image it creates, but to try to reflect Tolstoy's direct and precise, even if sometimes awkward or wordy, formulations.

lous creature Andrei accuses her of being. The use of diminutives to describe Lise's distinctive trait—"little lip" (*gubka*) and "tiny mustache hairs" (*usiki*)—and the narrator's frequent designation of her as "the little Princess" (*malen'kaia kniaginia*) contributes to readers' sense of her as not only small in physical stature, but rather limited in intellectual capacity. If she is perhaps overly concerned with trivial matters or herself, Lise is nevertheless unfairly and cruelly treated by the Bolkonsky men—Andrei and his father—because of what Andrei finally realizes is her quite innocent gaiety and exuberance.

When Andrei takes Lise to his family's country estate to stay with his father and sister, whom Lise has met only once before at her wedding, she is apprehensive and even fearful of being left to endure pregnancy and childbirth with relative strangers and far from the city. The detail of her little lip is repeated twice in the scene depicting her arrival at Bald Hills. It occurs the first time when the narrator reintroduces her to readers who have not seen her or Andrei for seventeen chapters:

> The little Princess had grown stouter during this time, but her eyes and her *short little lip with its tiny mustache hairs* and smile rose just as merrily and charmingly as ever when she spoke [1, 1, 23].

And we see the lip a second time as Lise launches into a whirlwind summary of recent events a moment after exchanging greetings with Andrei's sister, Princess Marya:

> The Princess spoke incessantly. Her *short little upper lip with its tiny mustache hairs* was continually flying down, where it ought to have been, to touch her rosy lower lip and opening again in a smile of sparkling teeth and eyes [1, 1, 23].

In both of these short passages the narrator makes a new association between Lise's lip and her smile. Her short upper lip is no longer just a sign of her charming beauty, which in fact begins to fade as her pregnancy advances, but of the garrulity and sociability that make it so difficult for her wholly to fit in or be genuinely accepted by the serious and reserved Bolkonsky family. Tightly bound up with her emotion, Lise's little lip becomes associated in the reader's mind with her habitual childlike happiness and frivolity. Tolstoy uses the evaluative word "childlike" frequently to describe the little Princess's behavior and facial expressions.

Also repeated in these chapters are details associated with Princess Marya's representation as a deeply thoughtful, spiritual, and kind individual whose negation of her own feelings and desires is a constant source of unacknowledged oppression. Marya's beautiful and luminous eyes and her heavy tread are repeated details that help to focus readers' impression of her and at the same time act as counterpoints to her sister-in-law's little lip and the vivacity and insouciance it represents. Lise's chatter is essentially ignored by Marya and Andrei, who are occupied with their own reunion. A moment later she bursts into tears, and all her anxiety surrounding her husband's "desertion" of her, which has been masked by her persistently delightful turned-up lip and smile, is revealed.

When months later news comes that Andrei is missing in action, Lise is within days of her delivery. Happy and deeply moved by the baby she feels inside of her, she places Marya's hand on her stomach in order to share her excitement and joy: "Her eyes smiled expectantly and her *little lip with its tiny mustache hairs* rose and remained lifted in childlike happiness" (2, 1, 7). Once again readers see the particular detail of Lise's lip in terms of the emotion she presently feels and communicates and at the same time are reminded of their earlier impressions of her. Ostensibly because of her sister-in-law's fragile condition, but also, clearly, because of her childlike joy and self-absorption, Marya decides not to tell Lise about Andrei's uncertain fate. But Lise is not oblivious to the gloom that envelops the household:

> *"Ma bonne amie"* [my good friend], said the little Princess on the morning of March 19th after breakfast, and her *little lip with its tiny mustache hairs* rose from long force of habit; but as sadness was manifest not only in every smile, but in every word, even in every footstep in that house since the day the terrible news had come, so now even the smile of the little Princess, who was influenced by the general mood—although without knowing its cause—was such as to remind one still more of the general sadness [2, 1, 7].

Lise's habit of turning up her lip so that her face seems always to be smiling acts as a constant reminder to readers that she is a stranger in this family of private and guarded individuals.

As it happens, Andrei returns home just as Lise begins labor. He goes to her room immediately to see her:

> The little Princess lay on pillows, in a white cap (the suffering had just left her); black locks of hair curled around her inflamed, perspiring cheeks; her rosy, charming little mouth with its *little lip covered with tiny black hairs* was closed, and she smiled joyfully [2, 1, 9].

Lise's mouth, usually open, is now closed, but as much pain as she has endured and has yet to endure, she still smiles "joyfully," not because Andrei is alive and has returned, but because that is the way she is. When the actual birth begins, Andrei is asked to leave the room and is only allowed to return after the baby is born and his wife is dead:

> She lay dead in the same position in which he had seen her five minutes ago, and the same expression, despite the fixed eyes and the pallor of her cheeks, was on that charming, childlike, timid little face with its *little lip covered with tiny black hairs* [2, 1, 9].

Up to this point references to Lise's little lip have been (in the original Russian) roughly identical: occasionally the word order has been reversed, a possessive pronoun has been inserted, or the adjectives "short" and "upper" have been added. But now in these two passages instead of the "little lip with tiny mustache hairs" (*gubka s usikami*), we read the "little lip covered with tiny black hairs" (*gubka pokryta chernymi volosikami*). Unfortunately and erroneously, English translations tend to ignore this significant, if subtle change and repeat the same "downy little lip." This deliberate change in words, however, reflects the fact that we now see Lise not from a generalized point of view expressed by the narrator, but from Andrei's particular point of view as it is expressed by the narrator. Even in death her little lip adds to the childlike quality of her face. Note that when Andrei first entered the room and looked upon her, he noticed both "childlike fear" and "childlike reproach" in her eyes. Ironically, it is only after she has died that Andrei and his father are able to express their emotion in a way that would have been familiar to her. At the moment of realization that he has become a father, Andrei begins to cry "as children cry," and old Bolkonsky "sobs like a child" when Andrei finally goes to see him after all that has happened.

Reminders of Lise remain: both Andrei and Marya notice that the sculpted angel in the chapel over her tomb seems to have the same raised upper lip as she (2, 2, 8), and Andrei remarks that his son, Nikolai, raises his lip when he smiles just as his mother used to do (3, 1, 8). The little Princess's raised lip, minus its little mustache hairs—perhaps because of the vitality expressed by this detail—becomes after her death a sign of the guilt and remorse Andrei feels for the way he behaved towards his pretty, young wife. This example clearly illustrates that the repeated physical attribute, in this case Lise's little lip, is not only a detail around which a coherent individuality is constructed, but a detail that provides insight into characters' interrelations. Similarly, the repeated detail of Hélène's impressive shoulders and bosom in *War and Peace* and her designation throughout as "a beauty" (*krasavitsa*) become most meaningful for readers when they are witnessed by and have a profound and disastrous influence on first Pierre and later Natasha.

These repeated details chart a course for readers' moral, aesthetic, and emotional responses, without dictating them. Meaning, knowledge, and understanding are generated instead by the connections and disparities readers observe among separate elements. Characters (and readers) all witness attributes which are visually essentially the same, but carry different emotional, psychological, and moral connotations depending upon the situational context and who does the witnessing. Recurrence of attributes at once reinforces readers' sense of the "reality" depicted in the novel and provides a point of focus for connections and comparisons that stimulate their cognition, insight, and awareness of human values and goals.

Tolstoy's many and diverse writings suggest that he considered the desire to achieve a harmonious and unitary view of the world and one's place in the world to be a most compelling, yet elusive goal. Throughout his life he worked at articulating his belief that a sense of harmony and unity is beyond the grasp of mere reason and logic exercised, as they tend to be, from a single, fixed position. Rather, he tried to suggest, harmony and unity are only discernible to a vision that can accommodate simultaneous yet different views: a multiperspectival vision. Tolstoy's story "From the Notes of Prince D. Nekhliudov, Lucerne," written in 1857, can be seen as an early extended meditation on this very subject. Here, Tolstoy's narrator wishfully exclaims:

> If only man would learn not to judge and not to think harshly and absolutely and not to give answers to questions that have been given to him only so that they may eternally remain questions! If only he understood that every thought is both false and true! False because of man's one-sidedness, his inability to embrace the whole truth, and true because it expresses one side of human aspiration. They have made for themselves divisions in this eternally moving, endless, endlessly intermixing chaos of good and evil; they have drawn imaginary lines over this ocean and they expect the ocean to divide itself just that way. As if there weren't millions of other divisions from a completely different point of view, on a different plane [5, 25].

And in the last lines of the story the humbled narrator observes:

> He gently looks down from His bright immeasurable height and rejoices in the endless harmony, in which you all contradictorily, endlessly move. In your pride you hoped to escape from general laws. No, even you with your small, trivial anger at the waiters, you, too, responded to the harmony-seeking need for the eternal and endless [5, 26].

Much later, in an 1875 letter to Strakhov, in which Tolstoy

shares with his friend what he calls "a sort of introduction to a contemplated philosophical essay," he explains what he considers to be the fundamental idea characterizing the philosophical, as opposed to the scientific, method:

> That fundamental idea is that any (and therefore my) philosophical view taken from life is a circle or sphere, which has no end, middle, or beginning, no most important or least important point—rather, everything is beginning, everything is middle, everything is equally important and necessary—and that the cogency and truth of this view depends on its inner concord, its harmony [62, 225].

As different as these formulations may be, both the passages from "Lucerne" and the passage from the letter suggest that for Tolstoy, a sense of harmony is possible, but only if one's perspective is broad enough: only if one's perspective can appreciate the multiplicity, complexity, and diversity of the parts. Unity, not as definitive arrangement, but as continual rearranging, is to be sought in diversity. Thus, in his artistic representations Tolstoy demonstrates that in perception, any conception of unity is a provisional construct in which the unstable and unfinalizable whole remains greater than the sum of its known parts. What counts for Tolstoy is the process of seeking, of development, of taking into account the endless rearrangement of details over time and across perspectives. In his short stories and novels, Tolstoy frequently depicts his characters creating stories, or narratives, about themselves or other characters. These stories are usually characterized by characters' attempts to achieve a sense of completeness, to see themselves and one another in terms of a kind of harmony and coherence among carefully selected details. But time and time again, characters are disappointed and disillusioned when they realize the disparity between their constructed vision and a complex and not wholly knowable reality that resists totalization. Repetition figures prominently in Tolstoy's depiction of both characters' persistent efforts and their inevitable frustrations.

2. The Structure of Characters' Experience

> The urge to prove that where we intuit unity there really is unity is a deep emotional motive to philosophy, to art, to thinking itself.
>
> —Iris Murdoch

Tolstoy presents us with characters whom we come to know as highly personalized complexes of habits, beliefs, and accumulated experience.[1] Over and over, even less reflective characters modify their concept of self in response to external events and encounters with other characters, and in terms of inner psychological, intellectual, and ethical issues and conflicts. The self for Tolstoy is always becoming, and this is so in part because situations are always changing. As Patricia Carden notes, an "emphasis on growth and formation and the consequent fluid image of the self become a keystone of Tolstoy's vision as artist."[2] And in reference to both Tolstoy's self-depiction in his diaries and his depiction of fictional characters, Boris Eikhenbaum asserts: "The fluidity of human experiences, the unceasing process of movements following and often contradicting one another, forms the essential ingredient in Tolstoy's

---

[1] As Morson notes, for Tolstoy individuals have no center or inner core: they are the accumulation of their habits and thoughts (*Hidden in Plain View* 201, 205).

[2] Carden, "The Expressive Self in *War and Peace*," p. 519.

method of portraying psychic life."[3] But even as he posits human experience as continual flux, Tolstoy insists upon the persistent efforts of human beings to structure and give meaning to that experience. Repetition, with its ability to emphasize, to remind, and to connect, is fundamental to the way we know or understand things. And Tolstoy uses this device, that is, he makes conscious literary use of this fundamental process, in the representation of characters' ongoing efforts to structure and give meaning not only to the separate moments of their lives, but to their experience as a whole that is never quite whole.

Repetition marks the inner speech and thought of Tolstoy's characters as well as the narrator's descriptions of their behavior and thought processes. These two types of repetition function in a variety of ways to achieve a variety of ends. Analysis of them helps us explore those aspects or characteristics of the mind that are implicit in Tolstoy's portrayals, as well as the literary techniques needed to depict those characteristics. Throughout his life Tolstoy sought to understand the nature of the mind and its processes: in his diaries, notebooks, and letters he sets forth models of the mind, considers the mental faculties, and attempts to clarify concepts pertaining to mental life, including consciousness, reason, and will.[4] By stud-

---

[3] Eikhenbaum, p. 40.

[4] For example, in an 1847 diary entry Tolstoy lists what he considers to be the five main intellectual faculties and then proceeds to come up with rules for their development (46, 271).

Faculty psychologies, which reached their greatest influence in the eighteenth century, are philosophical doctrines that ascribe a number of powers to the mind. Normally the mind is assumed to be unitary, but to function via multiple faculties. Already Aristotle worked out a comprehensive and systematic faculty psychology in his work *De anima*. Later Descartes assigned to the soul the sole function of thinking and assigned other faculties to mechanical brain functioning. By the time Locke enumerated the mental powers of the mind in *An Essay Concern-*

ying how Tolstoy uses repetition to represent, to make accessible to readers, the mental life of his characters, we gain insight into Tolstoy's intuitions and ideas about how the mind functions.

Repetition functions in characters' quoted or narrated monologue in several distinct ways. Quoted monologue refers to a character's mental discourse. Narrated monologue, variously known as *style indirect libre, erlebte Rede, nesobstvenno-priamaia rech'*, quasi-direct discourse, or interior monologue, has numerous definitions.[5] Basically, it refers to a type of discourse in which the voice of a character is experienced alongside of or in place of that of the omniscient narrator. Or as Dorrit Cohn explains in his study of narrative modes for presenting consciousness in fiction, narrated monologue is "a character's mental discourse in the guise of the narrator's discourse."[6] Oftentimes characters in Tolstoy isolate an element of their present or remembered experience, assign a verbal expression to that element, and then repeat that expression over and over again in the course of their thoughts—sometimes quoted, sometimes narrated—as they work to understand, define, structure their

---

ing Human Understanding (1690), the acceptance of the existence of faculties had become commonplace; arguments centered not on how many there were, but on whether they were innate or learned. Cf. *Baker Encyclopedia of Psychology* and *Concise Encyclopedia of Psychology.*

   In an 1857 letter to Countess A. A. Tolstaia, his relative and lifelong friend, Tolstoy details an imaginative and eccentric model of the mind, in which he conceives of the mind as a series of drawers, or boxes, all giving out onto a main corridor (60, 228). Tolstoy explains that the drawers on one side contain a person's positive memories and thoughts and those on the other contain the negative. The separate drawers open in response to particular stimuli.

   [5]For a clear and comprehensive discussion of narrated monologue and the confusion surrounding its appellations and definitions, see Rachel May's *The Translator in the Text.*

   [6]Cohn, p. 14.

present. Less frequently, but with equal significance, an element of a character's environment is repeated at the beginning and end of a narrated monologue conveying that character's inner thoughts. The repeated element, ambiguously poised between the narrator's discourse and the character's consciousness, thus acts as a frame for a depiction of the inward-turning mind. And finally, there is the repetition that occurs when characters recall details of past events and encounters recorded in earlier scenes. Repetition as memory joins two or more separate moments of characters' lives, giving Tolstoy the opportunity to depict how characters see and contemplate the continuities and discontinuities of their lives. Readers, too, observe these repetitions, which allow them to measure how a character has changed between two "identical" experiences.

Tolstoy's use of repetition in the narrator's discourse about characters tends most often to characterize their individual habitual manner or to trace explicitly and precisely the movement of their thought. Repetition in characters' own discourse also can communicate information about the pattern, the movement of behavior, thoughts, motives, memories, but only indirectly and never completely, simply because there are certain things human beings do not or cannot observe about themselves. Ordinarily we do not provide commentary on our actions and perceptions: we do not ordinarily say "now I am remembering," we simply remember, or rather, the two are quite different. Via his narrator, Tolstoy provides this commentary, which turns out to be somewhat repetitive.

The four paradigms of Tolstoy's use of repetition briefly sketched above—(1) repetition of a significant element of experience, (2) repetition as frame, (3) repetition as remembered experience, and (4) repetition in the narrator's discourse that records what characters do not observe about themselves—all play a role in the representation of how characters structure and give meaning to experience. The second and third paradigms are distinctive subsets of the first. All of these repetitions, it should be noted, call attention to and describe the form as well as the content of thought. That is important, because usually we do not apprehend the *form* of our thought, unless we are thinking *about* our own thought processes (in which case it is the content). Tolstoy inserts repeated elements into characters' quoted and narrated monologues and into the narrator's descriptions in order to represent, call attention to, and fashion the mental processes, conscious, semi-conscious, and not conscious, involved in creating structure and meaning.

Repetition of Significant Elements of Experience and Repetition as Frame

A Starting Point for Understanding

After his duel with Dolokhov, in the mistaken belief that he has killed his wife's rumored lover, Pierre tries to make sense of the storm of feelings, thoughts, and memories raging in his mind. He isolates his ill-chosen words *je vous aime*, spoken on the night of his engagement to Hélène, as the main cause of his present unhappy situation:

> "But of what am I guilty?" he asked. "Of the fact that you married her without loving her, of the fact that you deceived both yourself and her." And he vividly pictured that minute after supper at Prince Vasilii's when he spoke those words which were not natural to him: *Je vous aime*. "It all started from that! I felt even then," he thought, "I felt then that it was wrong, that I did not have the right to say that. And so it has turned out" [2, 1, 6].

He asks himself repeatedly why he spoke those words *je vous aime*, which he knew "were a lie and still worse than a lie." Reflecting upon that night Pierre feels these words to be worse than a lie because with them he deceived not only Hélène, but himself as well. Attracted by Hélène's physical beauty and sexual charm and knowing the vulgar rumors that surrounded her, Pierre had been unable to sort out his actual feelings before being pressed into marriage. He had preferred to interpret her lack of intelligence and interest as evidence of a special kind of wisdom in the hopes of convincing himself that she was not a "bad" woman, especially since he felt himself helplessly and forcefully joined to her by forces beyond his control. In the end Pierre passively accepted what he saw as the inevitability of his marriage to Hélène:

> [H]e knew that he was bound to say "the one word" that would join him to her irrevocably. Hélène had always been an enigma to him, and now in the aftermath of the duel as his impulsively uttered words sound again and again in his memory, Pierre tells himself, "The whole solution was in this terrible word, that she is a depraved woman: now that I've said this terrible word everything has become clear!" And a moment later he repeats, "I knew she was a depraved woman, but I didn't dare to admit it to myself."

In both these scenes—the initial declaration of love and the recollection of the fateful declaration—Pierre attributes great and independent power to particular words. He seems to feel himself the speaker but not the originator of the words *je vous aime* and "depraved." And in one sense he is right since in both cases he has borrowed these words directly from society's lexicon in an effort to make some sense of his confused thoughts, memories, and feelings. On the night he succumbs to the will of those anxious to see him marry Hélène, Pierre gropes for the appropriate words: "'There is something special they say *on these occasions*' [*v etikh sluchaiakh*], he thought, but could not at all recall what it was they say *on these occasions*" (1, 3, 2). The narrator's repetition of Pierre's exact words seems to suggest the endless replay of this question in Pierre's mind. Repetition here also suggests the idea of fixed expressions even as Pierre looks for one. Thus, there is a shade of irony in his search. Finally he blurts out *je vous aime*, "having recalled what had to be said *on these occasions*."

For Pierre, the scene acted out between him and Hélène becomes one of "these occasions" that requires the words *je vous aime*. But what exactly does Pierre envision when he refers to "these occasions"? He seems deliberately to blur the moral line between a sincere declaration of eternal love and a statement of expediency meant to secure a momentary pleasure. Here, sexual desire has love as its "eulogistic covering."[7] Pierre has found a verbal fig leaf with which to cover the desires and motives he apparently considers unseemly. As Lydia Ginzburg observes: "Why does Pierre years later remember with shame and disgust saying to Hélène, 'Je vous aime'? Pierre torments himself because he, someone of complex spiritual life, used a hackneyed society cliché at a decisive moment; he used it precisely because it was impossible to translate into words what was actually taking place: sensual excitation on the one hand, crass calculation on the other."[8] Pierre immediately feels the inadequacy of these words and is ashamed. His almost frantic repetition of *je vous aime* in this chapter underscores the extent to which the

[7] Kenneth Burke in *A Rhetoric of Motives* defines "eulogistic coverings" as rhetorical concealments of motives (173).

[8] Ginzburg, p. 354.

phrase was at the moment of its utterance unnatural to him and unmotivated by genuine feelings of love for Hélène. For Tolstoy, words that can be cited over and over again, like *je vous aime* or the witty *bons mots* of Bilibin, are empty forms that have no correspondence to "authentic" experience.[9] Only to the extent that experience is free from self-deception and from the deceits and artifices of society can it be, according to Tolstoy, authentic. Pierre seeks temporary shelter from the lustful feeling of which he is ashamed in words proffered and condoned by society. Later, when he can acknowledge Hélène's coarseness and vulgarity, he seizes in the same way upon "depraved" as society's term for such a woman. Pierre's inner thoughts are subjective thoughts that bear the traces of societal and cultural influences.

The repeated words—*je vous aime* and "depraved"—whose social connotations reverberate at this moment with Pierre's inner emotion, memory, and thought suggest the extent to which Pierre's consciousness is not an internal but a boundary phenomenon, hovering uneasily between internal and external worlds. Bakhtin's exploration of the notion of consciousness, or the psyche, as boundary phenomenon has suggestive implications for Tolstoy's portrayals of the individual. As Caryl Emerson explains:

> In the Bakhtinian model, every individual engages in two perpendicular activities. He forms lateral ("horizontal") relationships with other individuals in specific speech acts, and he simultaneously forms internal ("vertical") relationships between the outer

[9]See Morson's discussion of Bilibin's mastery of languages and codes (*Hidden in Plain View* 257–62).

world and his own psyche. These double activities are constant, and their interactions in fact *constitute* the psyche.[10]

Even though Tolstoy may never have articulated the notion so common in our own day that thought is largely social,[11] he does explore in his fiction the relationship among forces external to an individual, forces related to the subjective association of ideas, and forces that remain elusive, and he demonstrates how all of these forces have an immediate influence on experience and a long-term influence on sense of self. Pierre's repeated phrase, *je vous aime*, is the nexus between the forces that act on and through him. The words are at the same time society's prescription for the occasion, Pierre's attempt first to make order and later to make sense of his experience, and an ironic expression of unacknowledged and imperfectly understood desires and motives he wished to quash. Repetition by characters in Tolstoy often functions in this manner. Other examples include Princess Marya's "temptations of the devil" (*War and Peace*), Irtenev's "like my own mother" (*Childhood*), or Ivan Ilych's "pleasant and proper" ("The Death of Ivan Ilych"). Discussing protagonists' use of language in *War and Peace* more generally, Michael Holquist writes: "The language of Tolstoyan heroes is always a kind of pidgin, a creolization of ideologies in which the self is a proportion constantly shift-

---

[10]Emerson, "The Outer Word and Inner Speech," p. 25.

[11]As Clifford Geertz writes, "Human thought is consummately social: social in its origins, social in its functions, social in its forms, social in its applications" (360). And L. S. Vygotsky in his study of the relation between language and thought asserts, "The true conception of the development of thinking is not from the individual to the socialized, but from the social to the individual" (20). Bakhtin in a later essay, "The Problem of Speech Genres," observes: "After all, our thought itself—philosophical, scientific, and artistic—is born and shaped in the process of interaction and struggle with others' thought, and this cannot but be reflected in the forms that verbally express our thought as well" (92).

ing between one's own language and that of others. The voyage of self-discovery on which Pierre is embarked is perhaps best understood as his attempt to find out which of the languages that surround him is his own, which most native to his voice."[12]

In an 1868 letter to his friend M. P. Pogodin, Tolstoy explained that he intended to explore in *War and Peace* the nature of people's freedom and their dependence on their surroundings·

> My thoughts about the boundaries of freedom and dependence and my view of history are not an accidental paradox which merely preoccupied me for a moment. These thoughts are the fruit of all the mental labor of my life and are an inseparable part of my contemplation of the world, which I worked out with a labor and a suffering God alone knows and [which] gives me absolute calm and happiness. And at the same time I know and knew that they will praise in my book the sentimental scene of the young lady, the ridiculing of Speransky, and other such rubbish, which is on their level, and the main thing no one will notice. You will notice and, please, read [it] and write [it] in the margins [61, 195].

And in his article "A Few Words About *War and Peace*," published in *Russian Archive* (*Russkii arkhiv*) in 1868, Tolstoy comments at length on the importance of this theme for his book. Tolstoy relates the theme mainly to how history and historical agents are construed and to the notion of heroism. Speaking, however, more generally, he observes: "To define the boundary of the spheres of freedom and dependence is very difficult, and the definition of this boundary is the essential and sole problem of psychology" (16, 14). Tolstoy's interest in this

[12]Holquist, p. 220.

theme had begun already much earlier and would continue throughout his life. For Tolstoy, a person's environment is determined as much by particular circumstance, events, and other people as by general social and cultural norms of behavior, speech, feeling, and thought. Human beings feel themselves to be free despite the existence of general laws of necessity to which they are subject, argues Tolstoy in the epilogue to *War and Peace.*

A person's words, then, bear the imprint of their socially and culturally determined meanings as well as that of the subjective significance attached to them by the associations, memories, emotions, and motives of the speaker. In using public phrases, or even clichés, we can still express our own thought; this paradox is a sort of linguistic parallel to the determinism/freedom paradox Tolstoy outlines. Repeated phrases in Tolstoy emphasize that what is spoken or thought by individual characters simultaneously conveys public and private meanings. By inserting repeated phrases into characters' speech or thought, Tolstoy illustrates the appropriation and transformation by individuals of public social, cultural, and historical forms and symbols. He depicts the largely unconscious (in the sense of not conscious) continual struggle between freedom and dependence that accompanies efforts to structure and give meaning to one's life.

As Pierre attempts to make sense of his experience, the social meanings of the words *je vous aime* and "depravity" give way to the subjective significance with which Pierre imbues them. For readers, the repeated words simultaneously evoke the emotion-laden and value-charged significance Pierre gives them and the equally value-charged, but not personally so, culturally conventional meaning society has given them. Pierre's repetitive thoughts demonstrate that he has not freed himself from the bonds of society's attitudes and habits. For although he is ready to admit that *je vous aime* was a lie, he continues to rationalize this lie by blaming his wife's "depravity." Pierre's focus on *je vous aime* as the single detail responsible for his unhappiness turns the phrase into a synecdoche for his troubled relationship with Hélène. Via this phrase, which gives expression to his feelings and thoughts as he confronts his present situation, he rationalizes his experience.

In the moments of recollection and self-castigation following the duel, the words *je vous aime* become the particular expression of Pierre's general feeling of anger, pain, and disillusionment. His attribution of all his problems to his having spoken these words is an example of the kind of false reasoning Tolstoy defines in *War and Peace* with his "law of reciprocity":

> A good player who has lost at chess is sincerely convinced that his loss was the result of his mistake, and he searches for that mistake in the beginning of his play, forgetting that at every step in the course of the game there were similar mistakes, that not a single one of his moves was perfect [3, 2, 7].

Tolstoy's point is that the real explanation for an event involves countless factors, many of which cannot or will not be noticed, so that although isolating one factor as the single cause may offer a measure of comfort to the human mind, responsibility and understanding are sacrificed. Because repetition offers the possibility of a syntax of pure emphasis—that is, making a thought, a memory, an emotion intense and solid through persistence—Tolstoy can use repetition to signal the efforts of his characters to determine a single cause or events. Tolstoy's characters frequently rely on repetition as a rhetorical means of persuading themselves of a certain view or explanation.

In Pierre's case every moment spent with Hélène, every glance exchanged, every word uttered or left unuttered is a factor in his present unhappiness. His irrational focus on this one phrase underscores his need to define, to explain at least to himself, his unhappiness. That is, he uses the repeated phrase to reduce the wealth of detail surrounding his courtship and marriage to what he feels is most essential. This narrow focus on one phrase functions, for Pierre, as a means of establishing a point of reference from which some kind of understanding can begin. But at the same time, the phrase continues to represent all the falseness of his relationship with Hélène. Pierre's reiteration of *je vous aime* involves simultaneously a narrowing of attention and an expansion of meaning: the phrase *je vous aime* becomes Pierre's symbol for his failed marriage. As L. S. Vygotsky points out, the basic characteristic of words is a generalized reflection of reality.[13] The words *je vous aime* are Pierre's synecdochic distillation of his own subjective reality. As part of his inner speech, that is, speech for himself, the words condense much thought and emotion into a single verbal phrase. A part of Pierre's initial experience becomes the sign of much more.

Vygotsky describes conceptualization as an intellectual process which "is guided by the use of words as the means of actively centering attention, of abstracting certain traits, synthesizing them, and symbolizing them by a sign."[14] Tolstoy uses repetition to illustrate this very process. In perception—that is, in attaining awareness or understanding—repetition focuses

[13] Vygotsky, p. 153.
[14] Ibid., p. 81.

emphatic attention on the repeated element to the near exclusion of an infinite number of other elements. This point takes us back to Tolstoy's notion of life as a "calculus" of moments, of which only a fraction are actually observable by the human mind.[15] Repetition obscures the heterogeneity of the elements of perception and has the effect of enhancing the significance of the repeated element at the expense of others. The iteration of a word or phrase in characters' speech or thought records their focus on a single element of their experience and its endowment with special significance for them.

Tolstoy's use of repetition also suggests that he knew there was something more to the flow of ideas than just association. For Tolstoy, the model that posits the mind as a bundle of associations could not account for the *growth* of consciousness. His use of repetition suggests the extent to which he saw mind as active in its own formation. Characters direct their mental processes with the aid of the repeated element, which becomes a sign. Thought for Tolstoy is analysis. Michel Foucault posits the reciprocal relation between sign and analysis in a way that Tolstoy might have approved of:

> if one element of a perception is to become a sign for it, it is not enough merely for that element to be part of the perception; it must be differentiated *qua* element and be distinguished from the total impression with which it is confusedly linked; consequently, that total impression itself must have been divided up, and attention must have been directed towards one of the intermingled re-

[15]In a number of ways Tolstoy's understanding of human psychology seems to anticipate that of William James. Here, for example, is what James has to say about the multiplicity of the objects of thought: "The mind is at every stage a theatre of simultaneous possibilities. Consciousness consists in the comparison of these with each other, the selection of some, and the suppression of the rest by the reinforcing and inhibiting agency of attention" (277).

gions composing it, in order to isolate one of them. The constitution of the sign is thus inseparable from analysis. Indeed, it is the result of it, since without analysis the sign could not become apparent. *But it is also the instrument of analysis, since once defined and isolated it can be applied to further impressions* [emphasis added].[16]

Perhaps most interesting of all, Tolstoy suggests that for Pierre not only do the words he repeats become a sign, but the *repetition itself* becomes a sign. Despite his misery, Pierre is not oblivious to the absurdity of his situation:

"Why did I say to her *je vous aime?*" he kept repeating to himself. And having repeated this question for the tenth time, a line from Molière came into his head: *mais que diable allait-il faire dans cette galère?* [But what the devil was he doing in that galley?], and he began to laugh at himself [2,1, 6].

This line that makes Pierre laugh is from Molière's *Les Fourberies de Scapin.*[17] Géronte, father of Léandre, repeats these words seven times in one scene as he incredulously questions Scapin about a misadventure that has befallen Léandre. Pierre has presumably recalled not only the line, which captures all of Géronte's frustration and anger, but the comically repetitive repetition of the line as well. Thus his own repetition becomes a sign of his own frustratingly absurd situation. In *Laughter: An Essay on the Meaning of the Comic,* Henri Bergson cites this

---

[16]Foucault, p. 16.

[17]The quotation is listed in Bartlett's *Familiar Quotations* along with three allusions to it in other works, including Tolstoy's. In Cyrano de Bergerac's *Le Pedant Jouie* one finds: "Que diable aller faire aussi dans la galère d'un Turc? d'un Turc!" [What the devil did he want on board a Turk's galley? A Turk's!] Bartlett next cites Tolstoy's use of the quotation in *War and Peace* and then adds that the quotation is often misquoted "in that gallery," as in Charles Dickens's *A Tale of Two Cities:* "What the devil do you do in that gallery there!"

very scene from Molière's play as an example of how repetition is used to create a comic effect.[18]

The remembered words *je vous aime* become for Pierre a sign of all that is wrong with his marriage, but they signified something else to him the first time he spoke them. His first utterance of these words was an act of desperation as he sought in vain to give definition to his relationship with Hélène, which others, it seemed to him, understood better than he. Having chosen the words because external circumstances seem to require them and not because they express his own inadequately understood desires, Pierre immediately senses the banality and conventionality of the formulaic expression. Later, after the duel, when he recalls his declaration of love, the words come to signify the artificiality and superficiality that characterized his relationship with Hélène from the start. The difference between Pierre's sense of these separate articulations is, for both him and the novel's readers, a sign of the changes he has undergone.

Repetition allows Tolstoy's characters and readers to measure how a person has changed between two experiences. By creating an explicit link between separate scenes, he provides an inducement to compare and piece together details. At the same time, Tolstoy demonstrates the importance, for both characters and readers, of a constant *double vision* backward and forward in order to achieve a sense of the continuity and wholeness of experience. Years later, Pierre again recalls the words *je vous aime* as he reflects upon the difference between what he thought he felt once upon a time for Hélène and what he feels now for Natasha:

[18]Bergson, p. 74.

He did not repeat the words he had spoken, as he had done then with sickening shame. He did not say to himself, "Ah, why didn't I say this and why, why did I then say *je vous aime?*" Now, on the contrary, in his imagination he repeated every word that he or she had said, pictured again every detail of her face and smile, and wanted neither to omit nor to add anything. *He wanted only to repeat* [4, 4, 19].

The impulse to repeat (but not to distill), to get at what for him is most essential, is once again felt by Pierre. In the earlier case, Pierre's repetition of his words destabilized their ostensible meaning so that he could come to terms with their real significance for him. Now Pierre's repetition affirms and preserves the significance of his exchange with Natasha. He does not want to add or improve on what has happened because, unlike the scene he played with Hélène, this moment with Natasha is not a performance. Because the event is in no way *cited*, he wants to cite it for himself.

Pierre uses *je vous aime*, his sign for false love, to analyze his feelings for Natasha, and he finds that they do not match: the old sign does not match the new signified. In the scene following the duel, Pierre repeats two expressions—*je vous aime* and "depraved woman"—in order simultaneously to punish and comfort himself for his marital situation. Now Pierre repeats numerous and varied details of his last exchange with Natasha in order to repeat, to relive, his happiness. Here, as before, repetition is the mechanism by which he conceptualizes his thought and feeling at this moment and incorporates the moment into his total conception of his life up to this point. But here, unlike before, the repetition safeguards the multiplicity of the details.

The articulations of *je vous aime* in three separate scenes suggest both the significant discontinuities and the essential continuity of Pierre's unique experience. In each of its separate articulations the expression is central to Pierre's representation of his thoughts, emotions, and motivations at a particular moment in a particular context. But the expression also becomes, for readers as well as for Pierre, a sign designating a constellation of related images and meanings. Repetition is one of the ways in which Pierre clarifies, conceptualizes, defines his experience: repetition both structures and semanticizes the chaos of his thoughts and feelings.

Tolstoy's use of repetition to suggest a model for how human beings create order and give meaning to their experience is not unique to *War and Peace*. Throughout his novels and short stories Tolstoy portrays the mental life of his characters in just this way. In *Youth*, for example, Irtenev repeats Kolpikov's insulting words "You are a boor, sir" (*Vy nevezha, milostivyi gosudar'*) in order to justify his deliberately rude treatment of him (2, 120–21). And in *The Cossacks*, having just arrived in the house of Grandma Ulitka and thinking over events since his departure from Moscow, Olenin is delighted by the prospect of a *new* (*novyi*) life: "The old life was obliterated, and a *new*, completely *new* life had begun, in which so far there had been no mistakes. Here, as a *new* person among *new* people, he could become worthy of a *new* and good opinion of himself" (6, 43). We have seen that in this method of portrayal, characters isolate an element of their present or remembered experience and, by simultaneously narrowing their focus and attributing greater significance to the single element, they establish a starting point, or a basis, for understanding. The repeated element, to summarize further, is the carrier of both public and private meanings and reflects, or at least suggests, characters' conscious and unconscious motives and desires.

Public and Private Symbols

When Tolstoy uses repetition as an element of characters' inner speech to call attention to and represent their mental life, that repetition is seen to have a local function, but the same repetition may also play a role in bringing out the main themes or general questions explored in the story or novel. In this next example various repetitions joining several scenes have to do not only with Prince Andrei's intellectual and emotional expectations for and responses to battle, but with the theme of conceptions of war and heroism in *War and Peace* as well.

"'It has begun! Here it is!' [*Nachalos'! Vot ono!*] thought Prince Andrei, feeling the blood rush to his heart. 'But where—and how—will my Toulon manifest itself?' he wondered" (1, 2, 17). Andrei's exclamations as the battle of Schongraben begins signal all the excitement and anticipation he feels both within and outside of himself at this moment. And it seems to Andrei that his feelings are shared by everyone around him:

> he saw everywhere the same rapid movements of soldiers forming ranks and examining their weapons, and he recognized on all their faces that feeling of excitement that was in his own heart. "It has begun! Here it is! Terrible and joyous!" said the face of every soldier and officer [1, 2, 17].

When Prince Bagration, the commanding officer, approaches, Andrei scrutinizes his face for some sort of sign acknowledging the situation:

The expression "*It has begun! Here it is!*" showed even on Prince Bagration's hard, brown face with its half-closed and lusterless, as if sleepy, eyes. Prince Andrei glanced with anxious curiosity at that *immovable* face, and he wanted to know whether this man was thinking and feeling, and what he was thinking and feeling at this moment. "Is there anything at all behind that *immovable* face?" Prince Andrei asked himself, looking at him [1, 2, 17].

As Andrei looks around him and shares with the soldiers and with Bagration a moment of presentness, the expression "It has begun! Here it is!" seems momentarily to fix the cutting edge of the present. A minute later and the heightened sense of excitement and anticipation will begin to ebb as new emotions and responses begin to assert themselves. By means of the repeated phrase Andrei both evaluates and labels his experience and makes a comparison between himself and the other men who are also preparing to enter battle.

Whereas the initial utterance of the expression "It has begun! Here it is!" is spoken by Andrei, the second two come from the narrator, who seems to speak through Andrei's consciousness. Note that both the narrator and Andrei refer to Bagration's "immovable face." From this brief passage set off by the repeated phrase it is difficult to tell with certainty whether the perception that all the soldiers share the same emotion originates in the mind of the narrator or in Andrei's own. Indeed, there is no clear line separating the voice of Andrei from that of the narrator. That the original utterance of "It has begun! Here it is!" belongs to Andrei suggests that it is indeed Andrei who finds confirmation of his own emotion on the faces of his comrades-in-arms. But does Tolstoy mean that Andrei is right to interpret the same (repeated) physical signs as indicating the same emotion, or is Andrei falsely interpreting everyone as a version of himself?

For Andrei this moment is important because it marks the starting point of what he imagines will unfold as the story of his heroic and glorious triumph as an officer of the Russian army. Andrei "tries to situate each present moment within an imagined narrative."[19] So to the extent that he seems to impose, rather than discover, a design on the battlefield, Andrei may err in attributing the same emotion to every soldier. At the same time, however, Tolstoy demonstrates in this scene and countless others that the subjectivity of perception is part of what makes judgment and understanding so difficult and uncertain. Andrei's initial impulse is in this sense a normal one, and a moment later he focuses less certainly, but more penetratingly, on Prince Bagration's "immovable face."

The ambiguity, which suspends the narrated monologue between the immediacy of quotation and the mediacy of narration, joins Andrei's subjective perception of a shared sense of excitement and anticipation to the narrator's apparent confirmation. As Cohn points out, the superimposition of two voices—the character's and the narrator's—in narrated monologue creates the "characteristic indeterminateness of the narrated monologue's relationship to the language of consciousness."[20] Whether or not this perceived reality is objectively true does not concern Tolstoy. In fact, here and in similar scenes (as we shall see), in which repetition underscores the coexistence of character and narrator within an ambiguous narrative passage, the message seems to be that what individuals observe and comprehend is what is "real" to them. Tolstoy sidesteps the

---

[19]Morson, *Hidden in Plain View*, p. 168.
[20]Cohn, p. 105.

philosophical problems posed by the "tree falling in the forest"—do things exist if they are not perceived and is knowledge possible beyond the contents of direct perception or experience?—in order to assert that awareness, consciousness, has the ability to envalue its object, to give meaning to experience, not definitively, but contextually and without precluding the possibility of change.[21] Meaning, in other words, arises from use. With the repetition of elements of characters' inner speech, Tolstoy makes a further point: the meaning of a word or phrase as it is used by a particular speaker has both a public and a private, a shared and an individual dimension. The scenes that involve such repetition figure as paradigmatic instances of the ongoing process of concept-building.

The words Andrei chooses to express his emotion on the threshold of battle—"It has begun! Here it is!"—indicate the impatience he has felt in waiting for the event which would transform his mundane life into a part of history, earn him glory, and establish him as a hero. Captivated by the figure of

[21]Cf. Bakhtin's description in "From Notes Made in 1970–71" of the opening up of the world's epistemological and ethical potential via awareness: "When consciousness appeared in the world (in existence) ... the world (existence) changed radically. A stone is still stony and the sun still sunny, but the event of existence as a whole (unfinalized) becomes completely different because a new and major character in this event appears for the first time on the scene of earthly existence—the witness and the judge. And the sun, while remaining physically the same, has changed because it has begun to be cognized by the witness and the judge. It has stopped simply being and has started being in itself and for itself (these categories appear for the first time here) as well as for the other, because it has been reflected in the consciousness of the other (the witness and the judge): this has caused it to change radically, to be enriched and transformed" (137). Pertinent here also is Kant's "transcendental a priori unity of apperception," which says that our perception, which is an act of judgment, is a process of organizing different elements into a whole and giving unity to them. It is a priori because it is given in advance of experience and it is transcendental because it is imposed on, not derived from, experience (Mead, pp. 43–45).

Napoleon, an acknowledged military genius, Andrei waits hopefully for his "Toulon," the military port and fortification where Napoleon first earned fame and status in a battle against the Royalists in 1793. Toulon becomes a symbol for Andrei of the military greatness which Napoleon found and which he is certain awaits him too. Already when he first learns of the upcoming battle of Schongraben from his friend Bilibin, Andrei imagines the heroic role he will play:

> "*Enough joking*" [*Polnote shutit'*], said Prince Andrei sadly and gravely.
>
> This news was distressful and at the same time pleasant to Prince Andrei. As soon as he found out that the Russian army was in such a hopeless position, the thought suggested itself to him, that surely he was the man destined to lead the Russian army out of this position, that here it was, *that Toulon*, which was to raise him from the ranks of obscure officers and set him on the path to glory! Listening to Bilibin, he was already imagining how on reaching the army he would give his opinion at the war council, the only one that could save the army, and how he alone would be entrusted with the execution of the plan.
>
> "*Enough joking*," he said [1, 2, 12].

Notice that Tolstoy uses repetition here to frame the narrated monologue of Andrei's daydream. This use of repetition is an example, then, of the second of the four paradigms of Tolstoy's use of repetition identified earlier. Whether the repetition signals that Andrei says the phrase twice or just once is not clear. We can imagine that Andrei brings himself out of a momentary state of preoccupation by reiterating the words he has just spoken, words that may in fact have brought on that state. It may also be possible that the spoken words and the unspoken thoughts occur somehow simultaneously, that "enough joking" is Andrei's public pronouncement on his private preoccupations. In any event, actual time is suspended as Andrei ventures forward in imaginary time, and actual space falls away as he pictures himself on the battlefield. Uspensky describes the phenomenon of framing as "an alternation between a point of view internal to the narrative and a point of view external to the narrative."[22] Tolstoy's use of repetition as a frame sets the inner thoughts of a character apart from the narrative flow and calls attention to a kind of reflective thinking that at a given moment takes as its object images of its own creation as opposed to the actual objects external to it at this given moment. These images are related to and even prompted by external circumstances, but have their source elsewhere: in the hopes, dreams, fears, desires, needs of the individual.

Thus, in another example of this framing device, Andrei, on his way to Brunn as a courier to announce the victory at Krems, fills in his recollections of the battle and anticipates the reception awaiting him at the Austrian court:

> It was a *dark, starry night*; the road loomed black in the glistening white snow that had fallen the previous day, the day of the battle. Now turning over in his mind impressions of the recent battle, now happily imagining the impression which he would make with the news of a victory, Prince Andrei sped along in a post chaise, experiencing the emotion of a man who has at last begun to attain a long-awaited happiness. As soon as he closed his eyes, the sound of gunfire merging with the rumbling of wheels resounded in his ears. Now he began to imagine that the Russians were fleeing, that he himself was killed; but he quickly woke up with joy, as if learning anew that this was not so, that, on the contrary, the French had taken flight. He again recalled all the details of the victory, his

[22]Uspensky, p. 148.

calm courage during battle and, feeling reassured, fell into a doze. ... The *dark, starry night* was followed by a bright, cheerful morning [1, 2, 9].

The placement of "dark, starry night" (*temnaia, zvezdnaia noch'*) at both the beginning and end of this passage marks the actual passage of time in the novel during which Andrei's thoughts and dreams travel backwards and forwards in imaginary time.

Returning to our original example, we observe that other clues, in addition to the frame, make it clear that both the thoughts and the emotion communicated in this passage belong to Andrei. These clues include the particle *imenno*, rendered by me in English as "surely," the deictic element *vot* ("here"), and the exclamation point.[23] When Andrei invokes the symbol Toulon again later—"But where—and how—will my Toulon manifest itself?"—his words not only remind readers of his daydream, but suggest that Andrei himself is recalling his earlier thoughts. The repeated element joins the two separate scenes in terms of details of plot, the thematics of war and heroism, and Andrei's feelings and expectations. Here, repetition of the word "Toulon" and the changing intonations with which it sounds mark Andrei's deepening understanding. An-

---

[23] In the original Russian the passage reads:

"—Polnote shutit',—grustno i ser'ezno skazal kniaz' Andrei.

"Izvestie eto bylo gorestno i vmeste s tem priiatno kniaz'iu Andreiu. Kak tol'ko on uznal, chto russkaia armiia naxoditsia v takom beznadezhnom polozhenii, emu prishlo v golovu, chto emu-to imenno prednaznacheno vyvesti russkuiu armiiu iz etogo polozheniia, chto vot on, tut Tulon, kotoryi vyvedet ego iz riadov neizvestnyx ofitserov i otkroet emu pervyi put' k slave! Slushaia Bilibina, on soobrazhal uzhe, kak, priexav k armii, on na voennom sovete podast mnenie, kotoroe odno spaset armiiu, i kak emu odnomu budet porucheno ispolnenue etogo plana.

"—Polnote shutit',—skazal on."

drei's expectations, however, are not fulfilled at Schongraben, and on the eve of the battle of Austerlitz thoughts of the role he will play once again fill his mind:

> And he pictured the battle, its loss, the concentration of fighting at one point, and the confusion of all the commanding officers. And here, that happy moment, *that Toulon* for which he had so long been waiting finally presents itself to him. He firmly and clearly expresses his opinion to Kutuzov, Weyrother, and the emperors. All are struck by the soundness of his views, but no one undertakes to carry them out, and so he takes a regiment, a division, stipulates that no one is to interfere with his orders, leads his division to the decisive point, and wins the victory alone [1, 3, 12].

Early the next morning as the Russian army marches into battle, "Prince Andrei was in a state of agitation, irritation, and at the same time controlled calm, as a man is when a long-awaited moment has come. He was firmly convinced that today would be the day of his *Toulon* or his bridge of Arcole" (1, 3, 15). The name "Toulon" becomes for Andrei a personal symbol of the glory and love he will earn via his shrewdness and courage under fire. Just as we saw Pierre do with the words *je vous aime* and "depravity," Andrei appropriates and then transforms the public meaning of the word into a private significance. With each repetition of the word, Andrei's images of war and bravery become more vivid and his desire for glory more intense: the word "Toulon" appears again and again as the expression of Andrei's emotion, evaluation, and expectation.

Throughout his novels and short stories Tolstoy uses repetition to depict characters whose interpretations of experience are built upon a single word or phrase that they have invested with great personal significance. The many particular instances of characters structuring their experience and creating meaning in this way suggest that by his portrayals Tolstoy is making a general statement about the necessarily repetitive nature of speech and thought directed toward understanding. But the underlying similarity of these depictions does not mean they are all the same. For as Tolstoy recognized, although the problem of creating meaning may be universal, every individual's solution is particular.

Rearranging Experience

When Andrei exclaims, "It has begun! Here it is!" his words become a general sign of the many particular images, thoughts, and feelings leading up to this moment. In the same way, Pierre's *je vous aime* brings together in a single phrase the wealth of details that constitute his thoughts and feelings concerning his marriage. But in this next example from *Anna Karenina*, instead of bearing witness to the progression and continuity of a character's thought, repetition emphasizes the break, the discontinuity, that results when preconceptions and expectations do not agree with actual experience. Once again Tolstoy uses repetition in narrated monologue to depict the subjective interpretive efforts of his character. This time, however, the narrator's repetitions play a role in the scene's development as well. Since repetition by the narrator is the subject of the third section of this chapter, I discuss the effects and implications of these particular repetitions only briefly.

Several days before the ball, to which she is very much looking forward, Kitty pays a visit at the home of her sister and brother-in-law. There she spends some time with Anna, whom she knows slightly and who has only just come to Moscow to help patch things up between her selfish and philandering brother and his wife, Kitty's sister Dolly. Enamored of Anna's beauty and grace and captivated by the poetic and mysterious aura that surrounds her, Kitty falls in love with the older married woman. Carried away by her naive and romantic imagination, Kitty tells Anna that she pictures her at the ball in a lilac gown. Anna's actual appearance in the ballroom in a black dress takes Kitty by surprise:

> Kitty had been seeing Anna every day, and was in love with her, and had always imagined her in *lilac*. But *now*, having seen her in black, she felt she had not understood all her charm. *Now* she saw her in a completely new and unexpected way. *Now* she understood that Anna could not have been in *lilac* and that her charm lay precisely in that she always stood out from her attire, that her attire could never be conspicuous on her [1, 22].

Restating Kitty's preconceived expectation of Anna in the first sentence of this passage, the narrator begins each of the next three sentences with the word "now," emphasizing the difference between what Kitty expected and what she actually sees and even comes to accept as entirely appropriate. But the more important repetition here is of the word "lilac." This word becomes the symbol of Kitty's naiveté and of her misjudgment of Anna.

As the ball gets under way Kitty is swept away by the festivity and endless dancing and does not give any more thought to Anna. But then, while dancing the last quadrille, Kitty suddenly sees her again in the same "completely new and unexpected way" (1, 23). This phrase, which earlier described Kitty's initial reaction to Anna's appearance, indicates that once again Kitty is confronted with two contrasting images of Anna. In horror and disbelief Kitty begins to realize that Anna's suppressed radiance, which she had noticed before the ball with admiring curiosity, has captivated Vronsky, who she thought was in love with her. Now as the mazurka begins Kitty cannot take her eyes off Anna and Vronsky:

> She *saw* them with her farsighted eyes, she *saw* them close-up too when they came together in the dance, and the more she *saw* them, the more convinced she was that misfortune had befallen her. She *saw* that they felt as if they were alone in that crowded ballroom. And on Vronsky's face, always so firm and self-possessed, she *saw* that expression of bewilderment and submission, which had so surprised her and which was like the expression of an intelligent dog when it feels guilty [1, 23].

The repetition of the verb "to see" (*videt'*) five times in this short passage emphasizes Kitty's complete absorption in watching Anna and Vronsky. Presumably, Tolstoy could have varied the verb with any of numerous possible synonyms. Whether or not variation was or is a stylistic convention or desideratum, an author as sensitive to word choice as Tolstoy—recall Strakhov's observation about his efforts to edit Tolstoy's writing—was surely attentive to the possible effects of nonvariation. Under the repetitive force of the verb, Kitty's visual impressions from nearby and from afar (note the irony of "farsighted," which suggests foresight or good judgment) converge into a feeling of distress. She continues to watch the pair, but then her eyes are drawn to Anna alone:

> She was *charming* [*prelestna*] in her simple black dress, her full arms with the bracelets were *charming*, *charming* her firm neck with its string of pearls, *charming* her curly hair now disarranged, *charming* the graceful, light movements of her little feet and hands, *charming* that beautiful face in its animation; but there was something terrible and cruel in her *charm* [1, 23].

Upon first seeing Anna at the ball, Kitty had noticed her

"charm." Now this "charm" is all she can see. The connotations of the word in both Russian and English, which suggest an ability to affect by or as if by magic or supernatural powers, are a comment upon Anna's unexpected effect on Kitty, and on Vronsky too.

Reiterated this way, as if it were an incantation and as part of Kitty's inner speech, the word "charming" becomes imbued for Kitty with tremendous personal significance: behind it are all of her collected recollections, impressions, and assumptions about Anna. The repetition of "charming" also suggests that Kitty is reassessing fundamental values. To be "charming" now is suspect and the life of balls, gallantry, handsome men and beautiful women, where "charm" is desired, seems bad, too. Spoken by the narrator, the passage, as an example of narrated monologue, communicates Kitty's point of view. But the superimposition of Kitty's language and the narrator's grammar manages to convey the narrator's identification if not identity with her mentality. As Cohn explains: "In narrated monologue, as in figural narration generally, the continued employment of third-person reference indicates, no matter how unobtrusively, the continued presence of a narrator. And it is his *identification*—but not his *identity*—with the character's mentality that is supremely enhanced by this technique."[24] The observation in the last line of the passage that "there was something terrible and cruel" in Anna's charm seems to be the assessment of both Kitty and the narrator. It lends support to the implicit link between the word "charm" and deceit. By the end of the mazurka Kitty explicitly connects Anna's charm with evil: "Yes, there is something strange, devilish, and *charming* about her" (1, 23), she concludes. As this passage makes clear,

[24]Cohn, p. 112.

narrated monologue allows for the penetration into the narrative of a character's inner speech. The repetition of "charming," by means of which Kitty's attention actively centers on Anna, is the first clue that Kitty is drawing this portrait of Anna. And the dropping of the verb, the word order, which gives emphasis to the word "charming," and the piling up of details that result in one colossal image are others. Tolstoy's use of repetition is critical here. Foucault was not the first to observe that "language cannot represent thought, instantly, in its totality; it is bound to arrange it, part by part, in a linear order."[25] But repetition can create the illusion of thought in its totality by representing impressions as durative and cumulative, as opposed to successive. Set off by a semicolon, the last clause, which restores the verb and concludes with the word "charm" (*prelest'*), both breaks Kitty's near-trance and serves as her final judgment of Anna.

For readers the ambiguous word "charming" becomes a sign of the transformation of Kitty's former love and admiration for Anna into an emerging awareness of the intoxicating power of Anna's desire and desirability. It becomes a sign capable of carrying conflicting tonalities of praise and blame at the same time. Here, as in the example with Pierre and *je vous aime*, repetition suggests the simultaneous narrowing of attention

---

[25] Foucault, p. 82. Note that in his *Laocoön*, published in 1766 and considered the first extended attempt in modern times to define the distinctive spheres of art and poetry, Gotthold Ephraim Lessing writes: "I reason thus: if it is true that in its imitations painting uses completely different means or signs than does poetry, namely figures and colors in space rather than articulated sounds in time, and if these signs must indisputably bear a suitable relation to the thing signified, then signs existing in space can express only objects whose wholes or parts coexist while signs that follow one another can express only objects whose wholes or parts are consecutive" (78). In other words, verbal description cannot provide the unified impression of a visible object and a painting or sculpture cannot successfully depict the various stages of an action.

and expanding significance of the word. In both cases, repetition also signals reconsideration. Finding herself in a situation in which all of the variables have unexpectedly changed, Kitty attempts to attach meaning, to fasten it down. She retakes control of the images before her. The isolated word enables her to articulate and make sense of her experience. Tolstoy illustrates once again the impulse to compress the separate details of experience into an intelligible whole. By portraying Kitty's attempts to give definition to her feelings and thoughts, he gives literary expression to what may be (can be felt to be, but not proven to be) a universal human drive to make sense out of experience, to give it form and order.[26]

The Persuasive Power of Words

Kitty's repetition of "charming" is rhetorically motivated. That is, she repeats the word not only to structure, but to confirm and convince herself of a certain point of view. Tolstoy frequently employs repetition both to exploit and to lay bare the rhetorical power, the persuasive power, of words, and nowhere is this function more evident than in the portrayal of Anna Karenina.

Once she begins her illicit affair with Vronsky, Anna is faced with what seems to her one impossible choice after another. In an effort to avoid making these painful decisions she repeatedly insists that she "doesn't understand" and repeatedly expresses her fear that others, especially Vronsky and Karenin, will not or do not understand her. Words become a barrier to communication between Anna and others. And even the word "words" becomes a repeated element that traces her self-

[26]See Geertz, who, following Max Weber, asserts that "the imposition of meaning on life is the major and primary condition of human existence" (434).

destructive immersion into a hateful world of her own making. From the beginning of her relationship with Vronsky, Anna is careful and even distrustful of the words that pass between them. When Vronsky tells Anna that his dalliance with Kitty was "a mistake, and not love," Anna becomes upset: "'You remember that I forbade you to pronounce that word, that vile word,' Anna said shuddering; but then she felt that by this one word which she forbade, she demonstrated that she claimed certain rights over him, thereby encouraging him to speak to her of love" (2, 7). Later the same evening in spite of her warning Vronsky mentions love again as Anna steps into her carriage: "'Love . . . ,' she repeated slowly in *an inner voice*, and suddenly, while unhooking the lace, added: 'I don't like that word, because it means too much for me, much more than you can *understand*,' and she looked him in the face. 'Good-bye'" (2, 7). Tolstoy points out that Anna's repetition of the word Vronsky has spoken is part of her inner speech, that is, speech intended only for her (and readers) and thus saturated with her associations, images, and feelings. As she utters this word inwardly it becomes wholly her own, and under the assumption that he is incapable of understanding, she does not even try to explain its meaning for her. The repetition in the two passages of "that word" and of the word for which "that word" becomes a euphemistic substitution, "love," not only suggests that Anna has thought about this subject before, but also demonstrates her inability to communicate verbally her innermost beliefs and values. This inability can also be seen in the same chapter in the incongruence, noted by the narrator several times, between the look in Anna's eyes and the words she speaks. Her difficulty in expressing herself has any number of possible underlying causes, such as distrust of Vronsky, unwillingness to face the consequences of her feelings, or hypocrisy. Still later the same evening Anna and Karenin have the first of many arguments over her public behavior with Vronsky. Three times she insists that she simply does not understand what Karenin is talking about. Repetition here becomes Anna's only means of defense. It also represents her inner denial of her feelings for Vronsky, or at least, of the possibility of true love and happiness he represents for her. But even here, repetition helps to organize the great diversity and multiplicity of sensations and impressions which is experience. Throughout the novel Anna speaks repetitively as if attempting to make things so, by wishing them so. That repetition makes it so is precisely the rhetorical logic behind incantation.[27] Here and elsewhere, too, Tolstoy exploits this logic to underscore the connection between repetition and the structuring of meaning. Pleading now with Anna to consider what he has said to her, Karenin declares his love for her. She dismisses his words derisively: "For an instant her head had drooped, and the mocking spark in her look had died out; but the word 'love' aroused her again. She thought: 'Love? Is he really capable of love? If he had not heard that love exists, he never would have used this word. He doesn't even know what love is'" (2, 9).[28]

[27] Cf. Bronislaw Malinowski: "In brief, a strong emotional experience, which spends itself in a purely subjective flow of images, words, and acts of behavior, leaves a very deep conviction of its reality, as if of some practical and positive achievement, as if of something done by a power revealed to man. This power, born of mental and physiological obsession, seems to get hold of us from outside, and to primitive man, or to the credulous and untutored mind of all ages, the spontaneous spell, the spontaneous rite, and the spontaneous belief in their efficiency must appear as a direct revelation from some external and no doubt impersonal sources" (81).

[28] Anna's thought paraphrases one of La Rochefoucauld's well-known maxims: "Il y a des gens qui n'auraient jamais été amoureux, s'ils n'avaient jamais entendu parler de l'amour" (There are people who would never have loved if they

Once again Anna sets her own sense of the word "love" as a barrier between herself and her interlocutor. The repetition calls attention to a tragic similarity between Anna's relationships with Karenin and with Vronsky: Anna cannot believe that either her husband or the man for whom she will eventually leave her husband could know or understand what "love" means. There is no close psychological contact between Anna and these men: their thoughts are not the same. Both Karenin and Vronsky are accustomed to solitary, independent thinking, cannot grasp another's thoughts easily, and are, in fact, overly partial to their own thoughts. And although Anna, like her brother Stiva, is good at guessing feelings when she allows herself to, she becomes less and less inclined to understand any point of view other than her own. Compare this situation with that of Kitty, who is able to apprehend Levin's marriage proposal by means of the initial letters of his words alone. Note, incidentally, that if the first letter of each word is enough, then the rest are redundant (repetitive). Because of their psychological and emotional compatibility, Kitty and Levin need not rely on the redundancy of the message to understand one another.

Anna can no more articulate her thoughts about the act of love than she could about the concept. After she and Vronsky

---

had never heard of love). Included in Tolstoy's plans and notes for the writing of *Anna Karenina* is a list of five maxims from La Rochefoucauld, including this one. Tolstoy was an admirer of the French writer and moralist, and collaborated with G. A. Rusanov in a translation of his maxims, which appeared in 1908. (The first translation of the maxims into Russian appeared in 1781.) As much as Tolstoy credited La Rochefoucauld with capturing thoughts in "living, precise, concise, and exquisite turns of phrase" (Preface to the maxims; 40, 281), Anna's reliance on another's words to refer to a subject she has such trouble talking about in her own words is poignantly ironic.

make love for the first time, she interrupts and silences his exclamations of happiness, but then abruptly silences herself as well:

> "What happiness!" she said with disgust and horror, and the horror was involuntarily communicated to him.
> "For God's sake, *not a word, not a word* more."
> She quickly got up and moved away from him.
> "*Not a word* more," she repeated, and with a look of cold despair, strange to him, she left him. She felt that at this moment she could not express in *words* the feeling of shame, joy, and horror at this entrance on a new life, and did not want to talk about it, to vulgarize it with inadequate *words*. But not even later, not on the second, nor on the third day could she find the *words* to express all the complexity of these feelings, and she could not even find thoughts with which to reflect by herself on all that was in her soul [2, 11].

This time words become a barrier to communication not only with Vronsky, but with herself. Thought is born through words, and thought unembodied in words remains a shadow.[29] With neither the words to share her feelings with Vronsky, nor the thoughts embodied in words to articulate her feelings to herself, Anna cannot understand or make sense of her experience. Whatever the underlying causes of this inability, the result is that her thoughts and feelings remain fragments unattached to a coherent self-image. By angrily repeating "not a word more," Anna fends off disturbing truths and hides her self from herself. Unable or unwilling to confront herself, Anna postpones thinking about what has happened between her and Vronsky:

[29] Cf. Vygotsky, p. 153.

She kept telling herself [*ona govorila sebe*]: "No, I can't think about this now; *later, when I am calmer*." But that calm, necessary for reflection, never came; every time the thought of what she had done, and of what was to become of her, and of what she should do, presented itself to her, terror came over her and she drove these thoughts away.

"Later, later," she kept telling herself, "when I am calmer" [2, 11].

Anna does not want even to discover the truth, let alone face it and act on it. Much later in the novel when Dolly visits Anna at Vronsky's estate in the country, Anna assures Dolly over and over again that "we will talk all about everything later" (6, 19). Here and elsewhere words for Anna become mere refrains and a means of avoiding confrontation, closing off communication, and fending off the truth.

Scenes in *Anna Karenina,* and other works by Tolstoy, in which characters reflect by themselves on where they have come from and where they may be going to in life are generally full of repetitions. These repetitions trace characters' thoughts and memories: they are the concepts around which characters' attention centers and with which characters construct an interpretation, an understanding, of their experience that satisfies their emotional and psychological needs. On the way back from the races Anna tells Karenin about her involvement with Vronsky. Later she tries to convince herself that with the truth in the open things will become easier for her:

After her husband left her, she told herself she was glad that everything would now be *defined*, and at least there would be no lies and deceit. There seemed to her to be no doubt that her situation would now be *defined* for good. It might be a bad one, this new situation, but it would be *definite*, and there would be no vagueness and lies. The pain she had caused herself and her husband by having said these words would now, she thought, be compensated for by the fact that everything would be *defined*. That evening she saw Vronsky, but did not tell him what had passed between her and her husband, although for the situation to be *defined* it would be necessary to tell him [3, 15].

The repetition of "defined" (*opredelitsia*) in this narrated monologue is Anna's attempt to clarify her position by insisting that it is clarified. But the final "defined," which no longer conveys her perspective, but the narrator's, undercuts her attempt: it is the narrator who notes that by failing to tell Vronsky about her confrontation with Karenin, Anna leaves a crucial condition for clarification unmet. This failure also suggests that Anna's claim—a claim she makes repeatedly from the beginning of her affair with Vronsky—that she hates lies and falsehood is itself a lie. Just what it would mean to Anna to have her position "defined" is left undefined. As part of her inner speech or thought, the word brings together any number of feelings and associations, which may even be indistinct to her.

Several other repeated phrases in *Anna Karenina* come to mind in connection with Anna's "defined." Throughout the novel Oblonsky repeats a phrase he picks up in chapter 2 of part 1 from his servant Matvei, who learned it from his wife, as we are told in chapter 7 of part 3. "It will all come right in the end" (*Vse obrazuetsia*), asserts Oblonsky, usually laughingly, whenever a dilemma presents itself. And likewise throughout the novel, Levin is annoyed every time he hears someone utter the phrase he first heard spoken by his vexatious steward: "as God wills" (*kak Bog dast*). Levin is critical of the attitude of resignation and lack of interest and initiative he believes the phrase expresses. By uttering any one of these three phrases—"everything will be defined," "it will all come right in the end," or "as God wills"—a speaker abdicates personal responsibility and clouds the truth. Not only Tolstoy's character Levin, but Tolstoy himself, is critical of such dehumanizing gestures.

Like Tolstoy before him, Freud also saw that repetition can signal the impulse to work over in the mind an experience in order to gain control of it. He explains what he calls "the compulsion to repeat" in *Beyond the Pleasure Principle*. Repetition coaxes associations and feelings into the conscious mind, helping the individual to make connections between past and present and to construct a more complete understanding of the experience. But if for Freud these associations and feelings are the repressed material of the unconscious, for Tolstoy they are what the mind is not yet focusing its attention on insofar as we cannot be paying attention to everything at once. Certainly Anna does not want to acknowledge all of the implications of her relationship with Vronsky, but in Tolstoy's psychology this denial is occasioned by social and cultural pressures that lie on the border between the private self and the public self rather than in the hidden recesses of the unconscious. Notice in this passage that when Anna reflects upon the pain both she and Karenin have suffered, she specifically thinks in terms of the "words" she spoke to him. These words seem to take on an independent existence as the sole factor which began and will determine the course of events:

> When she awoke the next morning, the first thing that came into her mind was the *words* [*slova*] she had spoken to her husband, and these *words* seemed so terrible to her that she could not understand now how she could have brought herself to pronounce these strange and coarse *words*, and she could not imagine what

would come of this. But the *words* had been said, and Alexei Alexandrovich had gone away without saying anything [3, 15].

Fearfully and pessimistically she thinks about Vronsky, about what will happen to her, and about how she will face her son and the other members of the household: "It seemed to her that those *words* she spoke to her husband, and which she was incessantly repeating in her imagination, had been said by her to everyone and that everyone had heard them. She could not bring herself to look in the eyes of those with whom she was living" (3, 15). Anna's repetition of these words in her imagination and the repetition of "words" in the text signal the disruption the affair has caused in her life and in her self as she finds herself speaking and behaving in ways previously alien to her. It is at this point in the novel that Anna feels for the first time, but not the last, that "everything in her soul was being doubled."

The Search for Meaning

Anna's repetition of "words" is part of the increasing emotional and moral circularity she experiences. Words to her seem wholly incommensurable with the task of expressing herself, of describing for herself, let alone for others, her feelings and thoughts. But at the same time her manipulation of certain words allows her to hide, to deny, painful truths. If Anna uses words to obfuscate truth, Levin uses them to the best of his ability to clarify it. Repetition can imply sameness, circularity, and stagnation, and these are the implications of repetition Tolstoy exploits in his portrayal of Anna as she comes to see her world in terms of more and more limiting and limited choices. Repetition, however, can also imply dissimilarity, linearity, and movement, and he exploits these in his depiction of Levin's development. Like Anna, Levin, too, struggles with words, but through them and in them he searches for meaning and truth.

In *Anna Karenina* Tolstoy continues to probe the limits of human freedom and dependence on one's surroundings, but this time he approaches the issue in terms of the potential negative influence of society on individual morality. "Society" for Tolstoy, as E. N. Kupreianova explains, "is not a scientific-philosophical concept, but only a historical and empirical given of the imperfection of human existence, its anti-human, unnatural element, which violates the laws and harmony of the universe by means of the antagonism and struggle of the egoistical interests of spiritually alienated people."[30] Both Anna and Levin experience conflict between their personal moral sense and society's moral view. Levin comes to frame the problem of morality in terms of philosophical conceptions of individual self-interest and the common good and in terms of psychological notions of heart and mind:

> Konstantin Levin considered his brother a person of great intellect and education, noble in the highest sense of the word, and gifted with the capacity to work for *the common good*. But the older he became and the more intimately he came to know his brother, the more often the thought occurred to him in the depths of his soul that this capacity to work for *the common good*, of which he felt himself entirely devoid, was not a quality, but on the contrary, a lack of something, not a lack of good, honest, noble wishes and tastes, but a lack of the power of life, of that which is called heart, that striving which makes a person choose one out of all the innumerable paths of life that present themselves, and desire that alone. The better he knew his brother, the more he noticed that

[30]Kupreianova, p. 76.

Sergei Ivanovich and many other workers for *the common good* were not led by their hearts to a love for *the common good*, but reasoned with their minds that to occupy themselves with this was a good thing, and only because of this occupied themselves this way. What strengthened this conviction for Levin was the observation that his brother did not take the question of *the common good* or of the immortality of the soul any more to heart than a game of chess or the clever construction of a new machine [3, 1].

First of all, Levin is absolutely right in his final observation. Several chapters later, Levin has spent the day in the fields, and Koznyshev, who has spent the day indoors, says to him upon his return: "Well, then, you are satisfied with your day. And so am I. First of all, I solved two chess problems—one, a very good one, opens with a pawn. I'll show you. Then I thought about our yesterday's conversation" (3, 6). Returning to the original quotation, we see that the phrase "the common good" (*obshchee blago*) is repeated five times in this passage that records Levin's opinion of his brother. Levin focuses on this phrase as the epitome, the very embodiment, of the difference between him and Koznyshev. Laden with great personal significance for Levin, "the common good" is also, as we shall see, a theme whose significance for the novel as a whole goes beyond Levin's experience. That is, the theme plays a role in the Tolstoyan linkages between sets of characters and plot lines in *Anna Karenina* of which only the author and readers can be aware. This type of repetition—repetition transgradient to characters' experience—is discussed at some length in Chapter 3 of the present study.[31]

[31]Elisabeth Stenbock-Fermor, too, in her study *The Architecture of "Anna Karenina,"* is interested in Tolstoy's linkages in *Anna Karenina*. Her concern is first and foremost with the four themes she identifies as providing the structure for the novel: the light of the candle, the railroad, the search for the meaning of

In this long passage that conveys his thought about his brother, Levin seems to anticipate the replies of an imagined interlocutor. The phrase "the common good" is itself heavily dialogized since clearly the phrase means one thing for Koznyshev and quite another for Levin. Levin's thought is the importation of outer conversation into the self, in which he takes the role of other as well as his own role. By repeating the phrase "the common good," Levin is able to construct an argument against his brother that concedes the nobility of his aspiration, but condemns its abstractness, that is, its disengagement from actual experience. Levin's repetition, via the narrator, structures not only his criticism of Koznyshev, but his understanding of his own experience. Later, in a philosophical discussion with his brother about the motives that underlie all human action, Levin tries to rationalize to himself, and to Koznyshev, his inability to work for "the common good." According to Levin "no activity can endure if it is not based on personal interest" (3, 3), and from this assertion it follows for him that moral action is not a mere hobby or philosophical exercise, but ought to describe one's practical and emotional, as well as intellectual, day-to-day activities and experience.

---

life and death, and the family. She argues that these themes and their linkages all lead to "the message" Tolstoy wished to transmit in *Anna Karenina*. My concern, by contrast, is with the repetition of particular phrases, which may contribute to the development of a theme in the novel, but which operate especially forcefully in a particular micro-, as opposed to macro-, context. In other words, I am less interested in the various elements or motifs that contribute to the development of a particular theme than in the repetition of a particular phrase in a particular context.

Although I find Stenbock-Fermor's study thought-provoking, I cannot go along with her reduction of *Anna Karenina* to four themes and a single "message."

Repetition as Remembered Experience

Over time a record of our day-to-day activities and experience is kept for us by memory. Memory, insofar as it re-evokes past feelings, thoughts, and actions, is itself a kind of repetition. As we have seen, Tolstoy depends upon repetition for the representation of characters' perception and understanding of immediate experience. But repetition plays a role in how characters perceive and understand their experience over time as well. Tolstoy uses repetition to explore and represent the role memory plays in the construction of images and concepts by which individuals give their experience form, continuity, and meaning. Life while lived is to a great extent random, but when recollected, or repeated, we give it more order. As Milan Kundera observes in his novel *The Unbearable Lightness of Being*: "Anna could have chosen another way to end her life. But the motif of death and the railway station, unforgettably bound to the birth of love, enticed her in her hour of despair with its dark beauty. Without realizing it, the individual composes his life according to the laws of beauty even in times of greatest distress."[32]

Memory as a mental phenomenon with both a passive and an active side is a subject that interested Tolstoy throughout his life. In a diary entry dated June 14, 1847, Tolstoy includes memory as one of "five main intellectual faculties"[33] and on April 21, 1905, he would write, "I think more and more often about memory, about recollection, and this faculty seems to me more and more important, more and more fundamental"

[32] Kundera, *The Unbearable Lightness of Being*, p. 52.

[33] Tolstoy writes: "We have five main intellectual faculties—the faculty of imagination, the faculty of memory, the faculty of comparison, the faculty of drawing conclusions from these comparisons, and, finally, the faculty of putting these conclusions in order" (46, 271).

(55, 136). Continually repeating and renewing the past so that it can live in and contribute to present experience, memory is a source of self-knowledge. For Tolstoy memory emerges as a key element of consciousness of self, other, and the experience or event of living. He saw in memory a record and a resource of experience demonstrating both great powers and significant limitations. Again, in his diary we read:

> If you want to know yourself, then notice what you remember and what you forget. If you want to know what you do consider important and what you do not, notice what you forget and what you remember. That which you remember, there, that is what can be the subject of an artistic work. For example: why does mention of one person remind one of another event or another person? Here in this connection lies what is most important in your world outlook. Through these signs you know yourself [Aug. 15, 1900; 54, 34].

Tolstoy recognized that when through memory we relate the details of our lives, give our lives narrative form, we are acting ethically, that is, we are making statements about ourselves and others that reflect the qualities—whether these are judged as good or bad—of our character or ethos.[34] In this context ethics has to do with the decisions people make whether as individuals or in groups that shape their identities and their lives, as well as the lives of other people, and the responsibility they assume for these decisions. It is when serving this func-

---

[34] See Wayne C. Booth's discussion of the ethical in *The Company We Keep*, in particular where he explains that "ethical" in the sense in which he uses it covers "all qualities in the character, or ethos, of authors and readers, whether these are judged as good or bad," and then explains that "[f]rom ancient Greece to the present, the word 'ethos' has meant something like 'character' or 'collection of habitual characteristics': whatever in a person or a society could be counted on to persist from situation to situation"(8).

tion that memory for Tolstoy becomes nearly inextricable from imagination. A close relation between memory and imagination is a literary and psychological commonplace, but in Tolstoy's case it suggests his understanding that artifice is an unavoidable part of remembering and counts as much as fact. Both memory and imagination allow us to conceive of things in their absence, memory with relation to the past.

Many have seen memory's attachment to the past as a limitation. Hume contended that with memory we are restricted or bound by reality, by the way we actually experience things, whereas with imagination we are free to alter and transpose.[35] Closer to our own time, Sartre maintained that what keeps memory and imagination distinct is that memory is determined by the nature of reality.[36] For Tolstoy, however, who was directly concerned with the individual's experience and thus was aware that the individual may not distinguish between veridical and ostensible memory, memory and imagination continually shade into each other. In his fiction Tolstoy rarely uses the word *pamiat'* ("memory") to refer to that part of the mind where memories or reminiscences (*vospomonaniia*) are, metaphorically speaking, awakened; instead, he uses the word *voobrazhenie* ("imagination"). When Natasha asks Pierre whether he thinks Andrei will forgive her for the incident with Anatol, Pierre begins to answer and then:

> By an association of *memories* Pierre was instantly carried back by his *imagination* to that time when comforting her he told her, that if he were not himself, but the best man in the world and free, then he would ask for her hand on his knee, and the same feeling

[35]Hume, *Treatise*, Bk. 1, Part 1, sec. 3.
[36]Sarte, p. 263.

of pity, tenderness, and love seized him, and the same words were on his lips [3, 1, 20].

This choice of words suggests that Tolstoy recognized the extent to which imagination and memory commingle in the recalling and retelling of past experiences. Memory and imagination together aid in the transformation of the separate moments of life into a unified, if unfinalizable, whole, at the same time that they make it possible to isolate and give meaning and value to these separate moments. When Pierre comforts Natasha and in so doing is reminded of the last time he gave her reassurance, the emotion he experiences is not recollected feeling but the emotion of the recollection. That is, he does not merely remember how he felt, he actually feels the same way again. For Tolstoy's artistic representations in general, the memory of a sensation can be hard to tell from the sensation itself. Compare, for example, the scene in which Nikolai Rostov remembers "the stench of corpse." Confused and upset by the alliance concluded between Napoleon and Alexander I in Tilsit, Nikolai recalls recent events, including his visit to Denisov in the hospital: "Then he remembered Denisov with his changed expression, with his submissiveness, and all the hospital with those amputated arms and legs, with that filth and disease. So vividly did it seem to him that he was at this moment smelling that hospital stench of corpse that he looked around to ascertain where the stench could be coming from" (2, 2, 21).

Pierre's memory of the words he spoke to Natasha a month or so earlier is prompted by the repetition of the circumstances: once again he finds himself alone with Natasha discussing Andrei. Certainly the repetition of Pierre's words in the two scenes, which occur in different volumes of *War and Peace*, functions as an aid to readers' memory by attaching reference points to the recollection and the recollected. But the repetition is also an indication of the extent to which the past moment has made itself tangibly felt in the present. In his portrayals of characters' remembered experience, Tolstoy shows how memories can help bring into focus a view of the present and secure a more or less coherent structure of convictions without resorting to a particular point of grounding, either transcendental or logical.

At the conclusion of volume two of *War and Peace*, which ends with Natasha's adventure with Anatol and broken engagement to Andrei, Pierre has a profound encounter with the sky not unlike Andrei's experience as he lay wounded on the Pratzen heights after the battle of Austerlitz. Staring at the sky, both heroes feel the unimportance and triviality of everything compared with what they feel in their souls at the particular moment. As he faces the possibility of his own death, Andrei finds in the quiet and infinite sky a correlative to the new sense of the incomprehensibility and at the same time the beauty and importance of life that grips him. And Pierre finds that the sky, specifically the comet, accords with, harmonizes with, the feelings of hope, renewal, and love that have been inspired by Natasha. For both Pierre and Andrei, a perception of the sky becomes a memory marking the onset of a new appreciation of life and to be recalled at some later moment. If Tolstoy relies on repetition to re-evoke each scene later in the narrative, he also uses it in the presentation and development of his heroes' original experiences: Andrei's realization of the mystery of life that is captured in the sky and that has nothing to do with conventional notions of heroism and glory, and Pierre's joy brought on by Natasha's trust and emotion and seemingly celebrated by the comet. That Pierre and Andrei have similar experiences is itself a kind of repetition that stimulates comparison of the two characters.

Wounded and lying on his back, Andrei hopes still to see how the battle has ended, but he cannot see anything:

> Above him there was no longer anything except the *sky*—the *lofty sky*, not clear, but nevertheless unmeasurably *lofty*, with gray *clouds quietly creeping* by him. "How quiet, calm, and solemn, *not at all like when I was running*," thought Prince Andrei. "*Not like when we were running*, shouting, and fighting; *not at all like* that do the *clouds creep* across the *lofty, infinite sky*. How is it I did not see this *lofty sky* before? And how happy I am to have finally discovered it. Yes! everything is empty, everything is deception, except this *infinite sky*. *There is nothing*, nothing at all, except it. And even that does not exist, *there is nothing* except the quiet, the peace. Thank God! [1, 3, 16].

This passage is saturated with repetitions all of which help to underscore Andrei's efforts to make sense of his experience by searching for meaning in the difference between the chaos and noise of battle and the peace and quiet of its aftermath. Still lying where he had fallen Andrei hears the voice of Napoleon nearby:

> His head was burning; he felt that he was losing blood, and he saw above him the faraway, *lofty and eternal sky*. He knew that this was Napoleon—his hero, but at this moment Napoleon seemed to him such a small, insignificant person in comparison with what was happening now between his soul and this *lofty, infinite sky* with the clouds sailing across it [1, 3, 19].

The image of the "lofty, infinite sky" becomes for Andrei the sign of all that is incomprehensible, yet indisputably important about life and death, and the locus of all the emotions, impressions, and thoughts that constitute his experience of the battle of Austerlitz. The repetitions in these passages also help to convey the subjectivity of Andrei's perception of the sky.

Like Andrei, Pierre, too, perceives the sky in terms of his inner state. I cite the following passage in its entirety despite its length, because published translations of *War and Peace* tend not to reproduce all of Tolstoy's repetitions. Having taken leave of the Rostovs, Pierre stands out in the street oblivious to the freezing cold and overcome by a feeling of love and tender emotion:

> Above the dirty, ill-lit streets, above the black roofs stretched the *dark starry sky*. Only as he gazed up at the sky did Pierre feel the insulting baseness of everything earthly in comparison with the heights to which his soul had been raised. At the entrance to the Arbat square an immense expanse of *starry dark sky* opened before Pierre's eyes. Almost in the center of this sky above the Prechistensky Boulevard, surrounded by and strewn on all sides with *stars*, but distinct from all of them by its nearness to earth, with its white light and long, upturned tail stood the immense bright comet of 1812, that same comet, which was said to portend all kinds of horrors and the end of the world. In Pierre, however, *this radiant star* with its long luminous tail aroused no feeling of dread. On the contrary, Pierre looked joyously with eyes wet from tears at *this radiant star*, which having flown with inexpressible speed though immeasurable space along a parabolic line seemed suddenly, like an arrow piercing the earth, to remain fixed in its chosen spot in the black sky, energetically raising its tail upwards and shining and sparkling with its white light among the countless other glimmering *stars*. It seemed to Pierre that *this star* answered completely to what was in his mollified and uplifted soul, now blossoming into a new life [2, 5, 22].

Once again, repetition not only conveys the strong and memorable impression an experience has had on a character, but seems intended to make a similarly strong and memorable impression on readers.

When Andrei sees the "lofty, eternal sky" again (2, 2, 12) and Pierre sees the "radiant comet" again (3, 3, 29), there is a direct link between their perception of the natural phenomenon and the emotions and thoughts associated with their original perception of it. That is, the repeated element, indicating an act of recognition, makes an explicit reference to memory, or to an act of recalling, by the narrator unnecessary and perhaps even unwarranted. Here repetition is both a reference to the past and an element of present experience: it signifies the interpenetration of past and present. Tolstoy invokes neither memory nor imagination in these perceptual experiences, but uses repetition metonymically to represent the mental activities that somehow account for them. The repeated elements that join these two sets of scenes demonstrate the continuity of the heroes' experience by providing a concrete link between events that are discontinuous and separate and yet similar in terms of the characters' state of mind, their thoughts and emotions. Repetition helps readers perceive the ongoing changes and developments in Pierre and Andrei's personalities (their attitudes, values, motives, and desires) as they try to achieve the happiness and contentment they believe accompanies greater understanding of life.

Pierre sees the comet for the second time while standing out in the street with Ramballe, the French officer who has occupied the house in which Pierre is staying and has just spent the evening enthusiastically and dramatically telling Pierre of his numerous romantic adventures. Pierre had responded to the Frenchman's stories by telling one of his own: the story of his love for Natasha. Gazing now for the second time at the comet, Pierre experiences the same feelings of love, happiness, and lack of fear as before:

> To the left of the house the glow of the first fire to begin in Moscow, in Petrovka, brightened. To the right a new crescent moon stood high in the sky, and on the opposite side from the moon hung that *bright comet*, which was connected in Pierre's soul with his love.... There was nothing frightful in a small, distant fire in a huge city.
>
> Looking at the *lofty starry sky*, at the moon, at the *comet* and at the glow, Pierre experienced a *joyous tender emotion*. "Well, how fine! Well, what else does one need?" he thought. And suddenly, as he remembered his intention, his head began to spin and he began to feel faint so that he leaned against the fence to keep from falling [3, 3, 29].

Now, as before, just thinking of Natasha seems to be all Pierre requires. Sharing with Ramballe good food, some wine and vodka, and conversation about love has made Pierre temporarily forget his intention to assassinate Napoleon. But all at once he recalls his plan. Since that night when his feelings for Natasha first ignited in him a sense of renewal and hope, Pierre has felt himself transported to a realm existing above human pettiness and absurdity:

> From that day when Pierre, leaving the Rostovs and remembering Natasha's grateful look, saw the *comet* fixed in the sky, and felt that something new had come to light for him, the question that had been perpetually tormenting him concerning the vanity and folly of everything earthly stopped presenting itself [*predstavliat'sia*] to him. This terrible question—why? what for?—which before would present itself [*predstavlialsia*] to him in the midst of any occupation, was now replaced not by another question and

not by an answer to the former question, but by her image [*predstavlenie*] [3, 1, 19].

In the weeks that follow, anxious about the course of the war and restless over his own inactivity, Pierre seeks to give his life some purpose. When one of his fellow Masons tells him of a biblical prophecy concerning Napoleon, Pierre sees his destiny. He now joins in his mind the image of Natasha and of the comet with the details of what has been revealed to him by the prophecy. Together, these elements give rise to his conviction that he is destined to play a role in Russia's salvation:

> His love for Rostova, the Antichrist, Napoleon's invasion, the comet, 666, the emperor Napoleon and *l'russe Besuhof*—all this together had to ripen, burst out, and lead him away from this spellbound, petty world of Moscow habits, in which he felt himself held captive, and guide him to some great exploit and great happiness [3, 1, 19].

Pierre interprets each one of these elements as a sign encouraging him to action. Natasha and the comet are recurring images by means of which Pierre finds some measure of coherence in his otherwise discontinuous and fragmentary experience. And to the extent that he invests these images with particular significance in determining the course of his life, they are also a means by which he endows his thoughts and actions with meaning.

For Andrei, the memory of the "lofty, eternal sky" he first glimpsed over Austerlitz is a sign of his thoughts about a higher, eternal plane of meaning that first came to him when he lay wounded on the battlefield. Since that time, Andrei has gone through the birth of his son and the death of his wife and has isolated himself in a world literally of his own making (his estate, Bogucharovo), over which he has complete control. Two years later, Andrei sees the "same" sky, a sky evocative of hope, aspiration, and eternity, after he and Pierre have shared their thoughts and feelings about the things that really matter to them. The two men have spent a long day together discussing their respective estates, present occupations, and mutual acquaintances. But it is only when they set out for Bald Hills that Pierre talks about his new commitment to Freemasonry and Andrei reveals, albeit obliquely, his remorse over the death of his wife. Even though he does not accept Pierre's beliefs, Andrei responds to the hope and faith his friend expresses:

> stepping off the ferry, he looked at the sky, which Pierre had pointed out to him, and for the first time since Austerlitz he saw that *lofty, eternal sky* he had seen while lying on the field at Austerlitz, and something that had long been slumbering, something that was best in him suddenly awoke, joyous and youthful, in his soul. The feeling disappeared as soon as Prince Andrei again entered the habitual *conditions of life*, but he knew that this feeling, which he did not know how to develop, lived in him. The meeting with Pierre was for Prince Andrei the epoch with which, though outwardly his life remained the same, inwardly a new life began for him [2, 2, 12].

Like Pierre, Andrei has a sense of something valuable outside life's normal, habitual conditions, which is connected in both their minds with the image of the sky. The expression "the conditions of life" (*usloviia zhizni*) becomes a repeated phrase in the narrative that not only links Andrei and Pierre, but connects them both with Natasha. In Natasha, both men discover a vital and untrammeled force that seems to lift her and them above the normal conditions of life.[37]

---

[37]For the "conditions of life" and Andrei see (3, 1, 8); and Pierre (3, 3, 8); and

Whereas on the battlefield it is the sky that seems to evoke in Andrei certain thoughts and emotions, on the ferry thoughts and emotions similar to those he experienced earlier seem to paint that same sky. But the sky is neither the cause nor the result of these thoughts and emotions. In both cases, the sky is the external, natural correlate to Andrei's inner experience. What is intangibly and ephemerally experienced in the mind can at least appear to become tangible and eternal when given figurative embodiment. The image of the sky Andrei retains in his memory accompanies and to a certain extent even guides him as he works to understand what is important in life and what is not. With repetition Tolstoy illustrates what seems like a Kantian notion that knowledge is essentially a whole in which separate events, ideas, and memories (or, as Kant might prefer, representations) stand compared and connected.[38] But if for Kant this unity is given in advance of experience and imposed on rather than derived from it, for Tolstoy it is a matter of direct experience and the line between the imposition and the derivation of meaningful structure is a thin one.

Andrei and the "lofty, eternal sky" and Pierre and the "radiant comet" are examples of Tolstoy's use of repetition to represent characters' efforts both to make sense of and structure their immediate experience and to find structure in their expe-

---

Natasha (3, 3, 13). The expression "simple and clear" (*prosto i iasno*) is another repeated phrase relating these three characters in terms of their different attitudes and approaches towards life. For "simple and clear" and Andrei see (3, 2, 24); and Pierre (4, 3, 15); and Natasha (2, 5, 10).

[38] See *The Critique of Pure Reason*, Part I, Bk. I, Ch. II, section 2, entitled "The *A Priori* Grounds of the Possibility of Experience," in which Kant concludes: "Thus all appearances stand in thoroughgoing connection according to necessary laws, and therefore in a transcendental affinity, of which the empirical is a mere consequence" (140).

rience over time. Tolstoy depicts each of these heroes searching for truth and happiness in his own way. And even if Andrei never attains the kind of understanding Pierre does, both are given moments of clear insight. But the subjective and idiosyncratic nature of emotion, thought, and memory means that sometimes people think in illogical and negative or pessimistic ways about themselves, their environment, and their future, and Tolstoy uses repetition to capture this aspect of mind as well.

Suicide enters Anna Karenina's mind as a possibility for the first time after she once again irrationally and unjustly provokes an argument with Vronsky. Convinced that Vronsky hates her and has fallen in love with another woman, Anna tells herself that the situation must somehow be brought to an end:

> *Thoughts* [*mysli*] about where she would go now—to her aunt who had raised her, to Dolly, or simply abroad by herself—and about what he was doing now alone in the study, whether this argument was final or whether reconciliation was still possible, and about what all her former Petersburg acquaintances would say about her now, how Alexei Alexandrovich would look at this, and many other *thoughts* about what would happen now, after the rupture, entered her mind, but she did not give herself up with her entire soul to these *thoughts*. In her soul there was some kind of vague *thought*, which alone interested her, but she could not grasp it. Again *remembering* [*vspomniv*] Alexei Alexandrovich, she also *remembered* her illness after childbirth and that feeling which would not leave her then. "*Why didn't I die?*"—she *remembered* the words she spoke then and her feelings then. And suddenly she understood what was in her soul. Yes, this was that *thought* which alone would solve everything. "Yes, to die!. . ." [7, 24].

In this narrated monologue, Anna's present thoughts and

feelings remind her that she had had similar thoughts and feelings following the difficult birth of her daughter. Her past experience helps her become fully aware of the thought that has lodged in her soul. The repetition of the words "thought(s)" and "remember" suggests the agitated and unrestrained activity of her mind. Anna's thoughts raced in the same way when she lay ill with both Vronsky and Karenin at her side and was certain that she would die. Her present belief that her death would solve everything is born from the words she recalls having spoken at that time, but after the fever and delirium had passed. "Why didn't I die?" (4, 20), she had cried out in bitter frustration directed at Karenin. Ironically, the thought that occurs to Anna now is the very thought that occurred to Karenin when he first received her telegram informing him that she was dying and wished his forgiveness. The explicit connection Tolstoy makes, by means of the repetition of Anna's exact words, between the scene in which Anna contemplates suicide and the scenes that deal with her near-death and recovery lets readers see the terrible course of Anna's increasingly hopeless and morbidly self-pitying thought. Repetition as mimesis, that is, repetition that represents present thought, and repetition as memory both play a crucial role in Tolstoy's portrayal of Anna, who, despite her irrational and desperate state of mind, is nevertheless able to make sense of her experience in her own twisted, pessimistic way. Unfortunately for Anna, the meaning she ascribes to "that thought" implies her own death.

In *Repetition: An Essay in Experimental Psychology*, Kierkegaard, in the person of Constantine Constantius, makes a deeply personal distinction between repetition and memory:

> Repetition and recollection are the same movement, only in opposite directions; for what is recollected has been, is repeated back-

wards, whereas repetition properly so called is recollected forwards. Therefore repetition, if it is possible, makes a man happy, whereas recollection makes him unhappy.[39]

For Kierkegaard repetition, which allows for a becoming by placing us wholly in the present, is a cathartic and transcendental experience. Tolstoy in his novels seems to make a similar distinction: he sees a qualitative difference between memory that carries the past forward into the present and memory that leads the present back to the past. Whereas Tolstoy demonstrates that the remembered experience of Andrei and Pierre is part of their becoming, that is, helps to propel them forward toward greater understanding of what one's relation to the world should be, he shows that Anna's grim return to the moment when she came closest to her death is an act of utter self-defeat.

Repetition in the Narrator's Discourse

Throughout this chapter we have seen the extent to which Tolstoy represents characters' thought as repetitive. For Tolstoy, the form of reflective thought, thought directed towards comprehension of an event, an idea, or a purpose, tends to be repetitive: associations, logical or intuitive, accrue around an initial image, which expands in significance even as it remains formally the same, and hence recognizable. By over and over again inserting repeated elements into the quoted or narrated monologue of his characters, Tolstoy is presenting his model of how human beings integrate the various details of experience into a coherent, if unstable, whole. But it is left to Tolstoy's narrator to describe what characters cannot or do not see

[39] Kierkegaard, p. 33.

about themselves. Human beings, let alone fictional characters, are not at every moment aware of or paying attention to their mental or physical activity.[40] And even if we are conscious of precisely how we are thinking or behaving, we do not usually share this awareness aloud with our interlocutors or observers, for whom this information remains inaccessible. In works of fiction authors often rely on their narrators to communicate such information. As Morson points out in a discussion of Tolstoy's narrator: "By definition, no one can focus attention on what he is not noticing. A description of what one does not notice can be offered only by someone else."[41] Significantly, in Tolstoy the narrator's discourse about the course of characters' thoughts as they reflect on what has happened or take in what is happening around them, and about their characteristic manner of coping with new or unexpected, but also familiar situations, makes frequent use of repetition. These repetitions, like those that characterize characters' quoted and narrated monologue, are critical to Tolstoy's representation of characters' efforts to order and give meaning to their lives.

Habitual Manner

While he and Anna are in Italy, Vronsky briefly takes up painting in order to occupy his time and energy:

> He had an aptitude for understanding art and for imitating art accurately and with taste, and he thought he had what it takes to be an artist, and, after wavering for some time over what *school of*

[40]Critiquing Locke's notion that the concept of personal identity consists wholly in the continuity of consciousness (*Essay Concerning Human Understanding*, Bk. II, Ch. 27, Sect. 10), Mary Warnock asserts: "It doesn't seem to be true that in perceiving or acting we have to be conscious at the time that we are perceiving or acting: I can't remember whether or not I turned off the oven" (59).

[41]Morson, *Hidden in Plain View*, p. 205.

painting [*rod zhivopisi*] to choose—religious, historical, genre, or realistic—he began to paint. He understood all the *schools* and could *be inspired* [*vdokhnovliat'sia*] by any of them; but he could not imagine that it would be possible to be quite ignorant of the different *schools of painting,* and *be inspired directly* by what was in his soul, without worrying about whether what he was painting belonged to some well-known *school.* Since he did not know this and was *inspired* not *directly* by life, but *indirectly* by life already embodied in art, he *was inspired* very quickly and easily and just as quickly and easily he was able to paint in a way that very much resembled the *school* he wished to imitate [5, 8].

The repetition in this passage of "school(s) of painting" and "to be inspired" suggests that Vronsky approaches art and painting just as he approaches any other activity, including love: wholeheartedly and purposefully with a set of rules and models to guide him. Already much earlier we learned of Vronsky's adherence to a "code of rules" for comporting himself:

Vronsky was particularly fortunate in that he had a *code of rules* which defined beyond all question what should and should not be done. This *code of rules* covered a very small circle of conditions, but the *rules* were beyond all question, and Vronsky, never going beyond that circle, never for a moment hesitated to do what had to be done [3, 20].

Sensitive to appearances, Vronsky's habitual manner is to seek out an already established method or viewpoint and adopt it as his own. Thus it is no surprise that he is well acquainted with the various schools of painting. There is more than a touch of irony in the narrator's explanation of Vronsky's source of inspiration: he is inspired by other artists' representations of life, rather than by the life within or around him. In his art, Vronsky is at a double remove from his ostensible subject: nature

and "real" life. Inspiration connotes a kind of divine or supernatural influence not governable by the one inspired and operating in the realm of the chance or accidental rather than the
expected. But in Vronsky's case inspiration becomes as ordinary as perception.

The vivid depiction of Vronsky as a skilled, but unoriginal
and imitative dilettante in art, which emerges thanks in part to
the repetition in these lines, stands in sharp contrast to the depiction of the genuine and passionate artist Mikhailov, with
whom Anna and Vronsky become acquainted. And if Vronsky's portrait of Anna is considered "successful" (*udachnyi*),
Mikhailov's portrait of her so completely isolates her "special,
particular beauty" (*osobennaia krasota*) that Vronsky believes
he has always known that "most sweet, soulful expression of
hers" (*samoe miloe ee dushevnoe vyrazhenie*) captured on the
canvas.[42] In this passage Tolstoy, via his narrator, uses repetition to describe Vronsky's approach to a newfound interest,
painting. Here, juxtaposed repetitions convey something essential about Vronsky's character and manner reinforcing his image as a person somewhat limited in his views, understanding,
and aspirations, but always striving to perform to the best of
his ability. The narrator's repetitions offer not only a description, but a critique of Vronsky's habitual manner. Vronsky's

[42]Csikszentmihalyi's distinction between more and less original artists seems
succinctly to summarize the difference between Mikhailov and Vronsky as depicted by Tolstoy: "The distinction between more and less original artists is that
the former start painting with a general and often vague idea of what they want
to accomplish, while the latter tend to start with a clearly visualized picture in
mind. Thus original artists must discover as they go along what it is that they will
do, using feedback from the developing work to suggest new approaches. The less
original artists end up painting the picture in their heads, which has no chance to
grow and develop. But to be successful in his open-ended process of creation, the
original artist must have well-internalized criteria for what is good art, so that he
can choose or discard the right elements in the developing painting" (252–53).

actions and thoughts with regard to Anna are viewed by readers in terms of the impression they have of him, an impression created not just by what Vronsky himself says and does or by Anna's perceptions of him, but by how and what the narrator communicates.

Because Tolstoy's narrator tends to remain impersonal and disembodied (except in his explicitly first-person narratives), his descriptions and commentary have an authority that readers are seldom directed by other aspects of the text to question. This covert or undramatized narrator imparts meaning to and information about characters without explicitly identifying a uniquely individual point of view for the narration and provides details and judgments that elude characters themselves. As Chatman explains: "Covert or effaced narration occupies the middle ground between 'nonnarration' and conspicuously audible narration. In covert narration we hear a voice speaking of events, characters, and setting, but its owner remains hidden in the discursive shadows."[43] Wayne Booth distinguishes between dramatized and undramatized narrators in his exploration of the forms the author's choice can take. Concerning undramatized narrators, he makes the important point that "something mediating and transforming has come into a story from the moment that the author explicitly places a narrator into the tale, even if he is given no personal characteristics whatever."[44]

The Movement of Thought

Having already spent two months in Moscow awaiting Kitty's delivery, Levin agrees one evening to join a group of

---

[43] Chatman, p. 117.
[44] Booth, "Distance and Point-of-View," p. 273.

friends and acquaintances for dinner at the club, where he has not been in quite a long time:

> He remembered the *club* [*klub*], the external details of its layout, but had completely forgotten the *impression* [*vpechatlenie*], which in former times he used to experience at the *club*. But *as soon as* [*tol'ko chto*], having entered the broad, semi-circular courtyard and gotten out of the cab, he entered the porch where he was met by a hall porter with a shoulder-belt who noiselessly opened the door and bowed; *as soon as* he saw in the hall the galoshes and coats of the members who realized that it was less trouble to remove one's galoshes downstairs than to wear them upstairs; *as soon as* he heard the mysterious ring of the bell announcing him and saw, while ascending the sloping, carpeted staircase, a statue on the landing and on the upper floor, a third hall porter, whom he recognized, though the man had aged, and who without haste or delay was opening the door for and looking over the guests, Levin was enveloped by the old, familiar *impression* of the *club*, an *impression* of repose, contentment, and propriety [7, 7].

The repetition of the adverbial expression "as soon as" in these lines traces not only Levin's passage from the doorway to the room where he is expected, but the piling up of images that recall to Levin's mind the feeling he had come to associate with the club as well. By repeating the words "club" and "impression" in such close conjunction at both the beginning and the end of the passage, Tolstoy underscores that each of these images contributes to Levin's total impression of the club. Although all that Levin sees seems to be described directly from his point of view and through his consciousness, the "as soon as," which requires a retrospective, narrative point of view, signals the narrator's voice. This voice helps to bring order to Levin's visual impressions and convey the increasing strength and vividness of his recollected impression until it can be articulated by Levin via the words "repose, contentment, and propriety."

In this passage Tolstoy uses the repetition of a temporal verb to suggest the movement and development of Levin's thought. At other times Tolstoy relies on the repetition of a verb of perception as a means of depicting both the analytic and the synthetic dimensions of mental activity. Recall the repetition of the verb "to see" in the scene where Kitty in disbelief and despair observes Anna and Vronsky together at the ball. An example from *War and Peace* would be the following passage in which Nikolai Rostov, who has just watched Napoleon bestow a medal on a Russian soldier, ponders the new alliance between Russia and France:

> In his mind an agonizing process, which he could not carry through to its end, was taking place. In his soul strange doubts were rising. *Then he remembered* [*To emu vspominalsia*] Denisov with his changed expression, with his submissiveness, and all the hospital with those amputated arms and legs, with that filth and disease. So vividly did it seem to him that he was at this moment smelling that hospital stench of corpse that he looked around to ascertain where the stench could be coming from. *Then he remembered* that self-satisfied Bonaparte with his little white hand, who was now an emperor liked and respected by Emperor Alexander. For what, then, were the severed arms, legs, the slain people? *Then he remembered* the decorated Lazarev and Denisov, punished and unpardoned. He found himself thinking such strange thoughts, that it frightened him [2, 2, 21].

Similar passages occur in other works by Tolstoy. Compare, for example, this passage from *The Cossacks* in which Olenin, having just set out from Moscow for the Caucasus, recalls the parting from his friends:

He *remembered* [*Emu vspominalis'*] all the sincere, it seemed to him, words of friendship spoken to him bashfully, as if accidentally, before his departure. He *remembered* the handshakes, the looks, the silences, the sound of a voice saying, *Good-bye, Mitya,* when he was already sitting in the sleigh. He *remembered* his own decisive frankness. And all this had touching significance for him [6, 7].

And note this passage from *Resurrection* in which Maslova, sentenced to hard labor and awaiting transport, ponders recent events:

And she *recalled* [*vspomnila*] how the defense attorney had stared at her, and how the president had stared, and how the people she met and who passed by her on purpose in the court had stared. She *recalled* how Bertha, who had visited her in jail, told her that the student whom she used to love when living at Kitaeva's had come there, asked about her, and was very sorry. She *recalled* the fight with the red-haired woman and felt sorry for her; she *recalled* the baker who sent her an extra loaf. She *recalled* a lot of things, but never Nekhliudov. Her childhood and youth, and especially her love for Nekhliudov, she never *recalled* [1, 37].

In each of these passages the repeated verb creates an image of the mind's continuous activity, in which a series of impressions and ideas is enumerated. These impressions and ideas can be seen to lead up to—and sometimes are explicitly shown to lead up to—a single essential idea. With the repetition of verbs of memory, Tolstoy shows that it is not single events, but many and varied details operating over a long time that shape and influence individuals' feelings, motives, and choices. Characters' original ideas and impressions are discontinuous in space and time, but the reiterated verb suggests that characters experience them in retrospect as somehow continuous. The narrator's repetitions underscore that knowledge and understanding are a matter of shaping separate and distinct parts into semblances of wholes.

Repetition that plays a role in the representation of how characters structure and give meaning to experience—(1) repetition of a significant element of experience, (2) repetition as frame, (3) repetition as remembered experience, and (4) repetition in the narrator's discourse that records what characters do not observe about themselves—also imposes on Tolstoy's fiction his vision of mental effort, of how thought, imagination, and memory cooperate in the ongoing process of relating different elements together and giving unity to them. Over and over again Tolstoy portrays characters who in trying to make sense of their experience focus their attention on what seems to them to be a crucial element of that experience. With each re-iteration of the isolated element, characters compel the formation of an interpretation that suits their individual motives and desires. These repeated elements become symbolic for characters, but as Tolstoy makes clear, they make better signposts than hitching posts. That is, they can better direct attempts to achieve understanding, acting as means to an end, than serve as a final statement on a subject, acting as ends in themselves. Symbols, according to Tolstoy, can help us simplify and clarify complex or confused situations, issues, or ideas, but because they are by nature reductive and limited, placing too much faith in them, Tolstoy warns, may endanger critical inquiry and honest self-evaluation.[45]

In moments of self-evaluation and self-reflection, Tolstoy's characters often picture themselves in different times and

[45] Cf. Dan Sperber's assertion that the symbolic "is not a means of encoding information, but a means of organizing it" (70).

places and bring together—logically or associationally—all kinds of details. When Tolstoy provides a frame for such moments with the repetition of an element of a character's consciousness, he underscores the internal point of view of the narrative at that point. He emphasizes that in the midst of whatever may be taking place externally, a character's mind may be engaged elsewhere. By momentarily bringing objective time to a halt, these framed scenes also call attention to the subjective experience of time, or time "as the immediate datum of consciousness."[46] The dynamic interpenetration of past, present, and future that can occur in the mind's time allows for the subjective re-ordering and re-valuing of events that are part of the process of understanding.

Tolstoy may have recognized the randomness and contingency that characterize the world,[47] but he also recognized the continual efforts of individuals to give meaning and value to their own lives. The lives of Tolstoy's characters as depicted in his short stories and novels suggest the extent to which past experiences, feelings, and thoughts influence and shape them in the present. Life's meaning and value, Tolstoy seems to suggest, are directly related to the way we incorporate our past into our present. Repetitions that mediate the matching of past and present reveal connections and themes in characters' experience. Tolstoy demonstrates that these connections and themes provide us with a sense of the continuity of our lives, but he also shows that understanding and self-worth depend not upon the quantity of these connections and themes, but upon their quality. Repeated elements in characters' discourse reflect the content of their consciousness and also a particular

[46]Meyerhof, p. 6.
[47]Cf. Morson's *Hidden in Plain View*, especially pp. 84–88 and pp. 128–29.

organization of their impressions and ideas. Repeated elements in the narrator's discourse describe this organization from an external point of view. From this external point of view, Tolstoy's narrator records mental processes and habits not accessible to characters themselves and these descriptions suggest the unconscious structuring of experience that takes place continually in the human mind. In both cases Tolstoy's depictions demonstrate the critical role repetition plays in perception, which for Tolstoy is a process of organizing different elements into a whole whose unity, because of its unpredictability and changeability, is more than the sum of its parts.

3. Relationships Among Characters

The truly apocalyptic view of the world is that things do not repeat themselves.

—Ludwig Wittgenstein

Tolstoy uses repetition to penetrate the complexities of subjective human experience. He also uses it to demonstrate just how inextricably joined to the lives of others each individual life can be. Thus, repetition plays a critical role not only in the structure of characters' experience, but in the structure of their interrelationships as well. Sometimes the repeated element sheds light on the dynamics—the motive and controlling forces—of a group of individuals and sometimes it becomes a means for exploring the relationship between just two or three characters. In both cases repetition serves to define and illuminate particular themes or ideas in the book. By repeating the same thematic phrase in a number of contexts, Tolstoy depicts differing perspectives on the same question or issue, and reminds readers that understanding begins with a discriminating awareness of the diversity of viewpoints. Like those repetitions that structure characters' experience, these repetitions also depend on a dynamics of parts and wholes. Repetition is a tool of both analysis and synthesis: it can be used to resolve a whole into its constituent parts or to create a whole from separate parts. And here, too, repetition functions pragmatically in terms of readers' experience; aesthetically in terms of qualities such as balance, rhythm, and unity; and semantically in terms of both content and expression.

The main difference between repetitions that function in characters' individual inner experience and repetitions that create links among characters is that those in the latter category are transgradient to the experience of characters. That is, these repetitions are not experienced as such by characters; they are part of Tolstoy's representation of the unsystematic, unpredictable, and unrecognized connections that occasion, even guarantee, their participation in a whole greater than themselves. How repetition functions transgradiently to characters' positions to structure and give meaning to interrelationships among characters is the subject of this chapter.

Group Dynamics

Society

Tolstoy devotes the opening chapters of *War and Peace* (1, 1-9) to the description of an exemplary Petersburg social gathering at the home, and under the direction, of the deliberately enthusiastic and artfully officious Anna Pavlovna. The narrative in these chapters is dense with description of characters' facial expressions, gestures, and voices; striking, or de-familiarizing, similes; conversation among characters; and vital—in terms of readers' orienting themselves—commentary from the narrator. Guests at the soiree, and the hostess herself, perform their roles ably and in conformity with social conventions. Only Pierre Bezukhov, who is attending his first soiree ever in Russia, seems out of place, and his "intelligent and at the same time shy, observant, and natural look, which distinguished him from everyone else in that drawing room," causes Anna Pavlovna some anxiety.

As the narrator records the manner and conversations of the numerous and various guests, a certain similarity begins to emerge. Prince Vasilii makes a clever remark to Anna Pavlovna "smiling" (*ulybaias'*). She draws in closer to him to continue their conversation on a more intimate level "smiling affectionately" (*laskovo ulybaias'*). The Viscount, one of the guests of honor this evening and anxious to relate a story he has heard, "smiled subtly" (*tonko ulybnulsia*). Princess Hélène attends to his story "with that same unchanging smile of the perfectly beautiful woman with which she had entered the drawing room" (*s toi zhe neizmeniaiushcheisia ulybkoi*). After a time Prince Vasilii prepares to take his leave, but is stopped in the anteroom by Anna Mikhailovna Drubetskaia, who seeks his help in attaining a position for her son and smiles "with the smile of a young coquette, which at one time must have looked natural on her but which now did not suit her careworn face" (*s ulybkoi molodoi koketki*). Later, when Pierre's view of Napoleon as a hero provokes a debate, the ever-gracious Princess Bolkonskaia opposes him "smiling" (*ulybaias'*). Pierre, too, smiles, but "his smile was not like that of the other people, which merged with what was not a smile" (*Ulybka u nego byla ne takaia, kak u drugikh liudei, slivaiushchaiasia s neulybkoi*).

In the course of this one evening and these five chapters, everyone "smiles" quite a bit. Perhaps it should not be surprising that people at a party should be smiling. Yet the descriptions of characters and of the manner in which they smile, in addition to what they say, ironically suggest the artificiality and superficiality of the majority of these smiles and the falseness of the entire situation so carefully arranged by Anna Pavlovna.

Tolstoy's ubiquitous repetition of various forms of "smile"

underscores the willingness of almost everyone present to submit to an atmosphere of cordiality and propriety that inhibits genuine exchange of heartfelt ideas or opinions. Pierre and Andrei are the two exceptions: Pierre because he is too naive and uncorrupted by society to know how to behave "properly," and Andrei because he has utter contempt for what he considers empty social forms and hypocrisies. The repetitions also set up comparisons among the different characters: the apparent similarity of each smile belies differences in motivation, mood, and genuineness that become clear as we begin to notice and compare the instances of repetition.

Initial descriptions of Prince Vasilii's voice, manner, and appearance portray him as a self-satisfied, disdainful, and bored nobleman seemingly protected from emotion by an impenetrable veneer of affectation. But when Anna Pavlovna questions him about his sons, his demeanor changes and he admits, "*smiling* more unnaturally and animatedly than usual," that they are a constant source of worry to him. His pained smile at the thought of his children connects him with Anna Mikhailovna, who, as noted earlier, also smiles unnaturally when she speaks to the Prince about her son, Boris. Like Anna Mikhailovna, Prince Vasilii wants to secure a position for his son. In fact, both parents have come to the soiree expressly in order to make inquiries on behalf of their children. As the first to arrive Prince Vasilii finds an opportunity early to speak to Anna Pavlovna alone: "'Tell me,' he added as if only just casually recalling something when in fact that which he was asking about was the main reason for his visit, 'is it true that the Dowager Empress wants Baron Funke to be appointed first secretary of Vienna?'" Anna Mikhailovna has to wait longer for her chance, but after she has spoken to Prince Vasilii, "she returned to the circle where the Viscount continued to tell his story and having completed her business, again pretended to listen, waiting for an appropriate moment to leave." Both anxious parents resort to pretense in order not to call attention to their manipulations: the Prince *pretends* to have just recalled the news about the secretarial post in Vienna, and Anna Mikhailovna, having accomplished her mission, *pretends* to listen to the Viscount's story. But if Prince Vasilii and Anna Mikhailovna have in common a concern for the future of their children, they do not share the same motives. Prince Vasilii recognizes Anna Mikhailovna as the sort of woman who out of a self-deprecating love and devotion would stop short of nothing to attain success for her only son. A number of chapters later, he runs into her again in Moscow at the home of the dying Count Bezukhov. Relating this encounter, Tolstoy writes: "Evidently the Prince understood, just as he had understood at Anna Sherer's soiree, that it was difficult to get rid of Anna Mikhailovna" (1, 1, 12). Both in Petersburg and in Moscow, the Prince takes note of Anna Mikhailovna's maternal tenacity. On the other hand, a pragmatic view of paternal responsibility devoid of all affection or love is what prompts Prince Vasilii's concern for Ippolit and Anatol.

Like Anna Mikhailovna, Anna Pavlovna, too, has a girlish smile that is out of place on her aging face: "The discreet *smile*, playing constantly on Anna Pavlovna's face, although it did not suit her worn features, expressed, as in a spoiled child, a constant awareness of her charming defect, which she neither wished, nor could, nor found it necessary to correct." If Anna Mikhailovna and Anna Pavlovna represent the old guard among society ladies, Lise Bolkonskaia, "known as the most bewitching woman in Petersburg," and "the beauty" Princess

Hélène represent the younger generation. With their "radiant" (*svetlaia*) smiles both young women captivate their male audiences. But whereas Princess Hélène is deceitfully affected and manipulative, Princess Bolkonskaia is like a child simply enjoying a childish pleasure. And even though she is pregnant, Princess Bolkonsksaia continues to attract admirers: "Whoever spoke with her and saw at every word her *radiant smile* and flashing white teeth, which were continually visible, felt that he was in an especially amiable humor that evening. And this was true of everyone" (1, 1, 2). The narrator's final assertion resounds ironically when in the next chapter we find that the exception to this rule is the Princess's own husband, Andrei, who responds with a "grimace," not a smile, to his wife: "Of all the faces he found boring, the face of his pretty wife, it seemed, bored him more than any other. With a *grimace* that spoiled his handsome face, he turned away from her" (1, 1, 3).

Princess Hélène passes among the men at the soiree "*smiling on all as if politely granting each the right to admire the beauty of her figure*" (1, 1, 3). Pierre in particular is struck by her beauty: "Princess Hélène, gently holding the folds of her gown, passed among the chairs, and the *smile* shone still more *radiantly* on her beautiful face. Pierre looked with almost frightened, rapturous eyes at this beauty as she walked by him" (1, 1, 3). Tolstoy's repetition of the image of the smile calls attention to both a love gone sour between Lise and Andrei and a love not yet begun between Hélène and Pierre. Later, when Pierre begins to see Hélène regularly in society, he quickly becomes accustomed to her unchanging smile, which now "expressed so little for him" (1, 3, 1). He is unable, however, to resist her tantalizing body, and her seductive beauty convinces him that he must marry her. Sexually attracted to Hélène's body, Pierre ignores, with disastrous consequences, what her vapid smile implies about her personality. The smiles of Hélène and Pierre place them on opposite ends of Tolstoy's moral spectrum. The narrator refers repetitively to Hélène's "unchanging smile," whereas Pierre's smile is described as "agreeable" (*priiatnaia*), "joyful" (*radostnaia*), and "light-hearted" (*veselaia*). His genuine and artless smile contributes to his characterization as someone whose natural sincerity and enthusiasm make him an anomaly in Anna Pavlovna's salon. Even when he causes a stir with his unpopular view of Napoleon, his smile says to everyone, "Opinions or no opinions, you see what a good and nice fellow I am" (1, 1, 5). Princess Hélène, on the other hand, with her statuesque shoulders, exposed bosom, and immutable expression and tone of voice, is the epitome of the artificiality, superficiality, and triviality that characterize high society in Tolstoy's Petersburg. Although beautiful, she is lifeless, and her "unchanging smile" becomes an emblem of the stagnant and immoral existence led by society's elite.

Significantly, it is Pierre who prompts a look of warmth and friendliness from Andrei, who otherwise appears tired and bored: "Prince Andrei, without looking around, wrinkled his face into a *grimace* expressing vexation at whoever it was who was taking his arm, but seeing Pierre's *smiling* face, he *smiled* an unexpectedly kind and pleasant *smile*."

Tolstoy uses the repetition of a seemingly unremarkable detail to bring out differences among the personalities of his characters and at the same time to synthesize a point of view which exposes the narrowly inflexible standards of conduct that prevail at a typical Petersburg social event. Because repetition allows for the joining of separate moments by similarity rather than contiguity, the scattered references to the smiles of various characters create an impression of simultaneity. In these five chapters narrative sequence is less important than the pattern of references and relationships that structure them. Tolstoy produces a tableau, as it were, with its own internal dynamic, and we find what Joseph Frank calls the "spatialization of form in the novel":

> For the duration of the scene, at least, the time-flow of the narrative is halted; attention is fixed on the interplay of relationships within the immobilized time-area. These relationships are juxtaposed independently of the progress of the narrative, and the full significance of the scene is given only by the reflexive relations among the units of meaning.[1]

For Tolstoy the forces of propriety and conformity that operate among people in social situations lead to inauthentic behavior and a false unity in diversity. Unity in diversity in Tolstoy's fictional world has to do with the apparently shared thought, emotion, and motive among a group of people all engaged in a single effort or goal in spite of the varied and various thoughts, emotions, and motives that characterize each of these people as individuals. Tolstoy values sympathy and love not just as emotions, but as paths to knowledge and understanding. In an 1893 diary entry, for example, he writes:

> There are two methods of knowing the external world.... The other method consists in first having known yourself by loving yourself, then knowing other beings by loving these beings, by transferring yourself by thought into another person, animal, plant, even a stone. By this method you know from within and form the whole world as we know it [52, 101].

[1]Frank, p. 15.

Sympathetic identification and understanding characterize unity in diversity for Tolstoy.

When Nikolai Rostov is under fire for the first time, his unique experience is depicted against the background of the general, shared experience of all the soldiers. Throughout this scene, Tolstoy calls attention repeatedly to the sameness of every soldier's experience with phrase such as "so thinks, or at any rate feels, every man," "all were looking," "their faces all so alike yet so different," "on every face," and "every one of the troops" (1, 2, 8). Tolstoy uses this technique of portraying one man's individual experience within the context of a shared experience in other battle scenes as well, and with it he makes us aware of the hidden diversity within an apparent unity. After the commotion dies down, Rostov, thinking he has shown himself to be a coward, realizes that no one seems to have noticed his difficulties: "And, indeed, no one had taken any notice, because each was acquainted with the feeling that the cadet under fire for the first time had experienced" (1, 2, 8). The sympathy and understanding that takes place wordlessly among soldiers in battle resulting in a certain uniformity of expression and mood is not the same, Tolstoy suggests, as the false or artificial uniformity that describes a social gathering. In social situations, individual motives tend to remain dominant: people regard one another as means not ends and adhere rigidly to more self-limiting roles.

When Princess Bolkonskaia, Mademoiselle Bourienne, Prince Vasilii, Anatol, and Princess Marya gather for tea at Bald Hills, each of them conceals his or her own thoughts, feelings, and motives, while engaging in "appropriate" conversation and conduct. Their talk is animated thanks to the seemingly effortless direction of Lise Bolkonskaia:

She greeted Prince Vasilii with that playful manner, which is often adopted by garrulous, *light-hearted* people and which consists in their assuming some long-established jokes and *light-hearted*, amusing *reminiscences* between themselves and the person they are addressing, when, in fact, no such *reminiscences* exist, just as there were none between the little Princess and Prince Vasilii. Prince Vasilii willingly gave way to this tone; the little Princess drew Anatol, whom she hardly knew, into these *reminiscences* of humorous events that had never occurred. Mademoiselle Bourienne also shared in the general *reminiscences*, and even Princess Marya felt with pleasure that she too was pulled into these *light-hearted reminiscences* [1, 3, 4].

The narrator's repetition of the word "reminiscences" (*vospominania*) five times in this short passage implicates all five characters in a social conspiracy based on admittedly trivial ("light-hearted" [*veselye*]) lies. For various and individual reasons, each of these characters wants to be accepted as part of the group. They are all more concerned with the impression they are creating than with the possibility of genuine and sincere communication. To the extent that each of them performs a role by joining in the invented reminiscences in accordance with the forms of social graciousness, each bears some responsibility for defining and maintaining a false situation. Like the word "smile," the word "reminiscences" here becomes an emblem for a false, or negative, unity in diversity, that is, a unity that compromises individual expression and choice.

The Battlefield

If for Tolstoy the salon provides the setting for trivial and false interaction among people, the battlefield is the place where natural instincts, genuine emotion, and significant, if fleeting, epiphany join men together in disarrayed, but unified effort. Tolstoy uses repetition to represent the positive unity in diversity that characterizes those moments of human interaction that are not so readily scripted by internally shared rules and conventions and are more vulnerable to circumstance and contingency operating externally.

Moments after a retreat under fire over the river Enns and just before the battle for the bridge begins, the Russian and French troops face each other across a barren expanse of about seven hundred yards:

> The enemy had stopped shooting, and that strict, formidable, un-approachable, and elusive *line* [*cherta*] that divides two enemy troops was all the more clearly felt.
>
> "One step beyond this *line*, which calls to mind the *line* that separates the living from the dead, and—uncertainty, suffering, and death. And what is there? who is there? there, beyond that field, and tree, and roof lit up by the sun? No one knows, and one longs to know; and one dreads crossing this *line*, and longs to cross it; and you know that sooner or later you will have to cross it and find out what is there on that side of the *line*, just as you will in-evitably find out what is there on that side of death. But you yourself are strong, healthy, cheerful and nervous and surrounded by equally healthy and nervously excited men." *This is what every man, even if he does not think, feels in the sight of the enemy* [1, 2, 8].

This concentration on the image of the line and the simultane-ous expansion of its significance recalls the mental process, in-volving both inner thoughts and feelings and external realities, that Tolstoy depicts with the repetition of *je vous aime* or "it has begun!" in the minds of Pierre and Andrei respectively (see Chapter 2). Here, however, Tolstoy describes what goes on not just in one individual's mind, but in the mind of "every man" at this particular moment. By universalizing this experience Tolstoy suggests that when confronting a disordered, chaotic situation, the ways of responding are sought and found within the self. There are no codes operating. People respond spontaneously, and yet they respond the same way. This situation bespeaks a fundamentally human bond rather than conventions. In recording what "every man feels in the sight of the enemy," the narrator starts out with an impersonal, indefinite third-person verb and then switches to the second-person verb form: at once the experience of every man becomes that of every reader. Now it is just "you" and the line that separates the living from the dead, and any strength or courage or hope comes spontaneously from within, from internalized ways or models of responding. These ways are imparted to human beings at least in part through processes of socialization as all human actions are, but they seem to suggest some kind of instinctual human response as well, and thus imply the existence of universal, immutable human qualities or virtues.

The repetition of the word "line" in this passage is Tolstoy's way of verbally conveying what the soldiers experience as mixed fear and anticipation not only at the sight of the enemy, but at the thought of their own death. The actual line separating the two armies becomes in the soldiers' minds a figurative line separating life and death. With this reiteration, Tolstoy creates the effect of affect, of the conscious subjective emotion experienced by the soldiers. Through affect, the soldiers constitute a community.

Gathered at Anna Pavlovna's soiree, Tolstoy tells us, are "the most heterogeneous people in terms of age and character, but identical in terms of the society in which they all lived" (1, 1, 2). The similarity in these people's faces—the smile they all wear—is a result of social prescription. By contrast, what makes the faces of the soldiers under cannonball fire similar is the naturalness, spontaneity, and genuineness of the feelings they are all experiencing. Tolstoy describes their faces as "similarly different" (*odnoobrazno-raznoobraznye litsa*) (literally, "similar-various faces"). Palpable among the soldiers and visible on their faces is a generalized mood or feeling born of the many individually shaded moods: "The soldiers, without turning their heads, glanced sideways at one another, looking with curiosity for the effect on their comrades. On every face, from Denisov's to the bugler's, there appeared around the mouth and chin one common *line* of struggle, nervousness, and excitement." Nikolai Rostov, about to have his first taste of battle, feels "completely happy," but even on his face "that same *line* of something new and stern showed involuntarily on his face" (1, 1, 8).

The line that literally separates the Russian and French armies on the battlefield, and figuratively separates life and death in the minds of the soldiers, now has a physical correlative on each of their faces. A sign of the shared feeling among the soldiers, the image of the line is sufficiently abstract to accommodate whatever varied thoughts and nuanced feelings the soldiers may have. Yet its repetition and transformation suggest that the unpredictable and uncertain circumstances of the situation have stimulated the same process of response among the men: an external threat prompts an inner sense of one's own mortality, which in turn manifests itself via one's involuntary and unconscious expression. Once again, the reaction of the soldiers surely bears the mark of socialization but, for Tolstoy, authentic life values come into play here on the battlefield as they can never in the salon.

The unpredictability and instability of military conflict and the fact that each battle unfolds in a new way seem to awaken in every soldier the same feeling of excitement mixed with fear and anxiety and intuition of mortality, of being both of this earth and vulnerable to death with all that this vulnerability implies. Morson may be correct when he characterizes Tolstoy's battlefield as utter chaos, but there is more to this chaos than the rule of contingency that Morson emphasizes. For within this disordered, externally determined phenomenon there is, in Tolstoy's view, fundamental and shared order in each man's soul. This common response, underscored by the repetition of the words "whole" (*ves'*) and "every' (*kazhdyi*) in phrases such as "the whole squadron" or "on every face," as much as by the repetition of the word "line," points to a *positive* unity in diversity: a unity which asserts that in spite of our individual and uniquely subjective experience of events, there exist certain universal truths we experience intersubjectively. "The true revelation of Tolstoyan genius is the depictions of certain general psychic states that exceed individual consciousness and connect [people] in the unity of jointly experienced life," asserts Lydia Ginzburg.[2]

In this scene Tolstoy's use of repetition brings into focus the individual experience of one soldier, Nikolai Rostov, without removing it from the context of shared experience. The repeated element means that the existential connection between Rostov and the other soldiers is never severed. His emotions and thoughts are brought into relief only to be placed back in a continuum that includes the emotions and thoughts of all the men:

[2]Ginzburg, p. 303.

"Well, so it is," thought Rostov; "he wants to test me!" His heart contracted and the blood rushed to his face.

"Let's see whether I am a coward," he thought.

Again on all the light-hearted faces of the men of the squadron there appeared that serious *line*, which had been on them when they had been under fire from the cannonballs [1, 1, 8].

The passage shows a sequence of thoughts in which the first are special to Rostov, the last common to everyone; and yet the common one flows naturally from the earlier ones specific to Rostov. And this flow makes us wonder: what uniquely individual processes in another person (in each person) have led to this common thought? In his study of Tolstoy's early experiments with various forms and methods of description, Boris Eikhenbaum cites "generalization" and "minuteness" as two methods Tolstoy found especially congenial. For Tolstoy, he explains: "The combination of generalization and minuteness determines the development of Tolstoy's artistic work. The first strives for simple and precise definitions, even at the risk of simplification. The main thing is logical clarity. . . . The second method—'minuteness'—virtually overthrows all these 'ratiocinations' and converts the psychic life into a kind of uninterrupted flow."[3] Repetition helps Tolstoy mediate between generalization and minuteness.

Rostov's experience is only part of a greater whole: he is everyone and himself at the same time. The image of the line, first presented as a metaphor for life and death, becomes a metonymy when it appears as a sign of great emotion on the soldiers' faces, and then metonymizes the consciousness of a single soldier. This manipulation of the figure by Tolstoy's narrator is equivalent to the movement we observed in the con-

---

[3] Eikhenbaum, p. 44.

sciousness of individual characters in Chapter 2 in the sense that in both cases the device of repetition allows simultaneously for the focusing of attention on particulars and the construction of a provisional, yet meaningful, whole.

Theme as Multiple Perspective

The three examples of repetition we have looked at thus far in this chapter—the "smile," "reminiscence," and "line"— demonstrate the role repetition plays in Tolstoy's representation and thematization of unity in diversity in *War and Peace.* Tolstoy's focus in each of these examples is on the ethical and psychological interactions and interconnections among people forming a group. And each scene offers a perspective on the theme of unity in diversity without directly naming it. In our next examples, however, theme is not just suggested by, but actually embodied in a repeated verbal element. The repetition of identical thematic verbal elements is not unique to Tolstoy. Nevertheless this type of repetition, too, allows for the movement between parts and an unfinalized whole that is so basic to Tolstoy's epistemology. That is, as readers attend to the various aspects of a theme as espoused by different characters, they are asked to piece together an understanding of competing values and motives, emotions and beliefs. The repeated verbal element becomes the vehicle for the representation of multiple perspectives.

Repeatedly in *Anna Karenina,* Tolstoy passes a single phrase through numerous perspectives, that is, through the consciousness of numerous characters. Each time these words pass through new contexts, they expand in significance. The senses they acquire from each separate context accrue and interact, and the word becomes a sign for readers of a whole constellation of motives and values. Readers experience a way of uniting words that Vygotsky labeled "influx of senses":

> The senses of different words flow into one another—literally "influence" one another—so that the earlier ones are contained in, and modify, the later ones. Thus a word that keeps recurring in a book or a poem sometimes absorbs all the variety of sense contained in it and becomes, in a way, equivalent to the work itself.[4]

Like elements that occur repeatedly in a single character's consciousness, repeated thematic elements gain in intensity in each of their recurrences both from the building up of associations and from the very fact of their repetition. But instead of depicting how one individual pieces together an understanding of experience, these repetitions allow readers to apprehend Tolstoy's thematic designs and consider multiple perspectives on complex ethical questions.

Ethical Laziness

Blaming his "silly smile" for exacerbating his wife's anger when she confronts him with his infidelity, Stiva Oblonsky asks himself in the opening pages of *Anna Karenina*, "'But *what on earth can you do? what can you do?*'" (*No chto zhe delat'? Chto delat'?*) (1, 1). He regrets Dolly's discovery of his affair with the children's governess, but recalls with vulgar glee the eyes and smiles of Mlle. Roland, and concludes, "But *what on earth, what on earth can you do?*" (1, 2). Oblonsky has a standard response for questions which he prefers to consider unsolvable, rather than to acknowledge that they require moral choices which he cannot give up his pursuit of pleasure long enough to deliberate. He simply forgets "inconvenient" obliga-

---

[4] Vygotsky, p. 147.

tions and "unpleasant" episodes. As Morson points out, it is not that Oblonsky has a bad memory; he has a good forgetery.[5]

Oblonsky's "what can you do?" is an expression born of his carefree and good-natured exuberance for life, which many readers and characters, including Levin, find appealing, but it also is an expression of a fundamental dishonesty that characterizes his relations with others. He repeats this phrase as if to assure himself that there is nothing that can be done so what is the use of worrying? Full of pity, but not love, for Dolly, who now reproves him bitterly, Oblonsky pronounces empty words more for his own consolation than for hers: "'But, *what on . . .* well, *what on earth can you do?*' he said in a pitiful voice, not knowing himself what he was saying, and dropping his head lower and lower" (1, 4). And as Dolly continues her reproaches, he laments, "This is *terrible! Terrible.*"

The phrase "what can you do?" or a near equivalent is spoken at least once by each of the main characters in *Anna Karenina*. In each case the character who utters these words is confronted by a moral conflict for which there are no immediate answers. While at least an acknowledgment that a problem exists, "what can you do?" at the same time conveys resigned acceptance and even lack of responsibility for its outcome. Like her brother, Anna Karenina is full of pity for Dolly. Somehow sensitive to what her sister-in-law may be thinking, Anna articulates the fundamental question Dolly faces: "But, Dolly, *what on earth can you do, what on earth can you do?* How is it best to act in such a *terrible* situation?" (1, 19). Anna's reenactment of Oblonsky's response to Dolly the day before suggests the extent to which sister and brother are very much

[5]Morson, "Prosaics in *Anna Karenina*," p. 6.

alike. Both display the same talent for saying what a person wants to hear and for knowing how to lie or to forget when it is convenient to do so. But whereas Oblonsky's dishonesty seems to cause him little pain, Anna's increasingly debilitates her thought and emotion. Anna's "what can you do?" seems to reiterate Oblonsky's view that what is done is done. And like her brother she places responsibility for the future of the marriage before Dolly, who has only to forgive and all will be forgotten. As Ruth Crego Benson points out: "One distinctly feels that, had Dolly bravely kept silent about Stiva's affair and kept up her duties as head of the household, the adultery would have neither attracted attention nor resulted in disaster. After all, Anna appeals to Dolly to forgive and forget, not to Stiva to stop having affairs" (96). The expression "what can you do?" is for Anna and Oblonsky a form of self-deceit: it minimizes the moral implications of an action by relegating its causes to an irretrievable past. Anna's misery becomes so great in part because she never confronts the causes of her actions, but only struggles with what seem like inevitable consequences. On the train just minutes before her suicide, Anna accepts the "truth" that human beings are created in order to suffer and asks herself rhetorically, "When you see the truth *what on earth can you do?*" (7, 31). This phrase at this moment expresses all the anguish her self-deceit has caused her. The moral impotence and hopelessness of "what can you do?" becomes finally for Anna an inducement to seek death.

Of all the main characters in *Anna Karenina*, Dolly alone rejects the consolation of "what can you do?" A loyal and good friend to Anna, Dolly cannot believe Karenin's accusations of infidelity. Not long after his meeting with a Petersburg lawyer to discuss divorce procedures, Karenin spends a few days in

Moscow, where he runs into Oblonsky, who persuades him to accept a dinner invitation at his home. Oblonsky informs Dolly about the estrangement between Anna and Karenin, and after dinner Dolly secures a moment to speak to Karenin alone. Hurt and unhappy, but prideful and bitter too, Karenin insists to Dolly that divorce is his only option. "There is nothing else I can do" (*Mne bol'she nechego delat'*) (4, 12), he tells her. Dolly cannot accept his finality: "'Nothing can be done, nothing can be done . . . ,' she uttered with tears in her eyes. 'No, not nothing can be done,' she said." She tries to dissuade him from divorce and finally he asks, "What then can I do?" (*Chto zhe ia mogu sdelat'?*). Karenin leaves Dolly with the same feelings of hate and vindictiveness towards Anna with which he arrived, but at least Dolly has gotten him to ask himself one more time what can be done. The first-person verb form inserted here, on Karenin's part, suggests engagement with, rather than detachment from, the problem.[6] Dolly's warning does have an effect, only not an immediate one. Karenin recalls her words later, and they are part of the sequence that leads to his forgiveness of Anna. Tolstoy is too good a writer to let him

[6] In her study of Nikolai Chernyshevsky's life and work, Irina Paperno points out that in *Anna Karenina* Tolstoy makes many references and allusions to the woman question, nihilism, and even Chernyshevsky's novel *What Is to Be Done?* (*Chto Delat'*) (154–55). Paperno identifies an "obvious" allusion in a draft version of this scene between Dolly and Karenin. In the draft version, Karenin says to Dolly, "Tell me, what is a husband to do?" (*chto delat' muzhu*) (20, 334). Dolly answers: "'What can you do? What can you do? [*Chto delat'? Chto delat'?*].' She opened her mouth in a painful smile and tears came to her eyes. She knew what to do—that which she had done—bear the cross." And Karenin replies, "It's impossible to live *à trois.*" In the final version of this scene, Dolly's negation of Karenin's assertion underscores the difference between Dolly and all the other characters who at one time or another ask themselves, "What can you do?" Ultimately, Tolstoy decides to give Dolly the moral strength to make a decision about how to handle a difficult situation without portraying her as a kind of pathetic martyr to womanhood.

change his mind immediately; so it is only over time that Dolly's words (or anyone's) could be effective.

Each time characters in *Anna Karenina* utter the expression "what can you do?" they are responding to the particular details of their individual situation. The phrase reveals something about their mood, motives, and moral understanding. But the repetition of the phrase enmeshes them in a universally human situation as well. Who has not been confronted with an accomplished fact—a word spoken, an action taken—that causes pain and unhappiness to someone else? The measure of our humanity, Tolstoy suggests, is the extent to which we consider, rather than dismiss, the moral implications of our words and deeds. Each utterance of "what can you do?" is motivated by the particulars of a given scene, but this theme that explores moral reaction gains in coherence as separate scenes accumulate and connect with one another. The linkages, however, are more complex than this statement suggests, for themes in *Anna Karenina* are closely interwoven. The theme of "what can you do?" is frequently joined with the themes of forgiveness and self-deception, which are similarly developed separately by means of repetition.

Forgiveness

In *Anna Karenina* Tolstoy explores the concept of understanding not just as a cognitive and intellectual faculty, but as an emotional, psychological, and moral force. Forgiveness, a special kind of understanding between two people because of the demands it makes on both of them, becomes a theme in this novel in which relations between man and woman are turbulent and uncertain even when love is present. Characters' decisions to ask for or to offer, or refuse to offer, forgiveness reflect the conscious and unconscious shifting and balancing of psychological and emotional factors and moral and axiological considerations that take place continually in their minds. The decision they make one day or the complex reasons behind it may not be the same on another. The development of this theme by repetition helps to focus attention not only on how different characters handle the question of forgiveness, but on how characters' views of their own situation and their attitudes towards others change.

When Dolly pleads with Karenin to reconsider his plans for divorce, she tells him it was Anna who saved her when her own marriage was in trouble and she urges him to forgive his wife as she has forgiven her husband. But he bristles at this suggestion:

> I cannot and do not want *to forgive*, and I consider it unjust. I have done everything for this woman, and she has trampled everything in the dirt, which is natural to her. I am not a wicked man, I have never hated anyone, but I hate her with all the forces of my soul and I cannot even *forgive* her, because I hate her too much for the evil she has done me! [4, 12].

Karenin's anger over his injured pride and insulted dignity precludes any kind of sympathy at this moment for Anna, or even for himself. Dolly's admission that she has forgiven Oblonsky seems particularly to upset him; he wants to set his own limits on how much he will endure.

The reference to Anna in this exchange between Dolly and Karenin recalls a much earlier exchange between Dolly and Anna. At that time, well before her involvement with Vronsky and subsequent rupture with Karenin, Anna assures Dolly that were she in Dolly's position she would forgive: "I would not be the same [woman], but I would *forgive* and would *for-*

give as if it had never happened, had never happened at all" (1, 19). At first glance, Dolly's response seems to echo Anna's words: "'Well, of course,' Dolly put in quickly as if saying what she had more than once thought; 'otherwise it would not be *forgiveness*. If one is *to forgive*, it must be complete, complete.'" Although Dolly does not contradict Anna and seems indeed to agree with her, her actual position is quite different than Anna's. Whereas Anna places emphasis on entirely forgetting the affair, Dolly is more concerned with entirely forgiving it, that is, forgiving it without harboring feelings of resentment, jealousy, or vengefulness. For Dolly, not forgiving entirely is the same as not forgiving at all. Her reasons for thinking this way are somewhat Dostoevskian: not to forgive entirely, not to relinquish entirely the "right" to judge, would set up the whole dynamics of superiority and humiliation, of the "benefactor" whose ostensible goodness is sure to cause resentment. True, complete forgiveness is an equalizer: it recognizes common human fallibility, as well as intrinsic human worth. Oblonsky takes advantage of the moral institution of forgiving and of the moral disposition of Dolly.[7] Many critics and readers have interpreted Dolly's forgiveness as a kind of self-deception. Perhaps in part it is, but she never denies that the transgression occurred. She is only guilty of trying to minimize the amount of pain it causes her in order to preserve what she can of all that she values. Anna, on the other hand, whose strategy from the beginning of her affair with Vronsky is denial and lies, gradually relinquishes all that she once valued, including finally her own life.

At the instant that Anna feels the impact of the train and

[7]Cf. Bernard Williams's discussion of the amoralist in *Morality: An Introduction to Ethics*, pp. 1–12.

comprehends the irreversibility of her action, she asks God for forgiveness: "Lord, forgive me everything" (7, 31). These final words could be an habitual gesture, like the sign of the cross she makes seconds before she throws herself under the train, or they could be an acceptance of personal guilt and responsibility she could never admit to herself or to anyone else. Habits, of course, develop by repetition; so that repetition can be seen to play yet another role in determining personal identity. Note that Levin, too, turns to a God he has not accepted since childhood when, like Anna, he faces one of life's transition points. During the long hours of Kitty's delivery, he repeats over and over again, "Lord, forgive and help me" (7, 13–14). His repeated prayer is more a measure of the helplessness and desperation he feels than of his religious faith, and his struggle to achieve some kind of understanding of God continues after the birth of his son. Anna's plea for forgiveness in death from a God we are not even sure she believes in is sadly ironic, since she has been unable to give or receive human forgiveness in life. Note that as Anna's paranoia, anger, and fear increase, she does not forgive Vronsky for words she knows he has not even spoken: "All the cruelest words that a coarse man could say, he said to her in her imagination, and she did not forgive him for them, as if he had really said them" (7, 26).

Anna came close to death once before at the birth of her and Vronsky's daughter. At that time she had sent a telegram to Karenin in Moscow requesting his immediate return and, more importantly, his forgiveness. Forgiveness presents itself to Karenin as the "proper" response, what Christian and social principles would require, if in fact Anna is telling the truth about her condition. Upon entering the room of his dying wife, Karenin hears her say, "Aleksei would not refuse me. I would forget, he would forgive . . . But why doesn't he come?" (4, 17). Wishing only to put an end to her misery, Anna says she would do exactly what she told Dolly she would do in such a situation: forget. Ironically, the positions of penitent and forgiver are now reversed, but that makes no difference to Anna.

Karenin, who is sensitive to the sufferings of others, is deeply moved by the tender and ecstatic look in Anna's eyes and by her emotional, confessional words. In response, he lets go of prescribed principles and allows, rather than forbids, himself to have his feelings: "He was not thinking that that Christian law which he had wanted all his life to follow was directing him *to forgive* and to love his enemies; but a joyful feeling of love and *forgiveness* towards his enemies was filling his soul." By means of the act of forgiveness, Karenin is able for the first time in his life to feel and express his emotions honestly, unmediated by the expectations or principles of others. Karenin understands forgiveness not only as something he does for Anna and Vronsky, but for his inner self and well-being as well:

> By his sick wife's bedside he had for the first time in his life given himself up to that feeling of tender compassion which the suffering of other people evoked in him and which formerly he had been ashamed of, as of a weakness; and pity for her and repentance for having wished for her death, and, above all, the very joy of *forgiveness* made it such that he suddenly felt not only the easing of his sufferings, but inward peace, which he never before had experienced. He suddenly felt that the very thing which had seemed unsolvable when he had judged, reproached, and hated became simple and clear when he *forgave* and loved [4, 19].

A key word in this passage is "compassion" (*sostradanie*). Karenin for the first time allows himself to enter into, to share

Anna's feelings. Unlike forgetting, forgiveness is an act of volition, and unlike legal procedure, it does not involve judgment and punishment. Forgiveness makes visible the moral capacity for both weakness and strength, capacities all human beings share. A freely willed act that takes as its starting point an essential equality and sameness among human beings, forgiveness is, for Tolstoy, knowledge of the unity to which all belong.[8]

Sadly, Karenin is not able to sustain this level of understanding and goodness. Instead he submits to the glances, gestures, and voices full of mockery, censure, and derision he senses all about him. Just as Anna feels a split within her being, Karenin, too, is conscious of the conflict between an inner "good, spiritual force" (*blagaia, dukhovnaia sila*) and a "coarse force" (*grubaia sila*) that governs the self he presents to others. His public image is most affronted by Anna's friend Princess Betsy Tverskaia, "who seemed to him the embodiment of that *coarse force*, which would rule his life in the eyes of the world and prevent him from giving himself up to his feeling of love and *forgiveness*" (4, 19). Forgiveness becomes an intolerable burden to his pride and dignity. With the repetition of "forgiveness" in this set of scenes that begins with Karenin's talk with Dolly in Moscow and ends with his confrontation with Betsy in Petersburg, Tolstoy escorts Karenin through a maze of conflicting thoughts and emotions. If at first he views forgiveness as a principle of conduct to be applied when appropriate, he comes to appreciate the profoundly human bond an act of forgiveness can forge, and for a brief time a sense of his own capacity for joy and goodness envelops him.

[8] Cf. Richard Gustafson's discussion of forgiveness as an aspect of Tolstoy's religious thinking and in terms of the role it plays in certain of his characterizations and works in *Leo Tolstoy: Resident and Stranger*.

The numerous repetitions of "forgiveness" in various contexts, as the expression of individual characters' capacity for moving outward beyond the self to extend sympathy, understanding, and love to others, stand in opposition to the novel's terse epigraph: "Vengeance is mine; I shall repay." For Orthodox believers, the ultimate power for both vengeance and forgiveness resides in God. Tolstoy himself seems to have accepted this truism, but he also knew that behind human acts of vengeance and forgiveness stands a vast array of individual moral and psychological attitudes and motives. In *Anna Karenina* vengeance remains for the most part an unstated, yet subtly present, theme. As Anna's fate demonstrates, vengeance can never be the starting point for understanding or love. At least in part, Anna's suicide is an act of vengeance, an act intended to punish Vronsky; with death, however, the possibility for any further communication ends. Forgiveness, on the other hand, sincerely felt and honestly expressed, begins with an act of understanding. The explicit repetitions of "forgiveness" testify to the positive potentials it contains even if these potentials are only rarely or briefly attained.

With the themes of forgiveness and "what can you do?" Tolstoy explores what the quality of characters' relations with other characters suggests about them as individuals. At times, acts of forgiveness and utterances of "what can you do?" become a form of self-deception, a way of structuring one's relation to another in terms of an established moral, religious, or social attitude, that relieves one of having to find one's own attitude. The repetition of these expressions not only establishes them as paradigms for viewing a conflict, but undermines their stability as such by illustrating various individual appropriations of the paradigmatic concept.

Moral absolutes and traditional values come under scrutiny in *Anna Karenina* as characters struggle to strike a balance in their lives between social and familial expectations and responsibilities, and personal happiness and fulfillment, between altruism and egoism. The task for Tolstoy's characters is to weave together a particular version of how to live (a morality, a set of rules, a narrative) both personal and tied to external (social, military, religious, novelistic) tradition. In a world where morality is not a matter of rules, cannot be generalized, a moral sense is developed by learning to make fine distinctions among apparently similar cases. Repetition reminds us of these similarities so we can attend to differences as part of our moral education. As with morality, so with authenticity, a life lived truly is a matter of sensitively appropriate responses to particular situations.[9]

Relationships Between Characters

With thematic repeated elements in *Anna Karenina* Tolstoy involves all of his major characters in his representation of certain shared human experiences which explore the range of human moral, psychological, and emotional response. But Tolstoy also uses repetition to call attention to and illuminate some particular bond shared by only two or at most three characters. Here we again get multiple points of view, but the

[9]Cf. Morson's example from Tolstoy in his discussion of ethics as a topic that concerned Bakhtin throughout his intellectual career: "In *Anna Karenina*, when Levin is challenged to say whether he would use violence to prevent a Turkish soldier from killing a Bulgarian baby, he replies that he does not know, that he would have to decide *at that very moment* on the basis of criteria he cannot enumerate in advance. His half-brother, a prominent intellectual, can only laugh at Levin's inability to state his principles, but for Tolstoy this sensitivity to real people and real particulars is the key to moral choice" ("Bakhtin and the Present Moment," 207; emphasis in original).

characters themselves, rather than any particular theme, are now the chief focus. This type of repetition, which sets up comparisons among characters that both provide insight into their relationships and illuminate them further as individuals, occurs in much of Tolstoy's fictional writing, including both *War and Peace* and *Anna Karenina*.

Pierre and Marya

Hesitating a moment in her room before going down to meet Anatol Kuragin, a possible suitor, for the first time, Princess Marya in *War and Peace* daydreams of love, marriage, and family happiness. Fearful that these may be "thoughts of the devil," Marya, whose spiritual life keeps her together psychologically, hears in her own mind God's words of consolation: "Desire nothing for yourself; do not seek, do not be anxious, do not be envious.... If it please God to test you in the duties of marriage, be ready to fulfill his will" (1, 3, 3). Marya enters the drawing room no longer concerned with her hair or her dress, nor worried about what she will say, because: "What could all that signify in comparison with the predetermination of God, *without whose will not a single hair falls from people's heads?*" says the narrator, paraphrasing from the Bible and speaking through Marya's consciousness. As it occurs in the Gospels of St. Matthew (10: 29–31) and St. Luke (12: 6–7), the image of the hairs on our heads is part of an argument about why God will not forget a single one of us: just as he remembers each sparrow, he knows each hair on our heads and thus remembers us, too. So in these verses the context is not really fate, or not only fate, so much as memory. Marya's choice of expressions is touchingly ironic, since the anxious efforts of Lise Bolkonskaia and Mademoiselle Bourienne earlier to improve her coiffure had resulted only in Marya's embarrassment and frustration. The metaphorical statement confirming God's ubiquitous presence and power seems to have an almost literal significance for Marya at this moment. More than five years, and seventy-five chapters, later, Marya offers her own words of consolation in a letter to Julie Karagina, whose brother has just been killed in Turkey. She empathizes with Julie's loss and grief by recalling her own experience when her sister-in-law, Lise, died in childbirth. In her letter, we read not only Marya's intention to comfort her friend, but her personalized understanding of why life unfolds as it does, as well:

Ah, my friend, religion, and religion alone, can—I don't say comfort but—save us from despair; religion alone can explain to us what without its help human beings cannot comprehend: why, for what purpose, good and noble beings able to find happiness in life, who not only have never caused harm to anyone, but are necessary to the happiness of others, are called to God, while wicked, useless, harmful people or those who are a burden to themselves and others are left to live. The first death I saw, and which I never will forget, the death of my dear sister-in-law, made such an impression on me.... She was irreproachable as a young wife; maybe she could not have been such a mother. Now ... she will in all likelihood receive there a place such as I dare not hope for myself. But not to speak of her alone, this premature and terrible death has had the most beneficent influence, in spite of all the grief, on me and on my brother.... I write all this to you, my friend, only to convince you of the Gospel truth, which has become a principle of life for me: *not a single hair of our heads falls without His will.* And His will is governed solely by His infinite love for us, and so whatever befalls us is for our own good [2, 3, 25].

At those times when she finds herself floundering a bit psychologically and morally, Marya turns God into a personal guide. Again we skip many years and scores of chapters to find Pierre convalescing in Orel with much free time for his thoughts, which the narrator relates:

> In the past he had been unable to see *the great, the unfathomable, and the infinite* in anything. He had only felt that it had to exist somewhere, and he had been searching for it. In everything near and comprehensible he had seen only the limited, *the petty, the commonplace, the meaningless.* He had armed himself with an intellectual telescope and had looked into the distance there where *the petty and the commonplace,* hidden in the fog of the distance, had seemed to him *great and infinite* only because it was not clearly visible. Such had European life, politics, Masonry, philosophy, philanthropy seemed to him. But even then, in those moments when he considered his weakness, his mind had penetrated that distance, too, and there he had seen once again *the petty, the commonplace, the meaningless.* Now, however, he had learned to see *the great, the eternal, and the infinite* in everything, and therefore, naturally, in order to see it, in order to enjoy his contemplation of it, he discarded the telescope, through which until now he had been looking over the heads of people, and joyfully contemplated the eternally changing, eternally *great, unfathomable, and infinite* life around him. And the closer he looked, the more serene and happy he was. The terrible question—why?—which had destroyed all his intellectual constructions in the past, did not now exist for him. Now to that question—why?—there was always ready in his soul a simple answer: because there is a God, *that God without whose will not a hair from a person's head falls* [4, 4, 12].

Neither Pierre nor Marya ever becomes aware that the other cites this biblical adage. When Marya and later Pierre evoke the image of God's power and ubiquity, they reveal something about themselves as individuals: readers learn not only what

they think but how they think. Each utterance of the adage
has its own significance for its speaker in its distinct context,
but repetition invites comparison. If readers notice the repetition of the adage, they may begin to think about differences
and similarities among the individual scenes and between
Marya and Pierre. So that in addition to three separate contexts, we discover a single inclusive context, as well.

To recognize this series of repetitions requires the perspective of the whole. The repetition is "transgradient" to the experience of the characters themselves and suggests the perspective
and values of the author. This notion of the surplus of the
author's vision vis-à-vis the characters from a position outside
them, which is the basis for the consummating or unifying aesthetic consciousness of the author, belongs to Bakhtin:

> The author not only sees and knows everything seen and known
> by each hero individually and by all the heroes collectively, but he
> also sees and knows *more* than they do.... And it is precisely in
> this invariably determinate and stable *excess* ["surplus," in Russian,
> *izbytok*] of the author's seeing and knowing in relation to each
> hero that we find all those moments that bring about the con-
> summation of the whole—the whole of each hero as well as the
> whole of the event which constitutes their life and in which they
> jointly participate, i.e., the whole of a work.[10]

The particular use of the "hair on one's head" quotation is in
the mind of each of the two characters, but the repetition is intelligible and visible as such only in the context of the whole,
which makes the same expression fit in three different contexts.

Both Marya and Pierre use the biblical aphorism to crystal-

[10]Bakhtin, "Author and Hero," p. 12. Emphasis in original.

lize their continually dynamic and interactive thoughts and memories, emotions and motives. Such crystallizations are the representation of what seems to be Tolstoy's psychological insight that at certain moments the complexity and instability of mental activity gives rise to apparently simple articulations. The attempt to put into words multiple, possibly conflicting, imperfectly or incompletely formulated thoughts and emotions is always in a sense misleading; any simplification emphasizes certain details at the expense of others. But articulation offers a starting point. Furthermore, in this particular example, and as perhaps often happens, a simplification borrows the rhetoric of an "other," in this case the Bible. Thus Tolstoy's insight has also to do with a psychological tendency to understand the self in terms of social and cultural attempts to understand human beings and experience.

For Princess Marya, the adage expresses her understanding and dutiful, if problematic, acceptance of the limitations and hardships that are part of life. This acceptance is paradoxically both the result and the cause of her attitude of shy reserve toward the possibilities and joys that she knows are also part of life. She accepts sadness and disappointment as part of God's world, whereas Pierre would like to eliminate these elements. For Pierre, the adage expresses his embracing at this moment of the knowledge that he possesses the freedom and the strength to recognize the infinite and eternal in everything and to realize happiness on this earth. Seven years earlier Pierre had shared his belief with Prince Andrei that "if there is a God and a future life, there is truth and goodness, and a person's highest happiness consists in striving to attain them" (2, 2, 12). His concern then was with a distant and future happiness. Now, in Orel, he understands the *presence* of this happiness, because he has learned that truth and goodness are not badges to be earned, but are characteristic of a certain way of living.

Pierre's new spiritual understanding echoes Tolstoy's own understanding, as expressed in an 1855 diary entry, of a religion "appropriate to the stage of development of mankind—the religion of Christ, but cleansed from faith and mystery, a practical religion, not promising future bliss but giving bliss on earth" (47, 37).[11] Marya, on the other hand, continues all her life to conceive of a separate existence that transcends life on earth and has its own happiness. In the final chapters of the book, the narrator describes Marya as she reflects upon happiness:

> Her face lit up with a smile; but at the same time she sighed, and there was an expression of gentle melancholy in her deep gaze, as though she felt that besides the happiness she was experiencing, there was another happiness, unattainable in this life, which she had involuntarily thought of at that moment [Epilogue, 1, 9].

Marya's humility keeps her from seeing her own life as an embodiment of "truth and goodness." Freed of the tyrannical love of her father and the condescending love of her brother, Marya nevertheless continues to invoke the command of God in her own strict self-judgment. If for Pierre at the end of the book, God is everywhere manifest including in himself, for Marya, God remains a guiding light, an ideal to follow, but never attain. Reflecting on the difference between her feelings for her

---

[11]This famous quote from Tolstoy's diary is usually taken to mean that even in 1855 Tolstoy had the idea for the religion without mystery he was to found decades later; but I take the line quite differently. In my view Tolstoy has in mind an ethical way of living that would concentrate attention on the particulars of the present, and thought and action in the present would be ends in themselves rather than the means to some future reward.

nephew, Prince Andrei's son, and for her own children, Marya "felt guilty before him and in her soul she promised herself to make amends and to do the impossible—in this life to love her husband, her children, Nikolenka, and all people as Christ had loved humanity. Countess Marya's soul was forever striving towards *the infinite, the eternal,* and the absolute, and therefore could never be at peace" (Epilogue, 1, 15).

Like Pierre, Marya thinks about God in terms of the infinite and the eternal. Pierre and Marya are both in a sense pilgrims, wondering about the nature of the journey through life and its final destination. The affinity between them is spiritual, rather than emotional or intellectual: they share an awareness of some unfathomable significance outside of themselves of which, not just in contemplation, but in their day-to-day activities, they are a part. The repetition of the biblical adage provides a concrete link between three separate scenes and quite different, yet in certain ways similar, characters. By means of this repetition Tolstoy provides not only an explicit provocation for readers' memory and thought, but awakens them to the qualities of detail, harmony, and coincidence that so frequently elude our detection in life.

Anna and Vronsky

Repetition that joins two or at most three characters is one of the ways Tolstoy creates the "labyrinth of connections" among men and women in *Anna Karenina* as well. These connections are not a matter of establishing polar opposites or rigidly symbolic contrasts, but rather represent the great diversity with which characters in Tolstoy, most of whom embody positive as well as negative traits, react and respond in human dramas familiar, to a greater or lesser extent, to us all.[12] One such connection is that Anna, Vronsky, and Levin, under the compulsion of their passions and ideas, all contemplate suicide, although with different consequences. Levin never actually attempts to take his own life, but Anna and Vronsky do and both, shortly before they make their attempts, believe they are losing their mind.

After Vronsky hurries away for what will prove to be the last time, Anna wanders into the nursery expecting somehow to see Serezha instead of Annie. Upset and disoriented, Anna leaves the child who reminds her too much of Vronsky and stands alone worrying about her appearance should Vronsky return:

"I'll go and wash up. Yes, yes; *did I brush my hair* or not?" she asked herself. And she *could not remember.* She felt her head with her hand. "Yes, *my hair is brushed,* but I don't at all *remember* when." She did not even trust her hand and went up to the mirror to see whether her hair was brushed or not. *Her hair was brushed* and she *could not remember* when she had done this. "Who is that?" she thought, looking in the mirror at the feverish face with the strangely brilliant eyes, frighteningly looking at her. "Yes, that is I," she suddenly understood, and looking at her whole self, she felt his kisses and, shuddering, moved her shoulders. Then she raised her hand to her lips and kissed it.

"*What is this, am I going mad?*" [*Chto eto, ia s uma skhozhu?*] and she went to her bedroom where Annushka was tidying up [7, 27].

---

[12]Barbara Hardy uses the phrase "common tests" to refer to these dramas or situations: "Levin's reaction to his child does not remind us of Karenin's, both are striking in themselves. It is rather that all the characters are subjected to similar tests, the common tests of fatherhood, profession, and faith, and that the parallelism is often scarcely noticeable" (890). Note that my point is the exact opposite of Hardy's; in my view it is precisely the parallelism, the repetition, that accentuates the differences.

The repetitions along with other words and images in this passage indicate Anna's agitation and confusion, which cause her to wonder whether she is going mad. Earlier in the novel, just after the birth of their daughter, Vronsky had experienced a similar, if more abrupt, disorienting shift in *his* self-perception. Whereas Anna's sense of humiliation and despair takes hold of her gradually, Vronsky is suddenly overcome with an overwhelming sense of shame after Karenin behaves magnanimously before him. Feeling humiliated and disgraced by Karenin's noble gesture and certain that he has lost Anna forever, Vronsky decides to shoot himself.[13] As drastic as this decision may be, it is in perfect accord with Vronsky's sense of honor and code of rules. It is as if denied the chance of a duel, which is what he had been hoping for earlier, Vronsky finds an equally chivalrous solution to his dilemma. Like Anna, although much less acutely, Vronsky suffers from a loss of identity: Karenin now seems right and decent, while he seems dreadfully wrong and deceitful. The overwhelming shock of his own humiliation and his inability to escape this feeling, because of the endlessly recurring memories and thoughts that flood his mind, cause Vronsky to believe he must be losing his mind:

> He still lay trying to fall asleep, although he felt there was not the least hope of this, and kept repeating in a whisper random words from some disjointed thoughts, wishing by this to prevent new images from rising. He listened to and heard repeated in a strange mad whisper the words: "Didn't know how to appreciate, didn't

[13] In a letter to Strakhov written in 1876 before he had completed work on *Anna Karenina*, Tolstoy mentions this scene depicting Vronsky's suicide attempt in connection with his conception of art as an "endless labyrinth of linkages." According to Tolstoy the idea to have Vronsky shoot himself came to him unexpectedly and suddenly as he was reworking the scene and, he asserts, "Now it turns out that for what follows this was organically necessary" (62, 269).

know how to use what I had; didn't know how to appreciate, didn't know how to use what I had."

"What is this? or am I going mad?" [*Chto eto? ili ia s uma skhozhu?*] he said to himself [4, 18].[14]

Not just this passage, but this entire chapter in which Vronsky is shown nearly possessed by his own riotous emotions and thoughts, is saturated with repetitions; even the words "to repeat" and "repetition" recur frequently. As with the passage in which Anna questions her sanity, the textual density of this chapter reflects extreme psychological conflict.

Vronsky's sense of madness and subsequent suicide attempt, as irrational as they may seem, are in defense of his own ego. Happily, his attempt fails and he begins to work at finding a new identity for himself, one that will include his relationship with Anna. Unhappily, Anna's successful suicide is the outcome of her complete loss of identity, personal as well as social. As she stands before the mirror and kisses her own hand, Anna experiences total and pathological abstraction from herself. She knows the moral impossibility of reconciling the passion she feels for Vronsky and the guilt she feels towards Karenin and Serezha. Her suicide is not a defensive action, but an attack: an attack on Vronsky, on all those from whom she feels alienated, including herself. She succumbs to that impersonal and evil force, of which Karenin and Levin are also conscious, because she has made her choices a certain way and has led herself to a moral impasse. When Anna unknowingly re-

[14] The words Vronsky repeats here are enigmatic, but it is perhaps noteworthy that in the scene that takes place immediately after Anna and Vronsky make love, Tolstoy uses one of these verbs, "to use" (*pol'zovat'sia*), in his description of a murderer's actions after a murder: "But in spite of all the horror of the murderer before the body of the one murdered, he must cut into pieces and hide that body; he must use what he has obtained by the murder" (2, 11).

peats Vronsky's words, questioning her sanity, as he once questioned his, we are somehow reminded of all that has happened between them since Vronsky shot himself and are acutely aware that Anna's mental and moral turmoil now is far more grave than Vronsky's was then. Like the dream they both have about the bearded peasant who mutters in French, these repeated words seem to be a sign of the unnatural and unhealthy bond between them that neither is strong enough to break.

Andrei and Nikolai

The repeated element that joins two characters is not always an expression that both happen to utter at different times under different circumstances. In this next example, the repetition of a silly joke in *War and Peace* provides the unlikely background noise for the expression of the deeply felt hopes and dreams of Andrei Bolkonsky on the eve of the battle of Austerlitz and Nikolai Rostov on the following day after the battle has been lost.

Pacing back and forth through the night fog in front of the hut where he is billeted not far from the field of Austerlitz, Andrei imagines the heroic role he will play in the next day's battle and anticipates the glory his heroism will earn him. At this moment nothing seems as important to Andrei as the praise, honor, and love of the other soldiers, the glory that would elevate him to a position of prestige and power. The lofty and detached tone of Andrei's thoughts is ironically undercut by the narrator's description of the "people" whose love and respect Andrei longs for:

> "Death, wounds, the loss of my family, nothing holds any terror for me. And as dear and as precious as many people are to me—my father, my sister, my wife, the people most dear to me; how

terrible and unnatural this seems—I would give them all up immediately for a minute of glory, of triumph over people, for the love
of people I do not know and will not know, for the love of these
people here," he thought listening to the sound of voices in Kutuzov's courtyard. In Kutuzov's courtyard the voices of the orderlies
who were packing could be heard; one voice, probably that of the
coachman, teasing Kutuzov's old cook, whom Prince Andrei
knew and who was called Tit, said: "Tit, eh, Tit?"
   "Well?" answered the old man.
   "Tit, go thresh a bit," said the joker.
   "Tfoo, go to hell," came a voice drowned by the laughter of the
orderlies and servants.
   "And nevertheless I love and value only triumph over all of
them. I value that mysterious power and glory that hovers above
me in this fog!" [1, 3, 12].

Late in the afternoon of the following day, Nikolai Rostov,
who has been sent to the front lines to deliver a message to the
Tsar and the Commander in Chief, discovers that the Russian
army has been routed. He comes upon the Tsar in gloomy and
solitary contemplation not far from a field strewn with bodies.
Although he has long imagined what, if ever he had the
chance, he would say to this figure, so revered and beloved by
him, Nikolai is now speechless and quietly rides away only to
watch in silent despair as the Tsar receives consolation from
another soldier bolder than himself. Upset at having lost the
opportunity to show his devotion to his Tsar, Nikolai heads
disconsolately back to the command post:

   In front of him walked Kutuzov's groom leading some horses in
   caparisons. Behind the groom came a vehicle and behind the vehicle walked an old bowlegged servant in a cap and a sheepskin coat.
      "Tit, oh Tit!" said the groom.
      "What?" answered the old man absently.

"Tit, go thresh a bit."

"Eh, fool, tfoo," said the old man spitting angrily. Some time passed in silence, and then the same joke was repeated again [1, 3, 18].

The contrast between Nikolai's sad and self-critical thoughts that are inspired by the Tsar and the inane joke at the expense of Kutuzov's bandy-legged old cook is actually tempered by the fact that we hear the same joke as before and, Tolstoy suggests, we would hear it again and again if we stayed on the road with this little caravan. Nikolai's thoughts, and Andrei's thoughts, too, are absorbed into the continuum of noise and activity that is history. But this observation does not mean these thoughts are unimportant, for they represent the effort of these two young soldiers to construct a concept of themselves that suits their emotional and psychological needs.

This repetition is an example of Tolstoy's dexterous use of trivial, even irrelevant, detail to create the impression of "real" life, where not everything that happens in the present has certain significance or relevance relative to "events" in the past or in the future. As Morson explains, Tolstoy's use of irrelevant details was part of his plan to write a book that would challenge the falsifying conventions of all narratives: "The unnecessary incidents and characters ... are as central to the structure and strategy of the work as they are irrelevant to its plot."[15] The fact that an ostensibly trivial detail occurs twice is bound to de-stabilize readers' conventional novelistic expectations for relevancy and significance much more than any single trivial detail could. Although the joke itself may be irrelevant, its repetition is significant insofar as it forges a link and encourages comparison between Andrei's thoughts and those of Nik-

---

[15]Morson, *Hidden in Plain View*, p. 147.

olai. As the threat of fighting draws near both Andrei and Nikolai are consumed by images of heroism and bravery, but their conceptions of these qualities are quite different. Nikolai, inspired by the proximity of the Tsar, dreams of total self-sacrifice in service to his Tsar and his country. When Tsar Aleksandr reviews the troops before Austerlitz, Nikolai is among the crowds of people caught up by an irresistible enthusiasm and love for the Russian Emperor. Andrei, on the other hand, dreams of distinguishing himself as a great individual; he longs to be ranked among those whom he believes "decide the fate of nations" (1, 3, 9).

The second utterance of the silly joke ironically underscores the ephemerality of Andrei and Nikolai's profound hopes and dreams. Their thoughts last only as long as the circumstances that prompt them do, even if their feelings and soon their memories linger on. But the endlessly repeatable one-liner has no particular context, nor even a single speaker. Tolstoy's juxtaposition of different types of human utterances is a reminder of the diversity of activity and response that are part of events that from a more removed perspective seemingly sweep everyone along uniformly. In conventional histories, as Tolstoy was well aware, such ostensibly trivial and inconsequential occurrences as the telling of this joke and its effect on Andrei and Rostov would never find mention. But for Tolstoy it is precisely the ordinary, the unnoticed details and particulars that constitute "real" life and thus "true" history.

When Tolstoy joins two characters by repeating a specific word or set of words, he is exploiting the economy of repetition: with a bare minimum of words a connection is made swiftly and explicitly. But repetition is economical not only because of the efficiency with which two characters are linked, but because of the munificence of significance, insight, and implication, which is the true substance of the link of which the repetition is only a sign. The pointedness with which repetition indicates a connection gives way to the complexity of that connection. Tolstoy uses the identity of two utterances to point to a relationship based on much more than this simple identity. Here we find starkly exposed one of the central paradoxes of repetition that makes the device so indispensable to Tolstoy's artistic rendering of life, which relies on processes of both analysis and synthesis. As Gregory Bateson asserts, "The essence and *raison d'être* of communication is the creation of redundancy, meaning, pattern, predictability, information, and/or the reduction of the random by 'restraint.'"[16] But at the same time repetition quickly ceases to provide new information, and it is precisely change and difference that give rise to new information.[17] Since a repeated phrase is both a fact of repetition with respect to another passage where the same phrase appears and a unique utterance with respect to the passage in which it occurs, the repeated phrase creates information by virtue of both its sameness and its difference.

Throughout this chapter we have been looking at repetitions in Tolstoy that are transgradient to characters' positions within the texts: repetitions that depict the dynamics that operate among people gathered together for some shared purpose, repetitions that pass a thematic phrase through numerous perspectives, and repetitions that act as links between two, or among at most three, characters. These repetitions that reveal

---

[16] Bateson, pp. 131–32.

[17] This commonplace of information theory has found useful application in the science of chaos, where it has prompted scientists to recognize that as a system becomes chaotic it generates a steady stream of information "strictly by virtue of its unpredictability" (Gleick, p. 260).

so much about character relationships crucial to the thematic and plot designs of Tolstoy's novels are of significance whether we are considering these narratives primarily as representation, communicative process, verbal structure, or psychological activity.

The double role of the repeated elements discussed in this chapter—their importance within a certain specific context and in the construction of a larger whole—is what gives the device of repetition its power to guide readers in seeing the design of the whole in terms of its parts. Repetitions that are transgradient to characters' experience, but critical to readers' experience, operate by exceeding the repeated with every reiteration: they become markers for the constellations of images and ideas that are the solid, but intangible fabric of Tolstoy's texts.[18]

[18] In his book *The Structure of "The Brothers Karamazov,"* Robert L. Belknap discusses the "structure of inherent relationships" that serves in Dostoevsky's novel (1) to establish connections between parts of the novel, (2) to maintain the reader's interest, and (3) to focus this interest on those parts of the novel which Dostoevsky considered important (44). Repetition is perhaps as important a device in Dostoevsky's oeuvre as it is in Tolstoy's, and Belknap points out that in *The Brothers Karamazov* repetition functions as an aid to the reader's memory and to establish the thematic foci of the "structure of inherent relationships." To make a thorough comparison of Dostoevsky's use of repetition with Tolstoy's would surely be an intellectually rewarding endeavor. For now, I merely observe that while for Dostoevsky repetition is certainly an important literary device, for Tolstoy repetition is much more than a literary device, because of the critical role he understood it to play in the way human beings structure and make sense of their experience.

4. Intertextual Repetition in Tolstoy

> She was a music I no longer heard, that rang in my mind, itself and nothing else, lost to all sense, but not perished, not perished.
> —Marilynne Robinson, *Housekeeping*

Up to this point my concern has been in*tra*textual repetition in Tolstoy. But readers more familiar with Tolstoy know the extent to which in*ter*textual repetitions—repeated themes, motifs, structural patterns, even characters—occur in his work as well. All writers will repeat certain devices and techniques throughout their career; people cannot recreate their whole personality or all their techniques with each work. So any writer will have certain characteristics, certain habits, certain particular and identifiable idiosyncrasies. Then there are writers—Tolstoy, Trollope, Zola among them—whose works not only contain these inevitable repetitions, but also reflect a deliberate, intentional reliance on the device of repetition to achieve certain ends.[1] In either case, repetitions in an author's oeuvre may be a key to his/her habits—stylistic habits and habits of thought—and this is true of Tolstoy.

Certain of Tolstoy's "habits" reflect his preoccupation with

---

[1] On repetition in Zola see Brown, *Repetition in Zola's Novels*. And on repetition in Trollope see Epperly, *Patterns of Repetition in Trollope*.

an epistemology and a psychology based on parts and the whole. Thus, once again, repetition becomes significant not just as a stylistic device, but as a supplier of both the form and the content of Tolstoy's ideas about how human beings structure and give meaning to their experience. Tolstoy's intertextual repetitions offer the careful, persistent reader a hypothetical text of his oeuvre: they suggest his persistent concern with particular kinds of experiences—experiences that involve conscious attempts at sense-making and self-shaping. Repetitions that occur across the boundaries of separate works belong to a perspective outside any one of them, that is, they are part of what readers construe as Tolstoy's authorial discourse. They tell us something about his authorial preoccupations, habits of thought, and associations. At the same time, intertextual repetitions may serve as clues to the fact that in addition to a given work there is a larger work in view. This larger work or whole consists of the combined significance that attaches to the repeated element in its separate contexts. When taken together by a reader the separate iterations can be seen to comment upon, embellish, or interact in some other way with one another. The well-read student of Tolstoy constructs an "as-if" model of the author, as if passages from his separate works were somehow intended to allude to, to anticipate, or to recall one another, whether or not they were, and as if his fiction were somehow designed as one large work, whether or not it was.

Each word, phrase, or idea that has an intertextual antecedent elsewhere in Tolstoy serves a particular function in its particular context, but it also signals that constellation of images, associations, and meanings that go beyond the immediate context. At the same time, an intertextual repetition becomes a marker of the connections, recognitions, and recollections triggered, often unexpectedly or involuntarily to be sure, in the mind of Tolstoy the author. These repetitions, if recognized as such by Tolstoy's careful readers, make them aware of an important element of continuity in his work and thought. Connections among works that are not readily apparent now become obvious. We can look to intertextual repetitions in Tolstoy's work in order to confirm the persistence of certain images or ideas in his thought, to follow the development of his thought, and to discover something about his authorial thought pattern. Repetition in Tolstoy's work taken as a whole contributes to our creation, our sense, of Tolstoy the author. Most typically, Tolstoy's intertextual repetitions consist of the repetition of a single topos or the repetition of a set of interrelated topoi. By looking at several representative examples of intertextual repetition in Tolstoy, I intend to demonstrate that by virtue of their appearance throughout his oeuvre, these topoi can be said to represent Tolstoyan universals. Furthermore, I intend to show that Tolstoy's conception of music provides a kind of model for how the repetitions that come to constitute a Tolstoyan universal interact.

Over his long career Tolstoy created many memorable characters drawn with great particularity. He immersed his sharply individualized characters in timeless moral and social situations and conflicts while at the same time managing to convey the particularity of the time (the season, the hour of the day or night, the year) and the place (the wheatfields, the battlefield, the courtroom) in which these characters lived. Through the myriad permutations of particular times, particular places, and particular characters, the Tolstoyan universals remain the same: those moments—signaled by a particular phrase or set of images—when characters self-consciously take stock of where they are, who they are, and how they ought to live occur again and again in Tolstoy's narratives. What changes over the course of Tolstoy's career is not the function of those universals, but the highly particularized context in which they appear. And this observation makes sense, for it seems to me that one of Tolstoy's ambitions was to dramatize, in an effort to make sense of, the paradoxical nature of human beings: in certain ways we seem to be essentially similar, but at the same time, we are undeniably radically different. A whole host of questions flows from this paradox: what accounts for the similarities? what accounts for the differences? are the similarities more than the differences, less important, or equally important? I do not claim that Tolstoy thought about these questions, only that his own wrangling with universals and particulars raises them. Tolstoy's intertextual repetitions offer readers who recognize them as such the opportunity to experience and observe the ongoing universal processes of sense-making and self-shaping.

Tolstoyan Universals

Tolstoy's intertextual topoi tend to describe or pertain to particular kinds of experience, which for character after character are invested with great significance. Tolstoy repeatedly establishes certain kinds of moments as paradigmatic instances of sense-making and self-shaping. At these moments cognitive, aesthetic, and ethical perception come together as characters invest otherwise ordinary moments with immense personal significance. These repeated moments may be thought of as Tolstoy's "mythic" offering, in the sense that they embody both the particular and the universal, concreteness and a generalizing force. They depict "universal imaginative experiences of dream, daydream, heightened consciousness, memory, hope, forgetting, sudden realization," as does myth.[2] Tolstoy offers readers representations of the efforts of the human heart and mind, the emotions and the intellect, to shape the self. The repeated element—that which links a number of passages from different stories and novels—is in each case the generalizing force that distills, from various, particular attempts at self-shaping, intimations of some universal, because recognizable or familiar, essence.

In my introduction I drew a connection between Socrates' belief in recollection as a source of self-knowledge and Tolstoy's use of repetition as a means of securing a sense of continuity and unity of the self that enables self-knowledge. Tolstoy's intertextual topoi reflect his absorption of Platonic theories.[3] The recognition, which involves repetition and remembering, of a repeated word or phrase as an intertextual topos occasions a kind of knowledge—a knowledge about the reenactment of a significant experience. At the same time, although the particular context of each repetition of a topos is crucial, its repetition alludes to a general form that posits universal, if not ideal, experience. Tolstoy relies on repetition to show the continuity between the world of ordinary human experience and the world of universal and eternal forms.

Tolstoy's early works reflect his preoccupation—discernible in his youthful diaries as well—with self-observation and self-expression. Both narrators of their own stories, Irtenev in

---

[2] This line that seems to me to describe Tolstoy's repeated moments so exactly is from Paul Friedrich's discussion of myth in *The Language Parallax*.

[3] In a fascinating article entitled "The Recuperative Powers of Memory: Tolstoy's *War and Peace*," Patricia Carden demonstrates that the Platonic doctrine of recollection underlies the shape that *War and Peace* took as a novel.

Youth (1857) and Masha in *Family Happiness* (1859) agonize over the apparent futility of turning a mental ideal in to a material reality. "Why is everything so beautiful, clear in my mind, and turns out so ugly on paper, and in my life in general, when I want to put something I have thought of into practice?" 16-year-old Irtenev asks himself in frustration. And 21-year-old Masha uncertainly confides to her husband that "Inside me everything is so incoherent, incomplete; I still feel I want something, but here it's so beautiful and peaceful." Like many of Tolstoy's characters, Irtenev and Masha experience the throes of the search for self-knowledge and order in themselves. And although Irtenev's difficulty lies in trying to express this order in word and deed, while Masha's lies in her sense of its absence, both characters crave a story that makes sense. For Tolstoy, identity and self-knowledge are achieved through reflections on one's past and present, and through making decisions on how to live and what to do with one's life; over and over again in his fictions he presents us with characters who struggle with these decisions.

Tolstoy often depicted the pitfalls of trying to construct a coherent narrative for oneself. Such attempts, he knew, are often based on misperceptions, incorrect assumptions, and unrealistic expectations, and inevitably lead to contradiction, falsehood, and unhappiness. In "A Landowner's Morning," published in 1856, the young and idealistic Prince Nekhliudov leaves the university and returns to his country estate in order to dedicate himself to improving the lot of his peasants. In his mind's eye he sketches himself as the generous benefactor of those in need. But the sanitized image in his imagination is much more pleasant than the actual grim evidence of poverty, which he guiltily realizes is all too easy to forget:

> Nekhliudov had already long known, not by hearsay, not by taking on faith the words of others, but actually, the extreme poverty in which his peasants found themselves; but this entire reality was so incompatible with his entire upbringing, his turn of mind and way of life, that against his will he would forget the truth, and each time he was, as now, vividly, palpably reminded of it, his heart would become unbearably heavy and sad as if the memory of some perpetrated, unexpiated crime was tormenting him [4, 134].

One year later, Nekhliudov is disillusioned and dissatisfied. His "story" has not had the happy end he expected, for from his point of view his peasants are still poor and uneducated. But rather than think about the reasons for his apparent failure, he takes refuge in idealized memories of his past life. The story ends with Nekhliudov wistfully imagining what are surely the carefree adventures of Ilya the peasant: adventures made possible by Nekhliudov, who has agreed to let the young man work off the manor this summer. Nekhliudov even imagines the dreams Ilya will have while on the road: "'Glorious!' Nekhliudov whispers to himself, and the thought—why isn't he Iliushka—also enters his mind" (4, 171). Note that Tolstoy does not use a first-person quoted-thought construction to record Nekhliudov's second thought: instead he uses a third-person reported-thought construction. This construction seems to emphasize that Nekhliudov sees himself as a character in a story that is his life. The use of the diminutive captures both Nekhliudov's wistfulness and the folktale-like quality of his musings. Of course, Nekhliudov does not envy Ilya's actual life: he envies an imaginary version of that life. Sadly, but not surprisingly, his "story" once again disappoints. In "A Landowner's Morning" Tolstoy seems to anticipate both Levin's continual frustrations as he tries to work out his relationship with his peasants and Kitty's futile efforts to imitate Varenka at the German spa. But whereas Kitty and Levin learn that life is not a script, Nekhliudov seems at the end still to wish it were.

Tolstoy also frequently depicted what he apparently conceived of as an inherent human urge to attribute special significance to specific personal events. Characters in Tolstoy often see certain moments or certain words as decisive. At these moments they experience a kind of epiphany, a realization that lets them glimpse the meaning in an event, if not life. Oftentimes these epiphanies are deceptive: Pierre's involvement with the Masons turns out to be a false path. Or they may have an undisclosed quality about them: perhaps Natasha falls in love so readily with Anatol because unconsciously she knows that marriage to Andrei would be a mistake. True epiphanies come when characters realize—and only the select ever do—the complexity of "peace." For Tolstoy "war," which posits a Manichaean view of the world that turns a myriad of individuals' needs and desires into a nation's sense of solidarity, is a metaphor for a simple understanding of the universe. And "peace," then, is a metaphor for the acknowledgment of the messiness, the randomness, the unpredictability of life. Tolstoy's intertextual topoi capture what are often only fleeting moments of epiphany.

"It has begun"

In a number of his works, Tolstoy uses the expression "it is beginning" (*nachinaetsia*) or "it has begun" (*nachalos'*) to signal characters' sense that something important, something that will significantly and irrevocably separate their past from their future, is about to happen. At these moments, characters believe they are encountering fate. Note, however, that such moments have an apparently momentous significance because characters, not Tolstoy, assign them significance. Tolstoy depicts the human inclination to stamp particular events and experiential details with special significance as a means of imposing structure on and finding meaning in their experience. But because our experience is ongoing and continuous, any beginnings, middles, or ends we identify along the way are provisional, and while they serve our particular intellectual and psychological needs at a particular time, they tend to be forgotten or transformed through the complex and inscrutable workings of our memory.

Morson explains Tolstoy's depiction of characters' impulse to structure in the context of Tolstoy's efforts to realize through narrative life as it is lived, given the constraints of narrative conventions and readers' narrative expectations:

> So long as novels depend on closure, Tolstoy believed, they will seem false. And so long as they try to combine closure with a depiction of free, choosing people, they will be temporally incoherent. Free people must live in a world without fatalism and completed structure, a world in which time is open and choices never end. This is the essence of Tolstoy's argument and the key to the most significant formal innovations of both *War and Peace* and *Anna Karenina*.[4]

To illustrate his assertion Morson discusses Anna Karenina's belief in omens and fatalism—a belief that makes her death by suicide seem inevitable. But the impulse to structure does not always have such tragic consequences; although a character's exclamation that "it has begun" may, from some overarching

[4] Morson, "Anna Karenina's Omens," pp. 135–37. See also *Narrative and Freedom*, pp. 42–81.

perspective, be erroneous, it nevertheless stamps an experience as meaningful for that character at that moment. The psychological experience depicted in these scenes is underscored and made memorable for readers by the repetition of the expression. That is, repetition helps to set these scenes apart from others in readers' memory so that if, or when, readers recognize the same repetition in another work, they are likely to reflect upon any possible connections. At the very least, they will recognize it as a Tolstoyan stylistic tic.

Repetition not only gives emphasis to the experience depicted in the scene, but facilitates recognition of a similar experience elsewhere. With each of its recurrences, the repeated phrase becomes increasingly emblematic of a specific psychological experience. Thus repetition both suggests connections among separate scenes in separate works and creates memorably effective individual scenes.

In *Youth*, the third in a cycle of three short works which record a man's own exploration of his intellectual, emotional, and moral development, Nikolai Irtenev lists the feelings that he says formed the basis of his dreams during the period of his transition from boyhood to the beginning of youth (*nachalo iunosti*). The first of these feelings, he writes, is "love of *her*, the imagined woman about whom I always dreamed in one and the same way and whom every moment I *expected* to meet somewhere" (2, 85). Irtenev sums up the second feeling—a desire that everyone love him—in just a couple of lines, before taking up a lengthier explanation of the third:

> The third feeling was a hope for some uncommon, vainglorious happiness so strong and firm that it turned into madness. I was so sure that very soon, following some kind of uncommon event, I suddenly would become the most wealthy and most distinguished

person in the world, that I continually found myself in [a state of] anxious *expectation* of something magically happy. I was always *expecting*, that here it *would begin* [*vot nachnetsia*], and I would achieve all that a person could wish for, and I was always in a hurry everywhere, supposing that it was *beginning* [*nachinaetsia*] *there, where I was not* [*tam, gde menia net*] [2, 85].

Irtenev's apprehension lest he miss the beginning, the onset, of his new life is similar to his obsession, which he describes in *Boyhood*, with the philosophy of skepticism:

In a word, I agreed with Schelling in the conviction that objects do not exist, but only my relation to them exists. There were moments when, under the influence of this *fixed idea*, I reached such a degree of absurdity, that sometimes I would glance quickly around in the opposite direction, hoping to catch unawares the void [*néant*] *there, where I was not* [*tam, gde menia ne bylo*] [2, 57].

The same preoccupation with his own awareness of his experience characterizes the younger and the slightly older Irtenev, but now impatient expectation rather than eager curiosity directs his thoughts. The irony is that the older Irtenev is *pursuing* what he takes to be his *fate*. This feeling of expectation interferes with his preparations for his university entrance examinations:

The consciousness of freedom and that vernal feeling of vague *expectation*, about which I already spoke, stirred me to such a degree that I absolutely could not control myself and I prepared for the examinations very poorly.... You would be sitting behind a book and concentrating all your attention with difficulty on what you were reading, when suddenly in the corridor you would hear female steps and the sound of a dress,— ... "Well, suppose it were suddenly *she*?" comes into your head,—well, what if now, *here it were to begin* [*vot i nachnetsia*], and I were to let it pass?" and you jump out into the corridor and see that it's just Gasha [2, 98].

When Irtenev is introduced to Dmitrii Nekhliudov's sister, Varenka, he ponders whether she could be the beloved he imagines and whether it is with her that love, and indeed life, will finally begin: "'Is it possible that she is *she*?' I wondered. 'Is it possible that it is *beginning* [*nachinaetsia*]?' But I soon decided that she was not *she* and that *it was not yet beginning*" (2, 154). But falling in love is not the only rite of passage Irtenev anxiously awaits. He is full of excitement when he is invited to his first drinking party: "Everyone without exception kept watching the door of the buffet room and, although they tried to hide it, they all wore an expression that said: 'Well, *it's time to begin* [*pora by i nachinat'*].' I, too, felt that *it was time to begin*, and I awaited the *beginning* [*nachalo*] with impatient joy" (2, 199). Finally the punch is ready and the lights are extinguished: "Many took off their coats (especially those who had fine and perfectly clean shirts). I did the same and understood that *it had begun* [*nachalos'*]."

In all of these passages Irtenev anticipates new experiences—sensations and thoughts—quite unlike those he had as a child and boy. But more importantly, he is intent on capturing, on being aware of, *the precise moment* at which these experiences begin, at which he becomes, in his own mind, a young man. That in fact there is *no* precise moment becomes an important theme in Tolstoy later. In *War and Peace* Tolstoy demonstrates that in life, causes are multiple and temporally extensive, not singular and located at a point in time. Every change, every moment is preceded by an infinite number of moments and changes all depending upon and influencing one another. This absolute interdependence of all the details of experience is the point of Tolstoy's "law of reciprocity": "A good player who has lost at chess is sincerely convinced that his loss was the result of his mistake, and he searches for that mistake in the beginning of his play, forgettting that at every step in the course of the game there were similar mistakes, that not a single one of his moves was perfect" (*War and Peace*; 3, 2, 7).

The repetition of the various forms of the expression "it is beginning" within scenes and throughout the book alerts readers to Irtenev's attentiveness not only to the content, but to the form, the stages, of his own experience, perception, sensation, and thought. Irtenev's first drinking bout proves a disappointment and he falls in and just as quickly out of love several times in the course of his account. His passage into adolescence is not punctuated with dramatic changes as he had hoped: it is fluid and continuous, and as the older narrator's effort and desire to record his development from childhood to youth attests, the past can never be left entirely behind. This truism could be the epigraph to Tolstoy's *The Cossacks*, as it is one of the lessons the novel's hero, Olenin, learns.

Anxious to leave behind the hypercivilized artificiality of Moscow society and a woman whose love he cannot return, Dmitrii Andreievich Olenin sets off for the Caucasus in search of a new life and a new and authentic self. As he parts from his friends he tells them, "But now everything is finished, you are right. And I feel that a new life *is beginning* [*nachinaetsia*]" (6, 5). Once in the Don Cossack country, Olenin's memories seem remote and his sense of anticipation increases. The story of a murder that has recently occurred on the road and the sight of armed men everywhere convinces Olenin that now he has entered a different world: "'*Here is where it begins!* [*Vot ono gde nachinaetsia*],' Olenin said to himself expecting at any moment to see the snowy mountains about which he'd been told so much" (6, 13). But it is not until the next morning that Olenin gets his first clear view of the immense and impressive mountains:

> As the troika moved rapidly along the level road, the mountains seemed to hurry along the horizon, their rose-colored peaks shining in the rising sun. At first the mountains only amazed Olenin, then they made him glad; but later, as he looked more and more intently at the chain of snowy mountains rising and escaping not from other black mountains, but straight from the steppe, he little by little began to grasp this beauty and he felt the mountains. From that moment on, everything that he saw, everything that he thought, everything that he felt took on for him the new, austerely majestic character of the mountains. All his Moscow reminiscences, his shame and repentance, all his commonplace dreams about the Caucasus, all disappeared and did not return again. "*Now it has begun* [*Teper' nachalos'*]," some sort of solemn voice seemed to say to him [6, 14].

The first two times Olenin uses the verb "to begin," he uses it in the present tense to assert that a new life, a new experience, something different is now under way and that the people and sights he encounters from this point on will also be new and different. Olenin's anticipation of novel sensations and experiences is similar to the anticipatory excitement Masha in Tolstoy's *Family Happiness* feels when as a young bride she enters Petersburg society for the first time:

> I suddenly found myself in such a new, happy world, so many joys enveloped me, such new interests appeared before me, that I immediately, if unconsciously, renounced all my past and all he plans of this past. "That was all nothing, child's play; it hadn't yet

begun [*eshche ne nachinaetsia*]; but here it is, real life! And what will it be like?" I thought [5, 116].

Whereas Olenin is trying to escape society's artificialities and constraints, Masha is eager to experience its diversions and frivolities. But like Olenin, she finds that happiness and a sense of one's own identity are not to be found in the adoption of what at first seems like an enviable and romantic role.

His third and final use of the verb, however, is in the past tense and is accompanied by the word "now," which as it is used here in Russian refers quite specifically to how things are presently as opposed to how they were earlier (*teper'* versus *seichas*).[5] With this declaration Olenin definitively marks this particular moment as the starting point, as the boundary separating his past from his future. The third utterance also differs from the first two in that the words seem to Olenin to be spoken to him rather than *by* him. That he should experience the words this way suggests his sense that they offer objective affirmation of what he feels to be true: a voice not his own also recognizes that something new has begun.

For Olenin, as for Irtenev, to state that something new is beginning (or has begun) is a means of distinguishing among values or ideals. By viewing their lives in terms of past and future, these characters can easily consign values they once estimated highly to a remote place in time from which they cannot reemerge. Their almost incantatory use of the verb "to begin" seems to hasten irrevocably the banishment of values and ideals they would rather now replace with new and "better" ones. Tolstoy uses this incantatory function of repetition again

---

[5] Of course, *teper'* means "now" when a comparison is being made with a previous state of affairs or when a transition from one action to another is indicated, and *seichas* means simply "now," "at this time."

and again throughout his fiction to suggest characters' belief or hope that words determine reality. Words used as if they were verbal charms and attempts to see certain moments as definitively decisive are only two of the many ways in which, Tolstoy shows us, human beings deceive themselves in their anxious efforts to create an acceptable narrative of their lives. As Tolstoy argues in *War and Peace*, there are no beginnings, because one event proceeds out of another continuously and because critical moments do not determine events, but the continuous succession of ordinary ones does. Another point he seems to make in his fictions is that what stops the movements of ordinary living is the mental act of noticing that you are noticing something.

When Prince Andrei pronounces the words "Here it is! It has begun!" three times as the battle of Schongraben gets under way (see Chapter 2 of this study), he, too, attempts to assign significance to a particular moment so that it can take its place in the narrative sequence he is constructing. In Tolstoy's *Khadzhi-Murat* (published posthumously), the words "it's beginning" (*nachinaetsia*) spoken by the young Russian soldier Butler, whose head is full of romantic images of heroism and battle, as he is about to take part in a raid against the Chechens, and the description of his thoughts and feelings leading up to the raid are oddly reminiscent of Andrei's experience.

Three impulses—a cognitive, an aesthetic, and an ethical one—merge in Andrei's verbal act. Simultaneously he seeks to know and understand something about this tense moment thick with the emotions and thoughts of countless soldiers just before battle; to fit his experience harmoniously into an emerging whole imagining in advance how it will turn out; and to establish his own identity, to belong to a role in life, but also to his own sense of self. Each of these impulses, or desires, depends on an interpretation of the part in terms of a projected whole. Over and over again Tolstoy demonstrates that the repeated phrase, as a meager, but purposeful distillation of the range and complexity of the conscious and unconscious feelings and thoughts that constitute an individual at any given moment, is an important means by which a part is brought into the whole. Repetition and the personal myth, story, or conception it voices are sources of empowerment giving the individual a sense of self-creation. Each of the scenes in which characters see a particular moment as a beginning essentially describes a moment of self-creation. At these moments characters have a sense of their lives taking shape, and it is this sense that sets these moments apart from others.

The scenes that are linked by characters' repetition of the phrase "it's beginning" (or "it has begun") represent characters who think they are in boundary positions, perched between the past and the future in a moment of presentness made rich by memory and expectation. Characters encounter their fate, their destiny, but the irony is that they themselves see (narrate) their experience that way. *Fabula* encounters *siuzhet*: the basic story stuff, the sum-total of events, becomes under the actor's gaze the story as actually told, the way in which events are joined. Dotting, as it were, Tolstoy's fictional landscape, these scenes evoke similar images, depict characters with similar feelings and thoughts, and thus probably elicit similar responses from readers who notice them. By comparing and contrasting the parallel experiences of various and distinct characters, readers receive an education in the nuances and particularities that save common or shared experience from becoming identical experience. Tolstoy reminds readers that each human being is at the same time a unique individual and part of a greater whole that is founded upon a union with other people, with ideas and entities beyond the self. This lesson on sharing comes not from each scene, but by their juxtaposition.

Nighttime Epiphanies

The juxtaposition of the passages discussed above is prompted by the repetition of the phrase "it has begun" or "it is beginning" in each one. In the following set of passages, a set of images and motifs, rather than a single phrase, prompts such juxtaposition. In other words, a strikingly similar scene, which is evoked by a particular set of images and motifs, appears in more than one work inducing readers to consider what the significance of the scene might be in terms of Tolstoy's larger oeuvre.

On August 10, 1851, Tolstoy recorded in his diary the following observation:

> The day before yesterday the night was glorious. I was sitting by the window of my hut in Starogladkovskaia and was taking pleasure in nature with all my senses except touch. The moon had not yet risen, but in the southeast the nighttime clouds were already beginning to turn red and a light breeze was bearing with it a scent of freshness. Frogs and crickets merged into a single vague, monotonous nighttime sound. The sky was clear and sowed with stars. I love to observe the star-covered sky closely at night [46, 82].

Other diary entries similar to this one suggest that Tolstoy regularly found a kind of pleasure and solace in contemplating the nighttime sky. Describing in writing these moments of peaceful absorption into the sounds and stirrings of nature at night often leads Tolstoy into further meditations on art, morality, memory, and other subjects which have become the very motifs of his life as he recorded it.[6] In his fictions, Tolstoy frequently seats his more thoughtful characters in the same position: in a state of affective reflection in concert with contemplation of the night. Each such scene recalls others like it because of certain images they share and because they all depict a character's experience of illumination concerning his or her identity or sense of self through a matrix of cognitive, aesthetic, and ethical awareness.

Tolstoy's Nikolai Irtenev, narrator and hero of the trilogy *Childhood, Boyhood, Youth* whom we encountered earlier, spends the summer of his sixteenth year on the family estate in the country. Here he indulges continually in the sensuous pleasures of nature and in fantasies of love, which at night merge powerfully together. In chapter 32 of *Youth*, Irtenev describes how he spent those days in the country. This chapter is itself entitled "Youth" as if to suggest that in the memory of the adult Irtenev, the thoughts and emotions that occupied him that summer are the essence of who he was during that period which he refers to in retrospect as his youth. A description of a typical day's activities is followed by a description of what the nights were like:

> When the moon was full I often spent whole nights sitting on my mattress looking intently at the light and the shadows, listening attentively to the silence and the sounds, dreaming about various subjects, mainly about poetic, voluptuous happiness, which seemed to me then the highest happiness in life, and grieving that so far it had only been granted me to imagine it [2, 178].

[6]Note Philip Kuberski: "The relationship between the galaxy of stars and some inner principle of the Self (the soul, destiny, conscience, the brain) would appear to be the metaphoric axis of any attempt to understand man's place in the universe" (63).

Gradually everyone in the household retires for the night and the lights are extinguished:

And that's when I would lie on my bed with my face to the garden and covering myself as best I could from the mosquitoes and bats, I would look into the garden, listen to the sounds of night, and dream about love and happiness.

Then everything assumed a different significance for me: the old birches with their leafy branches shining in the moonlit sky on one side and on the other darkly obscuring the bushes and the road from view with their black shadows, and the peaceful, luxuriant, increasing—uniformly like a sound—luster of the pond, and the moonlit luster of dewdrops on the flowers in front of the verandah, which also threw their graceful shadows across the gray flower bed; and the sound of a quail beyond the pond, and the voice of a person from the main road, and the quiet, barely audible scraping of two old birches against each other, and the buzzing of a mosquito over my ear under the blanket, and the fall of an apple—which had been caught on a twig—on dry leaves, and the jumping of frogs, which sometimes reach the edge of the terrace, their greenish backs shining somewhat mysteriously in the moonlight,—all this assumed a strange significance for me, the significance of beauty too great and happiness somehow incomplete. And then *she* would appear with her long black braid, her full bosom, always sad and beautiful, with bare arms, with voluptuous embraces. She loved me and for one moment of her love I would sacrifice my whole life. But the moon rose higher and higher, brighter and brighter in the sky, the luxuriant luster of the pond, uniformly becoming stronger, like a sound, became clearer and clearer, the shadows became blacker and blacker, the light more and more transparent, and as I looked intently and listened attentively to all this, something said to me, that even *she*, with her bare arms and ardent embraces, was still far, far from being all of happiness, and that even love for her was far, far from being all of goodness; and the longer I looked at the high full moon, the more true beauty and goodness seemed to me higher and higher, purer and purer, and closer and closer to Him, to the Source of all beauty and goodness, and tears of as if unsatisfied, but tumultuous joy would fill my eyes [2, 179].

The passage and chapter end with Irtenev's assertion that "it seemed to me at such moments as though nature and the moon and I were all one and the same" (2, 180).

This long passage, thick with the repetition of certain expressions, images, and syntactical constructions, effectively communicates not only the cognitive content, but the psychological form—a spiral of images of ever-expanding significance—and the emotional intensity of Irtenev's thought. His lyrical description captures especially the affective power of the play of light and dark at night: the night for Irtenev is not a time of obscurity and ignorance, but of focused illumination and heightened understanding. At night a youth's romantic dreams of love are eclipsed by equally ardent intuitions of his own relation to nature and through nature to God. Struggling to learn to know himself, to reconcile competing impulses for self-indulgence, moral goodness, and nobility of spirit, Irtenev finds some measure of reassurance on these summer nights when his sense of identity is strengthened by his identification with nature.

Only a year older than the youthful Irtenev when her story begins, Masha, Tolstoy's first-person narrator and heroine in *Family Happiness*, is similarly enchanted by romantic dreams of love. After a visit from her guardian, Sergei Mikhailovich, draws her out of a depression brought on by the death of her mother in the fall and the cold isolation of winter, Masha finds new hope and comfort in vague thoughts and wishes inspired by the coming of spring. Looking back on those days she recalls how:

> [s]ometimes all night long, especially on moonlit nights, I would sit by the window in my room until morning; sometimes in only a blouse, unbeknownst to Katya, I would go out into the garden and run through the dew to the pond; and one time I even went out to the field and alone at night walked around the entire garden.
>
> Now it's hard for me to remember and understand those dreams which then filled my imagination. Even when I remember, I don't believe that these were really my dreams, so strange and so far removed from life were they [5, 73].

Masha's reveries are those of a young girl just becoming aware of love and romantic self-indulgence. In her memory, she associates her immersion into the night with the influence and flourishing of her romantic hopes and desires. To the imagination of a young girl the nighttime and romantic love share a similar mystery and enchantment.

Marriage to Sergei Mikhailovich, however, turns out to be a disappointment to Masha. She had expected that the passion and intensity of their initial attraction would remain strong. Her enthusiastic, but naive and foolish foray into society keeps her illusions about love and happiness alive, and she begins to interpret her husband's disdain for the people and activities of society as coldness and a lack of love for her. Eventually, Masha comes to realize that she and Sergei Mikhailovich are still bound by mutual love: not the ephemeral love of romantic desire, but an enduring love based on their shared experience of everyday life. Her reconciliation with her husband and realization of a deeper love take place at nightfall. Masha recalls how desperate she was to make sense of her sadness and sense of loss:

> Again his presence, his simple, kind voice dissuaded me from thinking that I had lost something. What more was there to wish for? He was kind, gentle, he was a good husband, a good father. I did not know myself what I still lacked. I went out on the balcony and sat under the awning of the terrace on that very bench on which I had sat on the day of his proposal. The sun had already set, night was drawing on, and a dark springtime cloud hung above the house and garden. Only from behind the trees was a clear patch of sky with the dying sunset and a tiny evening star, which had just broken through, visible. Over everything there lay the shadow of the little cloud, and everything was waiting for a gentle spring rain shower. The wind had died down; neither a single leaf, nor a single blade of grass stirred. The scent of lilac and cherry blossom, so strong as if all the air was in bloom, filled the garden and terrace as if in waves, now suddenly weaker, now stronger, so that one wanted to close one's eyes and see nothing, hear nothing apart from that sweet scent. The dahlias and rose bushes, still without flowers, stretched out motionless along the dark, furrowed flower beds, as if slowly growing up their white supports of whittled wood. From the ravine came the sound of frogs shrilly croaking in unison, as if in a final outburst before the rain that would drive them into the water. All that could be heard above this clamor was a thin, uninterrupted sound of water. Nightingales called to each other in turn, and could be heard anxiously flying from place to place [5, 137].

Sergei Mikhailovich joins Masha on the terrace, and as the frogs croak and nightingales sing, the two talk openly and honestly for the first time about their relationship. Finally their discussion comes to an end:

And from the garden the scented freshness of night was rising ever more strongly and sweetly, ever more solemn grew the sounds and the silence, and in the sky more and more stars were lighting up. I looked at him and suddenly I felt easier in my heart, as if that painful moral nerve, which had made me suffer, had been removed. Suddenly I clearly and calmly understood, that the feeling of that time had irrevocably passed like the time itself, and that it was not only impossible to retrieve it, but that to do so would be painful and embarrassing [5, 143].

In these two passages, both from the last chapter of the story, nighttime is once again the occasion for thoughts and hopes about the self. But if as a girl, Masha was influenced by what she perceived as the mystery and enchantment of the night, as a woman just a few years older, she is enveloped by the sounds, smells, and forms of the natural world that seem to become more evident at night, when human activity is at rest. When Masha recalls her nighttime wanderings as a girl, she offers no real description of either the night or the content of her daydreams. From her perspective as narrator of her own story, these details are not important. What is important is that although her girlish fantasies may once have been appropriate, they could not provide a basis for a love that must change and develop over time. Her mistake was in believing that an imaginary life of romantic illusions could provide family happiness. Recounting her sincere and frank talk with Sergei Mikhailovich that takes place several springs later, Masha describes the night and her hopes and fears in much greater detail. It is as if her awareness of the stimulation of her senses by the natural world allows her to see the true nature of her relationship with her husband, whereas before her vision had been clouded by false expectations. Masha's apprehension of the night does not

cause the change in the couple's relationship; that change has
been taking place for some time. Rather, her attentiveness to
her senses and to the surrounding natural world that stimulates
them is a correlative to a new sense of herself and of her husband and children as part of this world. As Edward Wasiolek
observes, "[Masha] comes back to life when she touches what is
real and natural within her, and what is natural and real
changes with different periods of her emotional life."[7]

Here in *Family Happiness*, and elsewhere in Tolstoy's fictional worlds, nighttime is the right time for a special kind of
profound self-reflection, in which from within a matrix of
cognitive, aesthetic, and ethical strands of awareness, the individual achieves a clearer sense of his or her own identity. Sitting on the terrace beneath the stars, Masha is at once aware of
the apparent unity and harmony of nature that corresponds to
what is best in her; the development that must occur in the
love between husband and wife if it is to be a lasting love; and
a sense of how to live in family happiness.

Nighttime contemplation, unlike "it has begun" cannot be
said to be a motif unique to Tolstoy. But what *is* special to
Tolstoy is the subjective association he makes between nocturnal images—sounds, smells, and sights—and moral being, moral
identity. It is no surprise that Kant's epitaph, "The starry sky
above me, the moral law within me," struck a chord with Tolstoy. He repeats this phrase, which also figures prominently in
the conclusion to Kant's *Critique of Practical Reason*, at least
five times in his miscellanies—his compilations of the thoughts
and moral imperatives of famous people, past and present,
which he began in 1886 and continued until his death.[8] The

---

[7] Wasiolek, *Tolstoy's Major Fiction*, p. 44.

[8] For a discussion of the miscellanies, the chief of which are printed in volumes

significance of Kant's epitaph for Tolstoy is, I believe, that it brings together notions of the direct subjective experience of nature and an inborn moral sense. For Tolstoy these two distinct, but related notions establish starting points for knowledge and understanding. In the final scene of *Anna Karenina* Levin gazes up at the nighttime sky and senses some connection between his perception of the stars that appear to be moving and his apprehension of the law of goodness, which he feels within himself and shares with others:

> And just as astronomers' conclusions would be idle and precarious were they not founded on observations of the visible sky in relation to one meridian and one horizon, so my conclusions, too, would be idle and precarious were they not founded on that understanding of goodness, which was and will be the same for everyone and always, and which was revealed to me by Christianity and can always be verified in my soul [8, 19].

Levin realizes that his impulse to reason and analyze obscures a primary essential view of life: "To me personally, to my heart, has been revealed, without doubt, knowledge unattainable by reason, and I stubbornly want to express this knowledge by reason and in words" (8, 19). In Tolstoy, an individual's consciousness of the strength and potential of his or her moral and spiritual capacity becomes an element of the nighttime landscape. The self is absorbed into the natural world, and the moral and natural spheres of life are joined.

The natural world at night as Tolstoy conceived of it, with its powerfully affective quality that seems especially conducive to meditation on one's place in this world, takes on special sig-

---

40–45 of the Jubilee edition of Tolstoy's works, and Kant's presence in them see Jahn, "Tolstoy and Kant." See Kupreianova for a discussion of *Anna Karenina* and Kant (106–10).

nificance in *Resurrection* (1889–99), where it becomes first the backdrop for Nekhliudov's seduction of Maslova and only later an occasion for reflection and self-articulation. When Prince Dmitrii Ivanovich Nekhliudov is called to serve on a jury at the trial of a prostitute accused of murder, whom he recognizes as a girl he years before seduced and left alone to bear a child, he is conscience-stricken, and thus begins his moral scrutiny of himself and society and his spiritual regeneration. During a recess called by the president of the court, Nekhliudov takes a seat by the window in the jury room and thinks back to the night he took advantage of the beautiful young maid he knew then as Katiusha:

> He went out on the porch again. It was dark, damp, and warm outside, and that white fog, which in the spring drives away the last snow or is diffused by the thawing of the last snow, filled the air. From the river, which was a hundred paces down a steep slope in front of the house, could be heard strange sounds: this was the ice breaking [1, 17].

In the narrator's continued account of Nekhliudov's recollection of the seduction, certain words, including "fog," "strange sounds," and "ice," are repeated. These repetitions do more than describe the eerie weather conditions that night. They convey the negative light in which Nekhliudov now sees his actions: looking back he finds that the weather seemed already to be condemning him for his baseness. The repeated images communicate both the vividness and the onerousness of his memories. Tolstoy also repeats several times that Nekhliudov recalls that night while sitting by the window in the jury room. And Nekhliudov's first experience of that night was from the porch of the house. Both of these places—the window and the porch—are border positions, positions from which

Nekhliudov looks back to the past or forward to the future
and considers who he is and how he will behave. These are
border positions in a second sense as well in that they demar-
cate inner and outer realms. Within the court building, law,
order, and justice are held up as ostensible ideals, whereas outside its windows the city and even the countryside teem with
violations of these principles. There is also the absurdity of
Nekhliudov's sitting in judgment over Katiusha, whom he
once violated. Inside the house on his aunts' estate is the limited world of human invention, whereas outside is the infinite
world of nature. Irtenev, Masha, and Tolstoy himself in his diary entry also occupy literal and figurative border positions in
their respective meditations. The border positions they occupy
are liminal in both senses of the word: they find themselves on
a sensory threshold as well as on a threshold in time and space.
That is, these scenes record their increased attentiveness and
emotional-psychological response to the sounds, sights, and
smells of the natural world at a particular moment in a particular place.

Back in the courtroom Nekhliudov cannot detach his gaze
from Maslova's strange, squinting eyes: "He remembered that
terrible night with the *breaking ice*, the *fog*, and above all the
waning, upside-down *moon*, which towards morning had risen
and lit up *something black and terrible*. These two *black* eyes,
looking at him and past him, reminded him of this *something
black and terrible*" (1, 19). The italicized words in this passage
are words frequently repeated in the description of the seduction scene. These particular details are amplified in Nekhliudov's memory not because he is concerned about the suffering
he caused Maslova, although he is beginning to acknowledge to
himself his guilt before her, but because he fears she may rec-

ognize him. Neither Nekhliudov's original experience nor his recollection of that night involves an inwardly reflective experience of the kind had by Masha or Irtenev. But the similarities between the two sets of scenes make the differences even more significant. The scene with Nekhliudov carries special resonance for those readers who remember Tolstoy's earlier works and the other nocturnal scenes. The point is not just the difference between the sets of scenes, but readers' remembering the difference. If for Masha and Irtenev the night becomes the occasion for the realization of a correspondence between what is best in them and nature, for Nekhliudov the night provides the cover—the fog and the sound of the breaking ice—for his cruel and immoral act. Nekhliudov feels no kinship with nature, no gratitude for its apparent complicity; rather he seems in retrospect to see a host of evil portents in the behavior of nature that night. Later in the book, Nekhliudov has several nocturnal experiences that redeem the memory of his first one, which marks the lowest point of his moral descent, from which he can but rise.

Part of Nekhliudov's redemption, part of his quest to right the injustices he and society have committed, involves his relationship to the peasants on his estates. He travels first to his estate at Kuzminskoe, where first thing in the morning he intends to present a plan to the peasants that would allow them to rent his land. He goes to bed trying to suppress the doubts and questions that rise in his mind:

> But for a long time he couldn't fall asleep; through the open windows together with the fresh air and light of the moon flowed the croaking of the frogs, interrupted by the cry and whistle of far-off nightingales from the park, and one close by under the window in a bush of lilac in bloom. Hearing the nightingales and the frogs,

Nekhliudov recalled the music of the inspector's daughter; recalling the inspector, he recalled Maslova, how her lips trembled, like the croaking of the frogs, when she said: "You must just leave it alone." Then the German steward began going down to the frogs. He should have been held back, but he not only descended but turned into Maslova and began to reproach him: "I am a convict and you are a prince." "No, I will not give in," thought Nekhliudov, and he came to himself and asked himself: "Is what I'm doing right or wrong? I don't know, but it doesn't matter to me. It doesn't matter." And he himself went down there, where the inspector and Maslova had descended and there everything ended [2, 1].

In this passage the by now familiar sounds of the frogs and nightingales, light of the moon, fresh air, and scent of lilac coax Nekhliudov first to become lost in thought and then to slip into dream. Even when he emerges for a moment from his dream, he chooses to dismiss rather than confront at this time the crucial question he asks himself. The activities of the night do not again attract his attention, and he slips back directly into sleep.

Several days later, having signed an agreement with the peasants at Kuzminskoe, which leaves him and them dissatisfied, Nekhliudov arrives at his second estate, the estate of his aunts where he first met and later seduced Maslova. Here, he hopes to come to a more satisfactory agreement with the peasants. Before turning in for the night, Nekhliudov wanders to the porch even though at first he hesitates when he thinks of that other night which has become a guilty memory. In the rest of this chapter passages that describe nature—the air, the trees, the birds, the approaching storm—alternate with passages that record Nekhliudov's thoughts and memories:

He sat again on the porch and, breathing in the warm air filled with the strong smell of young birch leaves, looked for a long time at the dark garden and listened to the mill, the nightingales, and some other bird, too, that monotonously whistled in the bush right by the porch. The light in the bailiff's window went out; in the east, from behind the barn, the glow of the rising moon flamed; sheet lightning, brighter and brighter, began to illuminate the overgrown, blooming garden and the tumbledown house; distant thunder could be heard and a black cloud had moved across one third of the sky. The nightingales and birds became silent. Above the noise of the water at the mill, the cackling of geese could be heard, and, then, in the village and in the bailiff's yard the early cocks began to call to one another, just as they usually cry earlier on hot, thundery nights. There is a saying that when the crows cry early the nights are merry. For Nekhliudov, this night was more than merry. It was for him a joyful, happy night. Imagination renewed before him impressions of that happy summer he had spent here as an innocent youth, and he felt himself now to be as he had been not only then, but at all the best moments of his life. He not only remembered, he felt himself now to be as he had been when he was a 14-year-old boy praying to God so that God would reveal to him the truth, when he cried as a child on his mother's knees at parting from her, promising always to be good and never give her pain,—felt himself to be as he had been when he and Nikolenka Irtenev resolved always to support one another in living a good life and to try to make all people happy [2, 8].

But then his thoughts return to the present—the peasants here and at Kuzminskoe, the prison, Maslova. As he becomes more and more convinced that he must intensify his struggle against the injustices of society, the storm draws closer:

The black cloud had moved across the entire sky and the sheet lightning was no longer visible, but lightning bolts illumined the entire yard and the dilapidated house with its crumbling porches; thunder could already be heard overhead. All the birds quieted down, but to make up for it the leaves began to rustle, and the wind ran to the porch where Nekhliudov was sitting, stirring his hair. One drop, then another flew down; it began to patter on the burdock and on the iron of the roof, and all the air blazed up brightly; everything became silent, and before Nekhliudov could count three, something crashed terribly right above his head and went rolling along the sky.

Nekhliudov went into the house.

"Yes, yes," he thought. "The *work* that our life accomplishes, all the *work*, all the meaning of this *work* is not *understandable* and cannot be *understandable* to me: why my aunts; why did Nikolenka Irtenev die and I live? Why Katiusha? And my madness? Why this war? And all my subsequent dissolute life? To *understand* all this, to *understand* all the *work* of the Master—is not in my power. But to do His will, written in my conscience,—this is in my power, and this I know *without question*. And when I am doing this, I am *without question* at peace" [2, 8].

The Nikolai Irtenev mentioned in these two passages is, of course, the hero of Tolstoy's trilogy. Tolstoy's two fictional characters meet for the first time towards the end of *Boyhood* (1854). The two boys soon become close friends, and their friendship plays a significant role in *Youth*. Nekhliudov is the only one of Tolstoy's characters to reappear in more than one work.[9]

[9]This assertion is perhaps not entirely accurate since Nekhliudov's "sister" appears in both *Youth* and *Resurrection*. This sister, however, in *Youth* is named Varya, is younger than her brother, and is indifferent to Irtenev, whereas in *Resurrection* her name is Natasha, she is ten years older than Nekhliudov, and she is said to have been in love with Irtenev. Also note that in Tolstoy's play *The Living Corpse* (*Zhivoi trup*, written in 1900, but first published in 1911) a character named Anna Karenina appears, though it is obviously not the same Anna Karenina.

Nekhliudov's recollection of how he felt when he and Irtenev made their idealistic resolutions recalls the closing passage of *Boyhood*:

> It goes without saying that under the influence of Nekhliudov I involuntarily adopted even his manner, the essence of which was an enthusiastic adoration of the ideal of virtue and a conviction that the purpose of a man's life is continually to perfect himself. At that time to reform all of humanity, to destroy all human vices and miseries seemed possible,—and it seemed very easy and simple to reform oneself, to adopt all virtues and be happy . . .
>
> By the way, God alone knows whether these noble dreams of youth were actually ridiculous, and whose fault it is that they were not fulfilled [2, 75].

Irtenev's last sentence seems almost to anticipate *Resurrection*, in which Nekhliudov attempts to regain and make real some of those noble dreams. The mention of Irtenev is sure to evoke many associations in the minds of readers familiar with Tolstoy's trilogy: we remember Irtenev's struggle to learn to know himself, his tendency to philosophize, his romantic dreams. And we remember, through Irtenev's lens, Nekhliudov's serious, self-castigating nature and his constant efforts at self-improvement. With this single image, then, Tolstoy emphasizes that Nekhliudov is not trying to become a totally different person; rather he is rediscovering who he was and can be.[10]

In each of the long passages from *Resurrection* taken separately, and in the two taken as a kind of progression, nature is presented not as a static background, but as a dynamic presence of ongoing movements, overlapping sounds, and a continually

---

[10] Cf. Wasiolek, *Tolstoy's Major Fiction*: "What Nekhliudov discovers and what Maslova discovers, although perceived and understood only dimly by both, is that the process of true redemption is a return to what one has been" (197).

modulating array of tones, shades, and fragrances. The third-person narrative voice and the absorption of Nekhliudov into this dynamic presence establish the objectivity of the natural world that surrounds him. At the same time, his thoughts are somehow inspired by his subjective experience of this world. Objective reality and subjective experience of that reality are conflated in these passages, and Nekhliudov's absorption into nature's dynamism smooths a path to greater understanding of what is true and good in himself.[11]

For Tolstoy's characters, immersion in the nighttime world of nature may inspire, but does not end with awe at the infinite and eternal expanse of this world; instead it leads to profound reflection on the self. In his *Confessions* Augustine rhapsodizes about memory:

> The power of the memory is prodigious, my God. It is a vast, immeasurable sanctuary. Who can plumb its depths? . . . Yet men go out and gaze in astonishment at high mountains, the huge waves of the sea, the broad reaches of rivers, the ocean that encir-

---

[11]Cf. Kupreianova: "In Tolstoy's landscapes (and not only in his landscapes) the border between the 'representation' of the outer and the 'expression' of the inner is removed. It is removed to the extent that the outer and the inner, the subjective and the objective are mentally combined in the act and processes of direct contemplation and experience" (138). In her study, Kupreianova devotes a chapter to a discussion of the relation between nature and human beings in Tolstoy's fictions. Gustafson also discusses this relation at length. Gustafson's main point in this regard is that "the privileged moment in Tolstoy's fiction is the characters' encounter with the experience of nature. They discover the world in which they reside. Moments of movement outward and toward this expanse are emblematic of the characters' discovery of the Divine" (213). Unlike Kupreianova and Gustafson, with whose comments I for the most part agree, I see Tolstoy's nighttime descriptions as a distinct subset of his nature descriptions since the images and ambience that inform them are repeated over and over again, whereas other landscapes, the mountains in *The Cossacks* or the infinite sky in *War and Peace*, are specific to individual works.

cles the world, or the stars in their courses. But they pay no attention to themselves.[12]

And in *The Book of Laughter and Forgetting* Milan Kundera's
narrator comments: "While pondering the infinity of the stars,
we ignore the infinity of our father."[13] As different as these
two observers may be, both their observations lament the lack
of attention to precisely that which was one of Tolstoy's greatest concerns: the grandeur and potential that reside not just in
nature, but in human beings. It is as if feeling themselves a part
of this expanse frees, or encourages, characters to look upon
themselves—their memories, thoughts, and feelings—as objects
of attention. Every time the familiar images of night twine the
imagination and memory of a Tolstoyan character, the picture
of a unique person emerges. The process of remembering, classification, and integration of experience that shares the fore-
ground with the movements, sounds, and smells of night expresses the emergence of a sense of self and direction for the future.

That time after time another one of Tolstoy's characters sits
on a porch or a windowsill beneath the nighttime sky and
thinks about the pass to which his or her life has come suggests
the significance Tolstoy attached to these epiphanic moments
of self-renewal and self-empowerment. The same scene repeated over and over again nevertheless each time conforms to the
psychological and ethical needs and impulses of individual
characters. For readers who notice this type of repetition—the
repetition of a situation or scene—the scene portrayed assumes
an aura of universality even as it retains its particularity.

---

[12] Augustine, *Confessions*, Book X, p. 216.
[13] Kundera, *The Book of Laughter and Forgetting*, p. 165.

Music and Memory

Tolstoy's nighttime passages describe moments of intense immersion in the sensations, feelings, thoughts, and memories that together confirm both one's sense of self and sense of connectedness to another. For Tolstoy, perhaps as powerful an influence on the human psyche as nature is music. Tolstoy not only played, listened to, and enjoyed music his entire life, he reflected upon its qualities, its value, the nature of our response to it, and how it is able to affect us. Or as Ruth Rischin asserts: "Music never was merely a pastime with Tolstoy but was a way of experiencing the quandary of himself, of testing to the boiling point his own principles and aesthetic values under the emotional impact of art."[14] Rischin explores Tolstoy's use of Beethoven's music in his works as analogues of feeling. "In Beethoven's music," she concludes, "Tolstoy found the means to transcribe in fiction the mind's voice—memory, aspiration, desire. Musical metaphor contributed to the making of Tolstoy's personal mythology of the enchantment of art."[15] Rischin's insightful essay establishes Beethoven's music as a powerful and significant intertextual repetition in Tolstoy's oeuvre. More generally, Tolstoy's fiction is full of musical motifs that have nothing to do with Beethoven, but are nevertheless connected to Tolstoy's creation of psychological metaphor. Tolstoy gives many of his characters musical experiences, each representation a demonstration of the extent to which music is capable of arousing deep and meaningful emotions. More often than not in these representations, emotions called up by music are inextricably linked to the memories that are also called up. Throughout his life, Tolstoy was fascinated by what seemed to

[14]Rischin, p. 12.
[15]Ibid., p. 54.

him an actual and meaningful, if elusive connection between music and memory.[16]

As he recalls and retells the early years of his life in *Childhood*, Nikolai Irtenev records the many memories and musings he experienced already as a child. He remembers not only what memories he had as a child, but how these memories made him feel and still make him feel, and he readily attributes to his imagination a role in forming or coloring these memories, even if he is not able to explain precisely what this role is. One of his memories is of his mother at the piano and the feelings evoked by her playing. But Irtenev adds that even then he felt as if he were remembering feelings that never were:

> Mama was playing the second concerto of Field, her musicmaster. I was dozing, and in my imagination there arose some kind of airy, luminous, and transparent memories. She started playing Beethoven's *Sonate pathétique* and I remembered something sad, oppressive, and gloomy. Mama often played these two pieces and so I well remember the feeling they aroused in me. This feeling resembled memories—but memories of what? It seemed like remembering something that had never been [1, 31].[17]

The dreamlike state Irtenev enters as his mother plays is a state in which thoughts and feelings are almost indistinguishable

---

[16]Donna Orwin observes in an article entitled "Freedom, Responsibility, and the Soul: The Platonic Contribution to Tolstoi's Psychology" that in reflecting on the relation of feeling to music and memory, Tolstoy was undoubtedly influenced by Plato, whose works, including *The Republic*, he was reading in the early 1850s when his speculations in this area first began. Orwin's article is an illuminating account of the dynamics of Tolstoy's reception of Plato and the course of the Platonic strain in Tolstoy's art.

[17]In his discussion of *Childhood* as "pseudo-biography," Andrew Wachtel cites this passage as an example illustrating the dialogue that can take place between the child's recreation of past actions and the narrator's recollection of them (28–29).

from memories of thoughts and feelings. That they should seem like memories suggests they are familiar to him, that they are in some way repetitive of or continuous with something in his past experience. Tolstoy here hits upon two feelings induced by memories—pastness and familiarity—that Bertrand Russell later identified as the two feelings necessary for an image to be a memory.[18] Or as William James explained: "Memory requires more than mere stating of a fact in the past. It must be dated in my past.... It must have that *warmth and intimacy* ... characterizing all experience *appropriated* by the thinker as his own."[19]

Irtenev, however, questions the status of these images as memories. His uncertainty is Tolstoy's allusion to the Platonic doctrine that knowledge is remembered rather than acquired,[20] but it also indicates the special evocative power of music that works almost like suggestion under hypnosis. Here we are back to Tolstoy's infection theory of art: the idea that a work of art "infects" people with those feelings which the artist experienced while creating it. In his essay *On Art*, his last attempt to express his views on art before writing *What Is Art?*, Tolstoy

[18] Russell, p. 163.

[19] James, p. 612. Emphasis in original.

[20] Orwin, p. 505. Also, note that Pozdnyshev in *The Kreutzer Sonata* interprets the power of music in a negative light as the power to enchant by making us feel what we do not really feel: "And in general music is a terrible thing. What is it? I don't understand. What is music? What does it do? And why does it do what it does? They say music has an effect that elevates the soul—nonsense, it's not true! It has an effect, a terrible effect—I'm speaking for myself—but not at all one that elevates the soul. How can I put it? Music makes me forget myself, my true position. It transports me to some other position not my own: it seems to me that under the influence of music I feel what I do not really feel, I understand what I don't understand, I want what I don't want. I explain this by the fact that music has an effect like yawning, like laughter: I'm not tired, but I yawn when I see someone yawning; there is nothing to laugh at, but I laugh when I hear someone laughing" (27, 61).

himself links the ideas of infection and hypnotism:

> This feeling [the feeling of a person perceiving the work of art] has its source in imitativeness, or rather—in the property of infectiousness, in a certain hypnotism—in the fact that the spiritual effort of the artist to clarify for himself the subject that had been doubtful to him is communicated through the artistic work to the one perceiving it [30, 220].

Art, then, by means of infection, leads to a sense of community, of "universal unity" among people, which is, according to Tolstoy, its ultimate purpose in our time (30, 194–95). This purpose, he asserts, is most clearly discernible in music:

> A work of art is only a true work of art when to a person perceiving it, it seems—not just seems, but the person [actually] experiences a feeling of joy that he has produced such a beautiful thing. This is especially strong in music. Nowhere else is the chief significance of art so clear, the significance of unification. The *"I"* of the artist merges with the *"I"* of all those perceiving, merging into one [57, 132].

The experience of music in particular, and art in general, for Tolstoy, is the repetition by the listener, spectator, or reader, of the artist's original experience. For Irtenev, this repetition *feels* like a memory.

Tightly welded in Tolstoy's understanding of musical experience are the concepts of emotion and memory. During the time Tolstoy was working on *Childhood*, he wrote in his diary:

> Painting acts upon the capacity to imagine nature and its domain is space. Music acts upon the capacity to imagine your feelings. And its domain is harmony and time. Poetry acts upon the capacity to imagine both the one and the other, that is, reality or the relation of our feelings to nature.... Why does music act upon us

like memory? Music is superior even to poetry in that the imitation of feelings in music is fuller than the imitation in poetry, but it does not have that clarity which is the property of poetry [Nov. 29, 1851; 46, 239–40].[21]

Much later, in an 1897 diary entry, Tolstoy seems finally to attempt an answer to his own question about why music affects us like memory:

> When it happens that you were thinking about something and forget what you were thinking about, but remember and know the nature of your thoughts: sad, dismal, oppressive, gay, cheerful—you even remember their sequence—at first you felt sad, then were consoled, etc.—when you remember things that way, that's exactly what music expresses [July 16; 53, 158].

Music, according to Tolstoy, expresses feelings the way they reside in memory: as a sequence that makes sense to the person in whose memory they reside. Tolstoy seems to make a distinction between the cognitive content of a memory and its corresponding feeling: music more capably expresses the latter. This distinction is important in view of the value Tolstoy assigns feeling as the basis of communion among people in his *What Is Art?* Also, music, like memory, is capable of conveying feelings and meanings for which words provide an inadequate vehicle. Music and memory, unlike words, can have a play of

---

[21]Tolstoy's sober meditation on the different capacities of painting, poetry, and music may recall Gogol's essay "Sculpture, Painting, and Music," which appeared in his *Arabesques*, a collection of his essays and stories, in 1835. But the tone and agenda of Gogol's paean to the three "wonderful sisters" sent by God "to adorn and charm" the world distinguish it from Tolstoy's more matter-of-fact musings. In saving their greatest praise for music, both writers were probably influenced by German Romantic aestheticians who proclaimed the supremacy of music among the arts. On the relation between literature and music see Stephen Paul Scher, "Literature and Music."

contents, of shifting meanings and feelings. Writing on what music expresses, Susanne K. Langer explains that:

> The imagination that responds to music is personal and associative and logical, tinged with affect, tinged with bodily rhythm, tinged with dream, but *concerned* with a wealth of formulations for its wealth of wordless knowledge, its whole knowledge of emotional and organic experience, of vital impulse, balance, conflict, the *ways* of living and dying and feeling.[22]

The music Irtenev's mother plays evokes in him sad and oppressive feelings, but these are feelings in which he willingly indulges. Much later, readers learn of the death of his mother while he was still a child, and they realize that his recollections of her playing and of its effect on him are certainly colored by his knowledge that her death means these events can no longer actually be repeated, but can only return via memory. We might say that he narrates not memories, but re-memories insofar as time, events, and his imagination have continued to shape his recollection. In other words, the emotive and even the conceptual content of personal memories can change for a number of reasons, including the influence of subsequent experience, the pressure of individual needs and desires, or the presence of an audience. All three of these reasons are factors in Irtenev's retelling of his childhood. Irtenev says that his mother "often played those two pieces." So his recollection of this particular moment may actually be a generalized conceptualization of all the times he heard his mother at the piano. He remembers not just a moment, but a moment that contains many moments. Irtenev's memory of the many times his mother played the piano, particularly those two pieces, fuses

[22]Langer, p. 244. Emphasis in original.

the repetitions, the separate moments, into a single moment. Irtenev experiences a repetition that feels like a singularity. Memory fuses time rather than layering it, as in a palimpsest.

In a similar way, the readers' memory can seem to fuse time when readers notice intertextual repetitions. When a particular phrase or scene is recognized as a repetition, it becomes part of a new context, a new whole, which is constituted by other repetitions of the same phrase or scene. These repetitions form a kind of unity that is at once dynamic, semantic, and affective. As Oliver Sacks points out, this kind of unity is central to music, incantation, recitation, and all metrical structures, and, Sacks asserts, "It is typical of such flowing dynamic-semantic structures that each part leads on to the next, that every part has reference to the rest. Such structures cannot be perceived, or remembered, in part—they are perceived and remembered, if at all, as wholes."[23]

Tolstoy explores the link between music and memory further in *War and Peace*.[24] Left alone to occupy herself one winter afternoon after dinner, Natasha sits in a dark corner of the ballroom and plays her guitar. Thinking of her absent fiancé, Prince Andrei, she strums a tune from an opera the two of them recently attended in St. Petersburg. The music, whose significance would be unintelligible to any other listener, recalls to Natasha's mind still more memories associated with Andrei:

[23] Sacks, p. 59.

[24] If *The Kreutzer Sonata* (1889), in which music becomes a corrupting influence, represents Tolstoy's most negative view of the tremendous emotive and moral power of music, *Khadzhi-Murat* (1896–1904), in which song and singing permeate the hero's life, represents its celebration. In this short work published posthumously, music helps to reveal Khadzhi-Murat's character: who he is as an individual, a courageous leader, and a hero of almost mythic stature.

> That which came from her guitar had no meaning for outside lis-
> teners, but in her imagination there rose a whole series of memo-
> ries from these sounds. She sat behind the cupboard, directing her
> eyes at a strip of light that fell from the door of the pantry, lis-
> tened to herself, and remembered. She was in the mood for re-
> membering [2, 4, 9].

For Natasha, as for Irtenev, the music becomes inextricably associated with feelings and images given form by imagination
and memory. Music for Tolstoy's characters proves to be a
good bonding agent for personal memories.

In a diary entry for August 10, 1851, Tolstoy recalls with
satisfaction a night spent listening to the songs of gypsies and
comments:

> Anyone who has spent time with gypsies can't help acquiring the
> habit of singing gypsy songs; whether sung badly, whether sung
> well, they always give pleasure, because they bring back memo-
> ries. One characteristic feature reproduces for us many memories
> of occurrences associated with that feature [46, 82].

Here and in both the passages from *Childhood* and *War and
Peace*, Tolstoy suggests the proliferation of memories that music can inspire and color. Music has the capacity to join images,
feelings, and thoughts from separate moments in time into a
harmonious whole. This cooperation between music and
memory, which restores even as it adds to the whole, offers a
paradigm for how repetition functions intertextually in Tolstoy's work. Tolstoy identified harmony and time as the do-
main of music, but he might have added repetition too, since
memory, with which he links music so closely, is itself a kind
of repetition. When an intertextual repetition is recognized as
such, an array of related images, thoughts, and feelings is
evoked. This array constitutes a context outside the context of

any individual work, and as such focuses readers' attention on a particular set of questions and insights, allowing them to piece together some sense of a unity or whole. Intertextual repetitions function like music in that they fuse impressions.

The intertextual repetition of a topos or set of topoi that draws readers' attention to moments of sense-making and self-shaping establishes the universal quality of such moments without diminishing the particular import and resonance of the moment for the character whose experience is depicted. The larger whole, accessible only to those who recognize the repetition as a repetition, is essentially without beginning or end. By means of intertextual repetitions Tolstoy escapes the limitations of the conventions of narrative that require a beginning, middle, and end, and realizes his intuition that knowledge about the meaning of human life and death is not linear, but spherical. Recall Tolstoy's 1875 letter to Strakhov, quoted in Chapter 1, in which Tolstoy explained that philosophy is "knowledge that gives the best possible answers to questions about human life and death" and that any "philosophical view taken from life is a circle or sphere" (62, 225).

Different readers will notice different intertextual repetitions in Tolstoy's oeuvre, and not all of Tolstoy's intertextual repetitions have to do with moments of sense-making and self-shaping. But the ones that do, seem to me to be of special significance, because when readers recognize these repetitions as repetitions, they, too, become engaged in the task of piecing together parts into wholes. Understanding for Tolstoy is an aesthetic and an ethical phenomenon: human beings understand something about themselves or human life when the new and the old are integrated into a coherent, that is, familiar and repeated, ever-changing whole in accordance not with established rules and patterns, but with an ongoing process of seeking, of analysis and synthesis. Repeating, like remembering, brings about in people some kind of understanding about how things are. And this action is part of the point as well: it is not just the content of the ideas and beliefs which permeate Tolstoy's work that interests us as we are working towards an understanding of his epistemology, but the *processes* of remembering and piecing together. For Tolstoy, repetition, with its ability to emphasize, to remind, and to connect, is fundamental to the way we know or understand ourselves and the world we inhabit.

Afterword

It was one of those repetitions, one of those thematic "voices" with which, according to all the rules of harmony, destiny enriches the life of observant men.

—Vladimir Nabokov, *The Gift*

For Tolstoy, self-knowledge and knowledge of the world are made possible by the constant dialogue of past and present, of experience and reflection upon experience, and repetition plays a critical role in sustaining this dialogue. Repetition may be regarded as an avenue to Tolstoy's values, ideals, intellectual aspirations, to essential features of his moral and aesthetic activity. It is central to his style, to his understanding of characters' psychology, to the structure of his works, and to his interactions with implied readers. It defines much of what is "Tolstoyan" about Tolstoy. In his representation of characters' psychology, Tolstoy uses repetition to explore how characters perceive their immediate experience and structure their memories. Concerned with the shaping power of time, Tolstoy describes how memories form, how they endow life with continuity, and how, in giving meaning, they themselves change over time. For Tolstoy, memory, like art, is an active process. From the perspective of readers, repetition in Tolstoy's fiction operates in a variety of ways. Perhaps most fundamentally, it serves to activate memory and mold comprehension. Because repetition works as much by marking significant differences as by iterating similarities, it is also used to evoke readers' active participation in identifying the text's structure and comprehending its meanings. In so doing, readers become aware not only of characters' mental activity but also of their own. Tolstoy's novels are, in this way, doubly psychological. Readers observe characters as they work to make sense of their experiences. Simultaneously they themselves participate in a parallel process as they continually recast past knowledge of the text in the light of present experience and alter expectations of textual outcomes while responding to the passages they are reading. Without this process, in which memory and repetition play essential roles, Tolstoy believed that the world could only appear hopelessly contingent and experience could only fade into ephemerality.

I like to say that repetition in Tolstoy implies an ethical aesthetics of parts and the whole in the sense that for Tolstoy repetition evinces both ethical and aesthetic strands of life: both a longing for truth, insight, meaning and a desire for harmony, unity, clarity, and not as part-time impulses, but as ongoing, pervasive motives of our everyday activity. Tolstoy did not deny competing motives such as greed, revenge, or power. But even at their most petty, vicious, vindictive, or ignorant, human beings, Tolstoy believed, retained the potential to be better.

To allude here to the moral personality and competence of Tolstoy's characters and their artistic rendering is to anticipate the subject of a future study, one in which once again the approach would be rhetorical, focusing on both the construction and the perception of discourse in Tolstoy's art. How we use language as a means to an end is a question that can be posed over and over again in many different ways. Certainly the range and power of the literary uses of repetition and the variation and depth of its philosophical implications also remain rich topics for inquiry. The present inquiry, which now is ended, reveals that repetition is the key to and instrument of Tolstoy's insightful, provocative, and lifelong exploration of how human beings create and recover their experience for themselves and for others.

Reference Matter

Works Cited

Aristotle. *Poetics. Criticism: The Major Texts.* Ed. Walter Jackson Bate. New York: Harcourt Brace Jovanovich, 1970.

Augustine. *Confessions.* Trans. R. S. Pine-Coffin. Penguin Books, 1988.

Babaev, E. G. *Lev Tolstoi I Russkaia Zhurnalistika Ego Epokhi.* Moscow University, 1978.

Bakhtin, Mikhail. "Author and Hero in Aesthetic Activity." *Art and Answerability: Early Philosophical Essays by M. M. Bakhtin.* Ed. Michael Holquist and Vadim Liapunov. Trans. Vadim Liapunov. Austin: University of Texas Press, 1990: 4–256.

———. "Discourse in the Novel." *The Dialogic Imagination.* Ed. Michael Holquist. Trans. Caryl Emerson and Michael Holquist. Austin: University of Texas Press, 1981: 259–422.

———. "From Notes Made in 1970–71." *Speech Genres and Other Late Essays.* Trans. Vern W. McGee. Ed. Caryl Emerson and Michael Holquist. Austin: University of Texas Press, 1986: 132–58.

———. "The Problem of Speech Genres." *Speech Genres and Other Late Essays.* Trans. Vern W. McGee. Ed. Caryl Emerson and Michael Holquist. Austin: University of Texas Press, 1986: 60–102.

———. "The Problem of the Text in Linguistics, Philosophy, and the Human Sciences: An Experiment in Philosophical Analysis." *Speech Genres and Other Late Essays.* Trans. Vern W. McGee. Ed. Caryl Emerson and Michael Holquist. Austin: University of Texas Press, 1986: 103–31.

———. "Toward a Methodology for the Human Sciences." *Speech Genres and Other Late Essays.* Trans. Vern W. McGee. Ed. Caryl Emerson and Michael Holquist. Austin: University of Texas Press, 1986: 159–72.

Bartlett, John. *Familiar Quotations.* Boston: Little Brown, 1968 [1855].

Bateson, Gregory. *Steps to an Ecology of Mind.* Northvale, NJ: Aronson, 1987.

Belknap, Robert L. *The Structure of "The Brothers Karamazov."* Evanston, IL: Northwestern University Press, 1989 (The Hague: Mouton, 1967).

Benner, David G., ed. *Baker Encyclopedia of Psychology.* Michigan: Baker Book House, 1985.

Benson, Ruth Crego. *Women in Tolstoy: The Ideal and the Erotic.* Urbana: University of Illinois Press, 1973.

Bergson, Henri. *Laughter: An Essay on the Meaning of the Comic.* Trans. Cloudesley Brereton and Fred Rothwell. New York: Macmillan, 1914.

Berlin, Isaiah. *The Hedgehog and the Fox: An Essay on Tolstoy's View of History.* New York: Simon & Schuster, 1953.

Biriukov, P. I. *L. N. Tolstoi: Biografiia.* Vol. 1. 3rd ed. Berlin: Izd-vo I. P. Ladyzhnikova, 1921.

Bocharov, Sergei. *Roman L. Tolstogo "Voina i mir."* 4th ed. Moscow: Khud. lit., 1987.

Booth, Wayne. *The Company We Keep: An Ethics of Fiction.* Berkeley: University of California Press, 1988.

——. "Distance and Point-of-View: An Essay in Classification." *Twentieth-Century Literary Theory: An Introductory Anthology.* Ed. Vassilis Lambropoulos and David Neal Miller. Albany: State University of New York Press, 1987: 269–84.

——. *The Rhetoric of Fiction.* 2nd ed. Chicago: University of Chicago Press, 1983.

Brown, Calvin S. *Repetition in Zola's Novels.* Athens: University of Georgia Press, 1952.

Burke, Kenneth. *A Rhetoric of Motives.* Berkeley: University of California Press, 1969.

Butler, Thomas. "Memory: A Mixed Blessing." *Memory.* Ed. Thomas Butler. Oxford: Basil Blackwell, 1989.

Carden, Patricia. "The Expressive Self in *War and Peace.*" *Canadian-American Slavic Studies* 12 (1978): 519–34.

————. "The Recuperative Powers of Memory: Tolstoy's *War and Peace.*" *Modern Critical Interpretations: Leo Tolstoy's "War and Peace.*" Ed. Harold Bloom. New York: Chelsea House, 1988: 103–21.

Chatman, Seymour. *Story and Discourse: Narrative Structure in Fiction and Film.* Ithaca: Cornell University Press, 1978.

Chernyshevsky, N. G. "Detstvo i otrochestvo: Voennye rasskazy." *Literaturno-kriticheskie stat'i.* Moscow: Khud. lit., 1939.

Christian, R. F. *Tolstoy's "War and Peace": A Study.* Oxford: Clarendon Press, 1962.

Cohn, Dorrit. *Transparent Minds: Narrative Modes for Presenting Consciousness in Fiction.* Princeton: Princeton University Press, 1978.

Corsini, Raymond J., ed., *Concise Encyclopedia of Psychology.* New York: John Wiley & Sons, 1987.

Csikszentmihalyi, Mihaly. *Flow: The Psychology of Optimal Experience.* New York: Harper & Row, 1990.

Eikhenbaum, Boris. *The Young Tolstoi.* Trans. and ed. Gary Kern. Ann Arbor, MI: Ardis, 1972.

Emerson, Caryl. "The Outer Word and Inner Speech: Bakhtin, Vygotsky, and the Internalization of Language." *Bakhtin: Essays and Dialogues on His Work.* Ed. Gary Saul Morson. Chicago: University of Chicago Press, 1986: 21–40.

————. "The Tolstoy Connection in Bakhtin." *PMLA* 100 (1985): 68–80.

Epperly, Elizabeth R. *Patterns of Repetition in Trollope.* Washington, D.C.: Catholic University of America Press, 1989.

Fortunatov, N. M. "Avtor i chitatel' (iz nabliudenii nad avtorskoi pravkoi teksta romana L. N. Tolstogo *1806 god*)." *Filologicheskie nauki,* 1961 (1), Moscow: 66–74.

Foucault, Michel. *The Order of Things: An Archaeology of the Human Sciences.* New York: Pantheon Books, 1970.

Frank, Joseph. "Spatial Form in Modern Literature." *The Widening Gyre: Crisis and Mastery in Modern Literature.* New Brunswick: Rutgers University Press, 1963: 5–60.

Freud, Sigmund. *Beyond the Pleasure Principle. Standard Edition of the Complete Psychological Works of Sigmund Freud.* Trans. under the general editorship of James Strachey, in collaboration with Anna Freud, assisted by Alex Strachey and Alan Tyson. 24 vols. (1953–74).

Friedrich, Paul. *The Language Parallax: Linguistic Relativism and Poetic Indeterminacy.* Austin: University of Texas Press, 1986.

Geertz, Clifford. *The Interpretation of Cultures.* New York: Basic Books, 1973.

Ginzburg, Lydia. "Problemy psikhologicheskogo romana." *O psikhologicheskoi proze.* Leningrad: Khud. lit., 1977: 269–442. (In English: *On Psychological Prose.* Trans. and ed. Judson Rosengrant. Princeton: Princeton University Press, 1991.)

Gleick, James. *Chaos: Making A New Science.* New York: Viking, 1987.

Gogol, N. V. "Skul'ptura, zhivopis' i muzyka." *Polnoe sobranie sochinenii.* T. 8. Akademiia Nauk, 1952: 9–13. (In English: "Sculpture, Painting, and Music." *Arabesques.* Trans. Alexander Tulloch. Ann Arbor, MI: Ardis, 1982.)

Gustafson, Richard F. *Leo Tolstoy, Resident and Stranger: A Study in Fiction and Theology.* Princeton: Princeton University Press, 1986.

Hardy, Barbara. "Form and Freedom: Tolstoy's *Anna Karenina.*" *Norton Critical Edition of "Anna Karenina."* Ed. George Gibian. Trans. Louise and Aylmer Maude. New York: W. W. Norton, 1970: 877–99.

Harvey, David. *The Condition of Postmodernity.* Basil Blackwell, 1989.

Holquist, Michael. "Character Change as Language Change in *War and Peace.*" *Russianness: Studies on a Nation's Identity.* Ann Arbor, MI: Ardis, 1990: 212–26.

Hume, David. *A Treatise on Human Nature.* Ed. L. A. Selby-Bigge. Oxford: Clarendon Press, 1960.

Iser, Wolfgang. *The Act of Reading: A Theory of Aesthetic Response.* Baltimore: John Hopkins University Press, 1978.

———. "The Reading Process: A Phenomenological Approach." *Reader-Response Criticism from Formalism to Post-Structuralism.* Ed. Jane P. Tompkins. Baltimore: John Hopkins University Press, 1980: 50–69.

Ishchuk, G. N. *Problema chitatelia v tvorcheskom soznanii L. N. Tolstogo.* Kalinin, 1975.

Ivanits, Linda J. *Russian Folk Belief.* Armonk, NY: M. E. Sharpe, Inc., 1989.

Jackson, Robert Louis. "An Archetypal Journey: Aesthetic and Ethical Imperatives in the Art of Tolstoy, *The Cossacks.*" *Russian Literature* 11 (1982): 389–410.

Jahn, Gary R. "Tolstoy and Kant." *New Perspectives on Nineteenth-Century Russian Prose.* Ed. George J. Gutsche and Lauren G. Leighton. Columbus, OH: Slavica, 1982.

James, William. *The Principles of Psychology.* Vol. 1. Cambridge, MA: Harvard University Press, 1981.

Joravsky, David. *Russian Psychology: A Critical History.* Oxford: Basil Blackwell, 1989.

Kant, Immanuel. *Immanuel Kant's Critique of Pure Reason.* Trans. Norman Kemp Smith. New York: St. Martin's Press, 1965.

Kierkegaard, Søren. *Repetition: An Essay in Experimental Psychology.* Trans. and intro. Walter Lourie. New York: Harper & Row, 1964.

Knowles, A. V., ed. *Tolstoy: The Critical Heritage.* London: 1978.

Kuberski, Philip. *The Persistence of Memory: Organism, Myth, Text.* Berkeley: University of California Press, 1992.

Kundera, Milan. *The Book of Laughter and Forgetting.* Trans. Michael Henry Heim. New York: Alfred A. Knopf, 1980.

———. *The Unbearable Lightness of Being.* Trans. Michael Henry Heim. New York: Harper and Row, 1984.

Kupreianova, E. N. *Estetika Tolstogo.* Moscow: Izd-vo Nauka, 1966.

Kuzina, L., and K. Tiun'kin. *"Voskresenie" L. N. Tolstogo.* Moscow: Khud. lit., 1978.

Langer, Susanne K. "On Significance in Music." *Philosophy in a New Key: A Study in the Symbolism of Reason, Rite, and Art.* Cambridge, MA: Harvard University Press, 1942: 215–44.

Leahey, Thomas Hardy. *A History of Psychology.* 2nd edition. Englewood Cliffs, NJ: Prentice-Hall, 1987.

Lee, Dwight E., and Beck, Robert N. "The Meaning of 'Historicism.'" *The American Historical Review* 59 (1954): 568–77.

Lessing, Gotthold Ephraim. *Laocoön: An Essay on the Limits of Painting and Poetry.* Trans. Edward Allen McCormick. Baltimore, MD: John Hopkins University Press, 1984.

Magnus, Laury. *The Track of the Repetend: Syntactic and Lexical Repetition in Modern Poetry.* New York: AMS Press, 1989.

Malinowski, Bronislaw. *Magic, Science and Religion and Other Essays.* Westport, CT: Greenwood Press, 1984.

May, Rachel. *The Translator in the Text: On Reading Russian Literature in English.* Evanston: Northwestern University Press, 1994.

McLeish, John. *Soviet Psychology: History, Theory, Content.* London: Methuen, 1975.

Mead, George H. *Movements of Thought in the Nineteenth Century.* Chicago: University of Chicago Press, 1936.

Merezhkovsky, D. S. *L. Tolstoi i Dostoevskii: Zhizn' i tvorchestvo.* 4th ed. St. Petersburg, 1909. (In English: *Tolstoi as Man and Artist, with an Essay on Dostoevsky.* New York: G. P. Putnam's Sons, 1902).

Meyerhof, Hans. *Time in Literature.* Berkeley: University of California Press, 1955.

Miller, J. Hillis. *Fiction and Repetition: Seven English Novels.* Cambridge, MA: Harvard University Press, 1982.

Morson, Gary Saul. "Anna Karenina's Omens." *Freedom and Responsibility in Russian Literature: Essays in Honor of Robert Louis Jackson.* Ed. Elizabeth Cheresh Allen and Gary Saul Morson. Evanston, IL: Northwestern University Press, 1995: 134–52.

———. "Bakhtin and the Present Moment." *The American Scholar,* Spring 1991: 201–22.

———. *Hidden in Plain View: Narrative and Creative Potentials in "War and Peace."* Stanford: Stanford University Press, 1987.

———. *Narrative and Freedom: The Shadows of Time.* New Haven: Yale University Press, 1994.

———. "Prosaic Chekhov: Metadrama, the Intelligentsia, and *Uncle Vanya.*" *Tri Quarterly* 80 (Winter 1990/91): 118–58.

———. "Prosaics: An Approach to the Humanities." *The American Scholar,* Fall 1988: 515–28.

———. "Prosaics in *Anna Karenina.*" *Tolstoy Studies Journal* 1 (1988): 1–12.

Morson, Gary Saul, and Caryl Emerson. *Mikhail Bakhtin: Creation of a Prosaics.* Stanford: Stanford University Press, 1990.

Moser, Charles. *Esthetics as Nightmare: Russian Literary Theory 1855–1870.* Princeton: Princeton University Press, 1989.

Murdoch, Iris. *Metaphysics as a Guide to Morals.* Penguin, 1992.

Nabokov, Vladimir. "Introduction." *Eugene Onegin,* by Aleksandr Pushkin. Trans. with commentary by Vladimir Nabokov. Princeton: Princeton University Press, 1975: 1–88.

Olesha, Iurii. *Zavist': Tri tolstiaka, Ni dnia bez strochki.* Moscow: Khud. lit., 1989. (In English: *No Day Without a Line.* Trans. and ed. Judson Rosengrant. Ann Arbor, MI: Ardis, 1979.)

Orwin, Donna. "Freedom, Responsibility, and the Soul: The Platonic Contribution to Tolstoi's Psychology." *Canadian Slavonic Papers* 25 (1983): 501–17.

Paperno, Irina. *Chernyshevsky and the Age of Realism: A Study in the Semiotics of Behavior.* Stanford: Stanford University Press, 1988.

Poe, Edgar Allan. "Philosophy of Composition" and "Tale-Writing, Twice-Told Tales, Mosses from an Old Manse, by Nathaniel Hawthorne." *The Selected Poetry and Prose of Edgar Allan Poe.* Ed. and intro. T. O. Mabbott. New York: The Modern Library, 1951: 363–83.

Rischin, Ruth. "*Allegro Tumultuosissimamente:* Beethoven in Tolstoy's Fiction." *In the Shade of the Giant: Essays on Tolstoy.* Ed. Hugh McLean. Berkeley: University of California Press, 1989: 12–60.

Russell, Bertrand. *The Analysis of Mind.* London: George Allen and Unwin, 1961.

Sacks, Oliver. "The Last Hippie." *New York Review of Books,* Mar. 26, 1992: 53–62.

Sartre, Jean-Paul. *The Psychology of Imagination.* New York: Philosophical Library, 1948.

Scher, Steven Paul. "Literature and Music." *Interrelations of Literature.* Ed. Jean-Pierre Barricelli and Joseph Gibaldi. New York: MLA, 1982: 225–50.

Schultze, Sydney. *The Structure of "Anna Karenina."* Ann Arbor, MI: Ardis, 1982.

Schwartz, Regina M. "Joseph's Bones and the Resurrection of the Text: Remembering in the Bible." *PMLA* 103 (1988): 114–24.

Shklovsky, Viktor. *Lev Tolstoy.* Moscow: Progress Publishers, 1978.

———. *Mater'ial i stil' v romane L'va Tolstogo "Voina i mir."* The Hague: Mouton, 1970. Moscow: Federatsiia, n.d..

Silbajoris, Rimvydas. *Tolstoy's Aesthetics and His Art.* Columbus, OH: Slavica Publishers, Inc., 1991.

Sorokin, Boris. *Tolstoy in Prerevolutionary Criticism.* Miami University, 1979.

Sperber, Dan. *Rethinking Symbolism.* Trans. Alice L. Morton. Cambridge, Eng.: Cambridge University Press, 1975.

Steiner, George. *Tolstoy or Dostoevsky: An Essay in the Old Criticism.* Chicago: University of Chicago Press, 1959.

Stenbock-Fermor, Elisabeth. *The Architecture of "Anna Karenina": A History of Its Writing, Structure, and Message.* Lisse: The Peter de Ridder Press, 1975.

Sterne, Laurence. *A Sentimental Journey.* Penguin Classics, 1987.

Tannen, Deborah. *Talking Voices: Repetition, Dialogue, and Imagery in Conversational Discourse.* Cambridge, Eng.: Cambridge University Press, 1989.

Tolstoy, L. N. *Polnoe sobranie sochinenii.* 90 vols. Moscow: 1928–58.

———. *Anna Karenina.* Trans. Alymer Maude. New York: W. W. Norton, 1970.

Turgenev, I. S. *Pis'ma.* 8 vols. Moscow: 1958.

Uspensky, Boris. *A Poetics of Composition.* Trans. Valentina Zavarin and Susan Wittig. Berkeley: University of California Press, 1973.

Vivante, Paolo. *The Epithets in Homer: A Study in Poetic Values.* New Haven: Yale University Press, 1982.

Voloshinov, V. N. *Freudianism: A Marxist Critique.* Trans. I. R. Titunik. Ed. I. R. Titunik in collaboration with Neal H. Bruss. New York: Academic Press, 1976.

Vygotsky, L. S. *Thought and Language.* Ed. and trans. Eugenia Hanfmann and Gertrude Vakar. Cambridge, MA: MIT Press, 1962.

Wachtel, Andrew Baruch. *The Battle for Childhood: Creation of a Russian Myth.* Stanford: Stanford University Press, 1990.

Warnock, Mary. *Memory.* London: Faber & Faber, 1987.

Wasiolek, Edward. "A Paradox in Tolstoi's *What Is Art?*" *Canadian-American Slavic Studies* 12 (Winter 1978): 583–91.

———. *Tolstoy's Major Fiction.* Chicago: University of Chicago Press, 1978.

Williams, Bernard. *Morality: An Introduction to Ethics.* New York: Harper & Row, 1972.

Williams, Gareth. *The Influence of Tolstoy on Readers of His Works.* Lewiston, NY: The Edwin Mellen Press, 1990.

Wittgenstein, Ludwig. *Culture and Value.* Ed. G. H. von Wright in collaboration with Heikki Nyman. Trans. Peter Winch. Oxford: Basil Blackwell, 1980.

Index

In this index an "f" after a number indicates a separate reference on the next page, and an "ff" indicates separate references on the next two pages. A continuous discussion over two or more pages is indicated by a span of page numbers, e.g., "57-59." *Passim* is used for a cluster of references in close but not consecutive sequence.

Library of Congress Cataloging-in-Publication Data

Sankovitch, Natasha
    Creating and recovering experience : repetition in Tolstoy /
Natasha Sankovitch.
        p.   cm.
    Includes bibliographical references and index.
    ISBN 0-8047-3215-9 (cloth : alk. paper)
    1. Tolstoy, Leo, graf, 1828–1910—Philosophy. 2. Repetition
in literature. 3. Knowledge, theory of, in literature. I. Title.

PG3415.P5S26   1998
829.73'3—dc21   97-37651
                                                              CIP

This book is printed on acid-free, recycled paper.

Original printing 1998
Last figure below indicates year of this printing:
07   06   05   04   03   02   01   00   99   98